Preaching
from the
Old Testament

Elizabeth Achtemeier

Westminster/John Knox Press
Louisville, Kentucky

Scripture quotations from the Revised Standard Version of the Bible are copyrighted 1946, 1952, © 1971, 1973 by the Division of Christian Education of the National Council of the Churches of Christ in the U.S.A. and are used by permission.

Chapter 1 was originally delivered as the first in a three-part series of Lund Lectures, given at North Park Theological Seminary, Chicago, and then at numerous other seminary and ecclesiastical gatherings.

Excerpt from "The Waste Land" in *Collected Poems 1909–1962* by T. S. Eliot, copyright 1936 by Harcourt Brace Jovanovich, Inc., copyright © 1963, 1964 by T. S. Eliot, reprinted by permission of the publisher.

Book design by Gene Harris

First edition

Published by Westminster/John Knox Press
Louisville, Kentucky

PRINTED IN THE UNITED STATES OF AMERICA

9 8 7 6 5 4 3 2 1

Library of Congress Cataloging-in-Publication Data

Achtemeier, Elizabeth Rice, 1926–
    Preaching from the Old Testament / Elizabeth Achtemeier. — 1st ed.
        p.   cm.
    Bibliography: p.
    ISBN 0-664-25042-4

    1. Bible. O.T.—Homiletical use.   I. Title.
BS1191.5.A24 1989
251—dc19   88-35185
                                                                CIP

Preaching from the Old Testament

Other Books by Elizabeth Achtemeier

Preaching About Family Relationships
The Old Testament and the Proclamation of the Gospel
The Committed Marriage (Biblical Perspectives on Current Issues)

To my students
who, through thirty years of teaching,
have continually given me joy
and new insights,
friendship and inspiration

Contents

Preaching from the Old Testament

CHAPTER 1

A Personal Prologue
for Preachers

It is basic to the Christian faith that it is given to us in the form of a story, in the form of a history of happenings through which the holy God is revealed. We are not dealing in the Christian church merely with ideas, new or old, about God. The content of our faith is not an ideology—although some in the various movements about the country would like to turn it into that. But the content of our faith is not a set of ideals and goals by which we shape our public and private existence. The content of our faith is not a collection of ethical principles over against which we measure all our actions. Much less is the Christian faith simply a ritual by which we propitiate one or another deity or by which we magically coerce the powers that be to treat us kindly and favorably. The Christian faith issues in new understandings and dogmatic formulations, in ethical response and liturgical devotion, to be sure, but the final basis of all of these, and the center out of which they grow, is the story of what God has said and done in the human realm of time and space. Apart from that story, that holy history, there is no Christian faith. It stands or falls by its telling and retelling of the "old, old story."

The story is very clearly told to us in the scriptures. In the beginning—at the time of the big bang, if you prefer—God created the heavens and the earth, the cosmos, the galaxies, and all that is in them. He[1] created them good, full of order and life, running over and full of abundance. And he gave it all, in great love and esteem, to us, the creatures made in his image, that we might care for and keep his creation and enjoy it in our communities, as faithful stewards of his universe, subject to his lordship and kindly guidance.

Yet we human beings do not like to be servant to anyone, not even to God. And so daily we try to shake off our creaturehood and turn ourselves into our own gods and goddesses, with power over our own affairs, our own destinies, our own relationships. The result has been that we have corrupted God's world and despoiled its goodness, disrupting all the beauty of nature and all the loveliness of human community. Death now stalks our streets, which were intended to be full of life. Hatreds, suspicions, envies, greed now poison our commerce and our loves. Blood flows, polluting the ground. Loneliness sits in our living rooms. The scarred earth gives back thorns and thistles, and we walk in some awful twilight, where our feet stumble and the goal is uncertain and there is no meaning to it all. Such is the world we have created for ourselves by rebelling against God's lordship and by claiming that we are our own gods and rulers instead.

Yet God will not have done with us. He made us for life abundant. So he sets out in the second millennium B.C. to reverse the effects of our cursed rebellion. He sets out to make a new people in a new land, living in a new community of justice and love, under his guiding rule. He calls one man named Abraham out of Mesopotamia, to be the father of that new community. And then through all the vicissitudes and agonies of actual life in the ancient Near East, God guides the descendants of Abraham toward his good fulfillment of abundant life in the land—delivering them from slavery to the power of empire and world, pointing out the way they are to walk by his living presence in the covenant law, protecting them from the ravages of hunger and thirst and enemies, settling them in a good land flowing with milk and honey, constantly forgiving their pride and wrong, finally even giving them a Davidic king to be their protector of justice in peace and in war. And it is God's hope to draw all nations into that covenant community of Israel, that all peoples may live in peace and righteousness under his present lordship.

But Israel, like us, will have none of it. She is as rebellious and proud as we are. She whores after the gods of nature and nations; she forgets the One who has made her. She spurns God's commandments and corrupts his justice and relies on her own devices, to make her own fame and to secure for herself her own safety in the world of peoples. Thus she is rejected as God's people, and her national life is destroyed. Covenant, king, land, peoplehood, temple, blessing, life— all are done away in the holocaust of the Babylonian exile. Yet even in the midst of the ruins, the prophets cling to God's promises, peering forth into the future, to proclaim that God will yet make out of Israel's remnant a new people of Abraham and David. And then the centuries wait and wait in hope until the time is fulfilled, and there is born in a stable cave in the village of Bethlehem a son of David and of Abraham, who at the same time is the only begotten Son of God. Jesus Christ becomes, in his person, all that Israel was meant to be—the obedient and faithful Son of God, called out of Egypt; the cornerstone of a new community of righteousness and peace for all peoples, the Davidic ruler who knows how to protect the poor and to establish justice in society, the figure of the true human being who knows how to live in service to the lordship of God. In Christ, God once again sets out to establish his new covenant community and to restore to humankind the good life he intended for us all in the beginning.

But we will have none of that either. And so on the awful tree of Golgotha we think once more to do away with God's promise and purpose, and we bury his Son in the cold rock tomb of Joseph of Arimathea. But on the third day, at dawn, God raises his Son from the dead. He triumphs over all our attempts to defeat his lordship. Jesus Christ rises victorious over our wrong, our pride, our attempts to be our own gods. He rises triumphant over the death we seem determined to embrace. He rises once and for all in the power of the sovereign King, who is determined to forgive us, that we may have life and have it more abundantly. In short, Christ begins the final rule, the kingship, the kingdom of God on earth. And he promises, to all who trust his power and victory, strength to live an obedient and faithful life and participation in that new community of eternal life and good which will finally cover the earth as the waters cover the sea. The kingdom comes. It is begun in Christ. God's is the kingdom and power and the glory forever. Such is the incredible and yet historical outline of the true story we are given to tell.

From that sacred history, we learn the essential shape of reality. It shows us what is going on in the world, who the real power in our universe is, and what it is he is doing. The story reveals the purpose and direction of human history and the persons we are to become. Indeed, the sacred history itself conveys to us the power to grasp its truth as real and to live lives of faithfulness and obedience as citizens of God's new covenant people.

In short, the biblical history itself creates the new life and the new community within our world, and apart from that story there is no life and there is no coming kingdom. If the story be not true, if it has not taken place, then death has triumphed, our evil has won, God neither forgives nor rules. As Paul has put it, "If Christ has not been raised, your faith is futile and you are still in your sins" (1 Cor. 15:17). The Christian faith rests finally on the bedrock of a history that has taken place, and it follows therefore that unless we recount that history— unless in sermon after sermon, week after week, year after year, we tell that basic story, as it is given to us in the scriptures—our people will have no basis for their trust, no power to live the new life in Christ, and will finally remain pitable and futile creatures, living out desperate lives destined only for death. We must preach the story, we must preach the sacred history, in order to preach the gospel.

The truth is, of course, that we are not preaching the story very often, and that becomes clear when we consider the main types of preaching that are being carried on in the United States today.

Common to many of our evangelistic preachers is the type of sermon I have often called "propositional preaching." The gospel is framed in terms of propositions or truths: God is love; Jesus Christ died for our sins; we are washed by the blood of the Lamb. The good news is set forth in a series of propositions which are to be believed and intellectually accepted. The gospel remains an object "out there," an external authority to be imposed on the congregation, and of course there is great attention to saying just the right words or accepting the right version of the scriptures as evidence of belief.

I do not condemn such preachers. They sometimes have preserved the scriptures when others have been abandoning them in droves, and some evangelistic preaching has led its hearers to living faith in our Lord. But all other considerations aside, the thoughtful preacher cannot help wondering why we take a Bible which is full of stories and turn it into propositions. Do the propositions capture the height and breadth and depth of all that is in the story? God is love, to be sure—the statement is there in 1 John. But do we not need the story to sense the manner of his love? Do we not need the pictures of the passion story in the Gospel According to John to fill out the proposition—the scene in the garden across the Kidron; Judas and those Pharisees coming out with their lanterns and torches and weapons; Peter sitting beside the charcoal fire while the questioning goes on before the high priest; the crow of the cock, the whip, the crown of thorns, the purple robe, and the mockery; and finally the nails at the place of the skull, the thirst, the gambling for the tunic, the thrust of the spear in the side, and Nicodemus in the night with his myrrh? Do not all those vivid scenes from the sacred history bring home to our hearts more tellingly what it means that God is love? And so should the story not be the content of our proclamation of that marvelous mercy?

So often in our preaching, no matter what our theological position, we preach *about* the Bible, discussing its truths as principles from a petrified past. "The Bible says" is the phrase we use—"the Bible says our sins are forgiven"—and that remains an objective truth from a distant past, which may or may not appear to our congregations as expressing the reality they know in their everyday lives. How different is that indirect use of the Bible from a direct employment of it, in which its words are spoken immediately to the congregation—"Your sins are forgiven; take up your bed and walk"; "Come unto me, all ye that labor and are heavy laden, and I will give you rest"—all set in that gracious story of the man from Nazareth.

Stories have the character of allowing us to enter into them. We identify with the figures in them and find them telling the story of our lives. And this is one of the functions of the stories in the Bible—they let us enter into their events, to experience and feel what has happened, so that the story becomes our story and the happening an event in our situation. What a difference it can make really to preach the stories, rather than distilling out of them eternal truths and principles!

For example, God grieves at the beginning of the story of the flood: "I am sorry that I have made man on the earth." Could it be that is our story—he is sorry that he has made you and me? Or God remembers his dreams for the future in the book of Jeremiah (3:19): "I thought how I would set you among my sons, and give you a pleasant land. . . . And I thought you would call me, 'My Father,' and would not turn from following me." Could it be that we are those rebellious sons and daughters? But then could it be that God speaks further about the course our story will take? "Is Ephraim my dear son? Is he my darling child? For as often as I speak against him, I do remember him still. Therefore my heart yearns for him; I will surely have mercy on him" (Jer. 31:20). Even the prophetic words reflect a story between God and his people, and they come home most to our hearts when we see that the story is also ours, in Jesus Christ, when the preacher allows us to enter into it as participants and recipients of its action.

Most of the preaching that takes place in the United States is thematic preaching, preaching in which a theme or topic or moral lesson is distilled out of the text. The task of the sermon then becomes to prove that some thesis is true, or the task becomes one of convincing and exhorting our people to be good. We use all sorts of authorities to prove the truth of our statements, employing quotes from great thinkers or scientists or writers to back up our theses, appealing to reason and experience in all sorts of illustrations to support our theme. Sometimes we even appeal to fear, to greed for reward, or to self-righteous Pharisaism to talk our people into trying to live up to some legalistic moral code. Yet all the while it is the sacred history of God's words and acts that bear with them the gift and power of new life. And our people never know the truth and never become new creatures until they enter into that sacred story.

Because we do not often preach the sacred history, we especially do not often preach from the Old Testament, because page after page of it is made up of nothing but stories, and the whole is set within the framework of a history taking place. We are not very comfortable with the story of the Old Testament and its God who is always on the move

toward a goal. We are much more comfortable with truths, propositions, principles. We are much more comfortable with static themes
and moralistic exhortations. The result is that we have now lost in the
church large portions of the sacred history.

Some time ago Dean Lawrence Jones of the Divinity School of
Howard University told me about a sermon he heard, taken from the
tale of Balaam and his ass. How many of us have heard a sermon on the
Balaam stories recently? Those stories form the climax of the period of
the wilderness wanderings in Israel's history; theologically they are
very important. And thanks be to God, many black preachers still
preach the stories of Balaam and Joshua and Jezebel, of Hezekiah and
Nebuchadnezzar. But we white preachers no longer preach from
those texts in the Old Testament, and we now have lost in the
American pulpit great portions of the story.

The consequences of our loss of the stories of the Bible are dreadful
to behold. With the loss, first of all, we have lost their vividness and
power of language. It is a truism in the preaching field that the
preacher who reads well is often the one who can write and speak
well. And surely the first place to begin is with the stories of the Bible
itself. Who cannot learn from the artistry of the Elohist in that story of
the sacrifice of Isaac, in Genesis 22? The awful test of Abraham by
God: "Take your son, your only son Isaac, whom you love, and go to
the land of Moriah, and offer him there as a burnt offering upon one of
the mountains of which I shall tell you" (v. 2). And then the terrible
three-day journey, in silence, of father with his son; the arrival; and
then the acts spelled out more and more in detail:

> And Abraham took the wood of the burnt offering, and laid it on
> Isaac his son; and he took in his hand the fire and the knife. So
> they went both of them together. And Isaac said to his father
> Abraham, "My father!" And he said, "Here am I, my son." He
> [Isaac] said, "Behold, the fire and the wood; but where is the lamb
> for a burnt offering?" Abraham said, "God will provide himself
> the lamb for a burnt offering, my son." So they went both of them
> together.
>
> Genesis 22:6–8

Or have you read the stories of the wilderness wanderings in the
book of Numbers? What better place is there to find an analogy to our
ungrateful attitude toward God's acts of mercy than in the story of
Numbers 11:4–6?

> Now the rabble that was among them had a strong craving; and
> the people of Israel also wept again, and said, "O that we had
> meat to eat! We remember the fish we ate in Egypt for nothing,
> the cucumbers, the melons, the leeks, the onions, and the garlic;

but now our strength is dried up, and there is nothing at all but this manna to look at!"

Or would you like to learn how to picture character in a few brief phrases? Then read the beginning of the story of David's sin with Bathsheba, in 2 Samuel 11:1:

In the spring of the year, the time when kings go forth to battle, David sent Joab, and his servants with him, and all Israel; and they ravaged the Ammonites, and besieged Rabbah. But David remained at Jerusalem.

If we read this history, we may begin to learn something about the power of the language of story.

Because we have lost the language of these stories of the Bible, we have also lost the God they portray. For example, consider the covenant with Father Abraham, in Genesis 15:17:

When the sun had gone down and it was dark, behold, a smoking fire pot and a flaming torch passed between these pieces [of the sacrifice].

God's mystery, his utter impenetrable mystery, is pictured in those words! No wonder our people turn away from our rationalistic religion for the mysteries of the occult or of Eastern religions. We have lost the language of these stories and the mystery they carry with them.

Or the power of God! Look at it in the story of God's descent to Mount Sinai in Exodus 19:16–19:

On the morning of the third day there were thunders and lightnings, and a thick cloud upon the mountain, and a very loud trumpet blast, so that all the people who were in the camp trembled. Then Moses brought the people out of the camp to meet God; and they took their stand at the foot of the mountain. And Mount Sinai was wrapped in smoke, because the LORD descended upon it in fire; and the smoke of it went up like the smoke of a kiln, and the whole mountain quaked greatly. And as the sound of the trumpet grew louder and louder, Moses spoke, and God answered him in thunder.

Do our people know anything of that God of Sinai when they go to church to worship? It is through the language and pictures of these stories that we come to know who God is. And when we lose these stories, we lose our God of mystery and power and otherness. No wonder our secular age can live in a world in which it never sees God at work. As a man in a congregation in Pennsylvania put it, "Sure, I believe in God, but I don't think he does anything." Only a man who does not know these stories can carry around such a view of God.

Third, in relation to our loss of the sacred history, it is especially tragic in our time that we do not preach the story, because we are living in the midst of a society and a people who have lost the story of their lives altogether. How do we really receive our identity in this day and age? How do our people really know who they are?

We used to find an identity in our nation's story, but America's people have lost much of their knowledge of their history now, or they reject some parts that they do know. And so every little ethnic group starts searching out its own roots, in the attempt to find some story by which it may know who it is.

We also used to identify ourselves by our community's stories. But now we are a restless, mobile people, constantly on the move, isolated in our split-level homes, often not knowing even our neighbors. Or we used to find our identity by our family stories, but over half of all families now are disrupted and broken by divorce. One million more children each year are the victims of divorce and are shunted back and forth between separated parents, apartments, schools, with confusing arrays of stepparents, stepbrothers, and stepsisters entering and leaving their lives in the trauma and confusion engulfing their homes. Who has a family story by which to find self-identity in the midst of such chaos?

It is the character of stories that they have beginnings and endings, that the figures in them move from a past toward a future. But we have lost the past, or feel guilty about it, and when we look to the future it is very uncertain. The nation drifts steadily toward a regulated nightmare, in which our lives will be totally subject to the rules and whims of government bureacracies. The fruits of our labors are swallowed up by taxation, corruption, crime, change. Over the future hangs the threat of environmental pollution, machines still and rusting for lack of fuel, the menace of germicidal war or nuclear accident or holocaust. And in our homes we add alarms and bolts to the doors, and we fear even to go out at night.

The past is marred or nonexistent, the future uncertain and threatening. The only security is the now and looking out for our own survival. We have been called the me generation, but we could put it in other terms. We in the United States are people without a story. Stories have a past, present, future; beginnings and endings. Our stories have become static, frantic and fatalistic clingings to self-preservation in the moment. And so we invent imaginary stories, flickering out at us from those dramas we see on TV nightly. And we live in those and find there our fanciful histories.

Is it not absolutely important, then, for an age such as ours to hear the real story, the great cosmic drama that is going on, in which we all are players? There is a past: First Father Abraham and Moses and Miriam and the psalmists and the white-robed company of martyrs played their roles; Amos and Isaiah and Huldah and the goodly fellowship of the prophets; then Paul and Priscilla, Augustine and Anselm, Luther and Calvin and Knox, Bonhoeffer and King and Mother Teresa. And now you and I and Mrs. Jones are called onto center stage. We all are called to play the Christian before our Sovereign, to become the part, to add the next sentence to the drama, to form the future, while God from the throne, and his Son, and all the ministering spirits watch breathlessly to hear each line and to mark each movement, and the whole universe waits and waits, in hope, for the final triumphant curtain. There is a great cosmic drama going on, in which God is working out his purpose, and every action we take and every decision we make has significance in the framework of that story. Is that not what our people, who have lost their stories, need to hear, in order that they may know who they are and what meaning they have in this world?

God has brought salvation into our time and space through a series of concrete happenings, through a history, a story that now is told to us by countless faithful persons who experienced it. "That which we have seen and heard we proclaim also to you," those witnesses tell us in 1 John (1:3–4), "so that you may have fellowship with us; and our fellowship is with the Father and with his Son Jesus Christ. And we are writing this that your joy may be complete."

The story has been given us that our joy and the joy of our people may be complete. And we preachers have been called by God to tell that gladdening, saving story. We are stewards of the story, Paul tells us, stewards of its mysteries, and it is required of stewards that they hand on the story faithfully. As Bishop Charles Gore once told a group of ministerial candidates on the evening before their ordinations, "Tomorrow I will give you your ordination vows and will ask you, 'Do you . . . do you . . . do you?' But there will come a day when your Lord will say to you, 'Did you . . . did you . . . did you?'" It is required of us stewards of the story that we be faithful.

CHAPTER 2

Why the Old Testament Is Necessary for the Church

It is fair to say that the Old Testament is largely a lost book in many parts of the U.S. church. The people in our congregations have only the most limited knowledge of its contents. Many preachers rarely, if ever, preach from the Old Testament. Even the Psalter, which has been the treasury of devotion for the people of God for three thousand years, is, in nonliturgical denominations, fading into disuse and unfamiliarity. Our people may know or recognize a few lines from some psalms; they hear a number of prophetic promises at Christmastime; they can recognize the creation story when someone reads it to them. But beyond that, the Old Testament is unknown and unimportant to them, an unopened antique book from the distant past that can safely be left with the other antiques on the curio shelf.

Such an ignorance of the Old Testament has serious consequences. If we in the church do not know the Old Testament and do not teach and preach from it to our people, we leave them with no means for properly understanding and appropriating the Christian faith. When our forebears in the faith finally decided on at least the basic shape of the canon, they prefaced New Testament with Old as an essential part of the gospel. The last third of the Bible cannot be understood, they implied, without those first two thirds in the Old Testament. And if we ignore the first two thirds from the pulpit, we preach a truncated gospel. We and our people, for all practical purposes, fall into the heresy of Marcionism, and that has the most serious consequences for the church and for everyday Christian living.

In the first place, apart from the Old Testament, it is almost impossible properly to understand the nature of the world. We twentieth-century moderns see the universe as a closed system of cause and effect, in which everything operates automatically according to natural law, and we are now bending our efforts to harmonize with nature and not to upset its delicate ecological balances. We are the spaceship earth, we say, with limited resources and powers, called upon to guard what we have in order to preserve life in our float through the galaxies. But sometimes that is a terrifying prospect because we do not know if we have the wisdom to harmonize and guard and thus keep ourselves alive.

It is in the Old Testament traditions of creation, however, that we learn that the earth in its universe is not a closed system, but subject to a God who stands over and above it as its sovereign Lord. He sustains the world's processes of life and guards its order against the forces of chaos, and indeed he remains and takes us into an eternal fellowship with himself, though heaven and earth should pass away. And it is that God, that Creator and Sustainer of the universe, whom the New Testament presupposes.

Second, apart from the Old Testament, it is almost impossible properly to understand ourselves as human beings. Many in our culture would like to classify us as nothing more than animals, with instincts and drives that must be met, no matter what the human cost. Others try to dissolve our individual unique personalities into a oneness with some mystical Soul or Primal Matrix or great Being of life and nature. Marxists understand us totally in terms of economic forces. Sociologists classify us according to groups and cultures. The government has glibly made us statistics; the military talks about body counts and coolly reckons how many of us are expendable in a nuclear attack. For medicine, we may become nothing more than a liver, a kidney, a collection of cells to be fed from tubes. To advertisers, we are consumers to be manipulated with appeals to our pride or fear or greed. But it is in the Old Testament that we learn that we are fearfully and wonderfully made, like no other creatures in all God's good creation, made uniquely in his image, given dominion over the earth, and told that we were created for fellowship with one another and that it is not good that we be alone. Above all, it is in the Old Testament that we learn that we were created for relationship with God and that we cannot properly be understood apart from that relationship. And that view of human nature is presupposed by the New Testament.

Third, apart from the Old Testament, we also cannot properly understand who God is—that he is not identifiable with or found in anything in all creation, but that he is *holy* God, uniquely other than everything he has made. It is in the Old Testament that we learn that God is always personal, that he cannot be identified with an idea or process or emotional experience, and that he must be pictured, to be pictured rightly, in the metaphors of person, as Husband, Father, Savior, King, who loves and weeps, and speaks and sends, and whistles and calls and takes. The Judge who grieves, the Warrior who fights, the Redeemer who buys back his family member—such is the God whom we meet through the Old Testament's figures of speech. It is in the Old Testament that we learn we cannot know such a God except as he himself breaks into time and reveals his own person and nature, through the words he speaks and the deeds he does in particular places.

Indeed, it is in the Old Testament that we first learn such a God is working out a purpose in human history, which has a definite beginning in time and which will be brought to a fulfilled end. And the New Testament presupposes that kind of God and that historical purpose.

We cannot appropriate the New Testament view of the world and of human beings and of God unless we absorb those views first of all from the Old Testament. In many respects that last third of our canon in the New Testament is simply a final reinterpretation and summing up of the two thirds that have gone before in the Old Testament.

This is not to say that there is nothing new in the New Testament. There is much that is new. There is something greater than Solomon there, something greater than Jonah and Abraham. The prophets and kings and sages and psalmists desired to see what the New Testament sees, and did not see it. They desired to hear what the New Testament hears, and did not hear it. But who is this new figure who walks the roads of the New Testament story? Who is Jesus Christ?

The New Testament writers themselves were convinced we could not know him apart from the Old Testament. The first thing that Matthew can think to tell us about Jesus Christ, the first sentence in his gospel, reads, "The book of the genealogy of Jesus Christ, the son of David, the son of Abraham"—Christ can be understood only in terms of Abraham and David. For Luke, it was the Old Testament scriptures that illumined everything that Jesus did. After the meeting on the Emmaus road, the risen Christ appears to his disciples in the upper room and says to them:

> "These are my words which I spoke to you, while I was still with you, that everything written about me in the law of Moses and the prophets and the Psalms must be fulfilled." Then he opened their minds to understand the scriptures.
>
> Luke 24:44–45

Christ was understood by the New Testament writers as the fulfillment of the Old.

In fact, as the New Testament writers set forth their testimony to the nature of Jesus Christ, they framed that testimony in terms of the traditions and theologies of the Old Testament. I fully set forth that framing in an earlier book, *The Old Testament and the Proclamation of the Gospel.* Let me give a summary statement of it.

There is a great variety in the witness to Jesus in the New Testament. Some writers emphasize one thing, some emphasize another, but their total testimony gives us the definitive picture of our Lord, and every New Testament writer drew on Old Testament traditions and theology.

Some New Testament writers described Jesus Christ in terms of the royal traditions of the Old Testament. In that description, Jesus was variously the Messiah, the long-awaited son of David, the shepherd prince promised by Ezekiel, the High Priest after the order of Melchizedek, who had been designated Son of God and exalted to the right hand of the Father as the Lord over all enemies and powers. Jesus was the one to whom the Old Testament traditions of David and of the royal psalms pointed, the Ruler whose coming inaugurated the beginning of the kingdom of God.

For those New Testament writers who told the story of Jesus' earthly life and death, Jesus was described as a new Moses (Matthew), or as the prophet like Moses, who was to come (John; Acts); or as the Suffering Servant who gave his life as a ransom for many (Mark). He was the one who freed Israel from her final slavery (Galatians); the one who instituted the new Sinai covenant of the prophets in his blood (1 Corinthians; Hebrews); who made the perfect sacrifice for sin once for all (Hebrews). He was Psalm 118's stone which the builders rejected, which had become the head of the corner (1 Peter). He was Isaiah 8's rock of stumbling for the Jews and foolishness for the Gentiles (1 Corinthians). He was the ideal righteous man of the psalms, suffering and praising his Father from the cross (Passion stories). In short, the traditions of the exodus, Passover and Sinai, the Hexateuchal and prophetic traditions and the Psalter, and, as we shall see, the Wisdom writings, all found their goal in Jesus Christ, and that plan which God began with his first release of his people from Egypt was, according to the New Testament writers, brought to completion in the story of the crucifixion and resurrection.

For those New Testament writers who concentrated on the fullness of the incarnation, Jesus was, in various traditions, the new obedient son Israel (Matthew); the incarnate temple (John); Isaiah's cornerstone of the new congregation of faith on Zion (1 Peter). He was the incarnate covenant and light and lamb in his role as the Servant. He was the true vine (cf. Psalm 80; Isaiah 5), the true manna, the bread and drink of life. Jesus was the Word of the Old Testament made flesh, who gave the light that shone in the darkness (John). In Hebrews, he was even described as the incarnate promised land, that place of rest offered to all who faithfully held fast to him.

In other words, the New Testament writers were convinced that Jesus Christ was not some mysterious figure suddenly dropped from the blue, with no connection to the almost two thousand years of God's activity in history that had preceded him. Rather, Jesus Christ was the completion and fulfillment and final reinterpretation of that lively history, and so he can only be fully understood in terms of it. Unless we preach from the Old Testament, our people really cannot know who their Lord is.

In the same manner, unless our people are allowed to appropriate the Old Testament witness, they also cannot know who they are as the church of Jesus Christ. What is the church, according to the New Testament? It is the body of Christ, to be sure. It is the dwelling place of God in the Spirit, the "household of God" (Eph. 2:19). But it is "built upon the foundation of the apostles and prophets," with Christ as Isaiah's foretold cornerstone (Eph. 2:20). In Galatians, Paul calls the followers of Christ "the Israel of God" (6:16), the true children of Abraham (3:7), who have become the inheritors of the promise to the patriarchs (3:8, 29). It is the church now that is "the true circumcision" (Phil. 3:3), the new people of Yahweh envisioned by Hosea, the saved remnant foreseen by Isaiah (Rom. 9:25–27). We wild branches have now been grafted into the root of Israel (Rom. 11:17–20). We have become members of the commonwealth of Israel (Eph. 2:12).

The church is now the new Israel in Christ, according to the New Testament, but we cannot possibly understand what that means unless we know who the old Israel was. What does it mean to be Israel? Who was she? How was she created and ordered? What was she supposed to do? Our people can answer those questions only if we use the Old Testament in our preaching along with the New.

Most of the time we avoid preaching about the church in terms of Israel, because we rightly think that our people do not know anything about Israel and that therefore the use of such terminology would just confuse them. We employ every other metaphor of the church but that of the new Israel in Christ, and thus we foster our people's ignorance of the Old Testament and their feeling that the Old Testament is irrelevant for their Christian lives. We never fully, biblically proclaim to them who they actually are.

The story of Israel, in its long pilgrimage with God, can powerfully set forth the nature of our pilgrimage with him also. Look at the analogies between our life as the church and the life of Israel. Both of us are redeemed out of slavery, apart from any deserving on our part. Both of us have that deliverance as the sole basis of our peoplehood. Both Israel and the church are brought to the table of covenant and enter into an exclusive relationship with God, in which we agree to serve him alone as his elected people. Both of us are given a new beginning and a new life as a foretaste of the glorious liberty of the children of God. Both are set under commandments from God that are to be the sole basis of the guiding and ordering of our lives. Both of us are set on a pilgrimage toward a promised place of rest and fulfillment. Both are accompanied on our journey by the presence of God himself. Both are loved as the sons or children of God or as the bride of God. Both are to be a holy nation, set apart for God's special purpose and use. Both are to be a kingdom of priests, mediating the knowledge of God to the world. The history of the church, of the new Israel in Christ, recapitulates the history of the old Israel, as the prophets had promised it would. And how we impoverish our people, and their understanding of themselves as the church, if we do not let them enter into the full story of who they are—that story told over the two thousand years of struggle and temptation and defeat and redemption given us in the Old Testament! It is no wonder that our forebears included the Old Testament in our canon of scriptures, for the Old Testament is indispensable for understanding the nature of the world and of human beings and of God; and it is indispensable for knowing who Jesus Christ is and who we are as his new covenant people, the church.

We shall therefore investigate, in the chapters that follow, how one goes about preaching Christian sermons from various portions of the Old Testament. Let it be said right here at the beginning of that investigation that no book and no author can fully treat the possibilities of preaching from the Old Testament. The Book of the Old Covenant is a golden lode, whose riches are never exhausted and whose treasures are always surprising. Therefore, I never fully cover, in any one chapter, the sermon possibilities inherent in any one type of Hebrew literature. I simply try to give suggestions about what might be used and how. Some chapters deal more with the biblical content than they do with sermon suggestions, thus leaving the preacher to be stimulated to preach from that content. Other chapters go rather thoroughly into methodology and the use of specific texts. But it is my hope that from the various approaches used, the reader will be moved to mine and preach from this priceless lode of the Old Testament that has been treasured across the centuries and handed down to us as our own possession.

CHAPTER 3

The Approach to the Bible, the Community-creating Word

Before we move into a discussion of the actual process of developing a sermon from the Old Testament and then take up the homiletical treatment of various parts of the Book of the Old Covenant, it seems proper to examine in detail theologically some of the presuppositions that underlie this work. Only then can the reader have a clear view of the approach to the Bible that forms the foundation of this entire book.

The Creative Word

The word of God, by the scripture's definition, does not merely convey information, nor does it work its effects simply by producing new understandings. Those may result from the revelation of the word, to be sure, but the Bible's conception of the word of God is that it creates that of which it speaks. That is, the word of God is active, effective power, which brings about new situations in nature, in society, and in the lives of those who hear it.

The simplest example is found in Genesis 1. God says, "Let there be light," and light is created; a new situation comes into being. Thus, Psalm 33:9 can celebrate creation: "For he spoke, and it came to be; he commanded, and it stood forth."

The creative power of the word is not limited, in the Bible's view, to the world of nature, however. The word also creates that of which it speaks in the realm of history. In Second Isaiah, God clearly sets forth such working: "My word . . . shall not return to me empty, but it shall accomplish that which I purpose, and prosper in the thing for which I sent it" (Isa. 55:11). Thus when God utters a word of promise, of judgment, or of salvation, the view in the Old Testament is that the word works in events, shaping, influencing, motivating them, until the word is brought to fulfillment and what God has spoken has come to pass. Indeed, the whole Deuteronomic history, encompassing Deuteronomy through 2 Kings, is primarily an account of how God's words have worked their effects in Israel's life.

God remains always the Lord of his word, in the Bible's view. He can hold back its working until he sees what Israel will do, as in Ezekiel 12:26–28. He can recall the word and not let it work—which is the meaning of God's "repentance" in passages such as Amos 7:3, 6, or Exodus 32:14. But once God determines that the word shall go forth, it cannot remain unspoken by its human proclaimer (cf. Jer. 20:9; Amos 3:8) or be turned aside by human willfulness. The word will bring about the new situation in human life of which it speaks.

Paul's understanding of the word of God is no different. For him, too, the word is active, effective force which brings about events, and so he can say that the word of the cross is the *power* of God which *saves* those who believe (1 Cor. 1:18, 21), and if anyone lives in the power of that word by faith, that person becomes a new creation of God's (2 Cor. 5:17), with sinful past done away. That makes one very conscious of the active might of God at work in the world in the Word made flesh.

It is this understanding of the creative power of the word of God that defines history (or what we would call salvation history) for the biblical writers. A *Heilsgeschichte* or salvation history, for them, is history into which the word of God has been spoken, and which is then moved forward, shaped, and influenced by the working of that word, until the word is fulfilled. There are dozens of little salvation histories in the Old Testament (see, for example, 2 Kings 1:6, 17; 1 Kings 13:2 and 2 Kings 23:16–18; 1 Kings 14:16 and 2 Kings 17:21–23). But there is also one overarching salvation history, which awaits its fulfillment and which finally finds its completion in the New Testament. As Paul says, "all the promises of God find their Yes" in Jesus Christ (2 Cor. 1:20).

The working of the word of God is not confined within the span of the Bible's time, however. Its active, effective power continues to work through the medium of the biblical history to create new situations, and it is that working through the medium of the Bible's story that has created and continues to create the community of the Christian church. To be sure, the church has assembled the New Testament, put it together with the Old, and declared the whole to be its canon. But finally the reason for that assembling and declaration has been the fact that the church has learned, through the centuries, that the sacred story creates the church's life as Christian community. Through the word of both Old and New Testaments, the church has found itself redeemed out of bondage to sin and death, brought into covenant with its Lord, set on a pilgrimage toward the kingdom of God, and sustained, guided, judged, ever again forgiven, and renewed, every step along the way. To each new generation, the biblical word has spoken, to bring its transformation of women and men, old and young, into disciples of Jesus Christ, bound together in a universal community by their common allegiance to one Lord, one faith, one baptism.

Moreover, the church has learned, in its experience in every age with nonbiblically formed groups, that as soon as it deserts the community-forming word of the Bible, it ceases to be distinctively Christian and invents new faiths or begins to be absorbed into one or another cultural philosophy, ideology, or community; or it imposes on the culture around it imperialistic, non-Christian claims. The community of the Christian church is formed and sustained by the biblical word or it ceases to be Christian, and so the church has declared that the Bible, illumined by the Holy Spirit, is its one authoritative measure and guide of all faith and practice.

The Effects of Historical Criticism

What happens, however, when the community-forming word of the Bible is approached, no longer as the word of God that creates new situations but solely as a historical document from the past, to be studied by scientific, rational methods? Obviously, the word may be emptied of its power to create and be turned into an object to be analyzed. In one sense, this is exactly what happened with the rise of historical criticism of the Bible, beginning in the eighteenth century and continuing into the present.

I do not want to be misunderstood on this score. *Historical criticism was necessary and still is,* and it has contributed enormously to an understanding of the scriptures, as I think the rest of this book will demonstrate. Historical criticism freed the study of the Bible from the confining limits of dogmatic orthodoxy and showed the Bible to be a living, moving history of actual people, living in specific places at particular times. Biblical scholars have given us much more reliable texts of the scriptures; placed the biblical writings in their proper historical and cultural contexts; illumined the Bible's meaning from archaeology, linguistics, geography, history, sociology; taught us what types of literature make up the scriptures; deepened our understanding of countless passages in the sacred pages; and removed many obstacles that would hinder that understanding. In short, we cannot do without that scholarly past.

Historical criticism has, however, also brought with it some unfortunate results. First, because most clergy are trained in a critical approach to the scriptures and most laity are not, the feeling has been fostered in the modern church that only the clergy can properly understand the scriptures. The Bible is closed to the average lay reader until some critically trained "expert" tells the "uneducated" laity what the Bible "really means." It is no wonder, therefore, that few lay people read and study the Bible; they do not want to exhibit their "stupidity."

Second, because historical criticism approaches the Bible solely as a historical document, the truth of the Bible has come to be identified with its facticity. This has led to two surprising results. On the one hand, though the fundamentalists argue furiously against historical criticism, they nevertheless have adopted the critical criterion of "facticity" and must insist that every single statement in the Bible is fact—or at least that every single statement in the original manuscript of the Bible was fact—whether geologic, geographic, zoologic, or whatever. Rationalism and scientism rule supreme. On the other hand, some naïve historical critics have maintained that what is true in the Bible is only that which can be shown scientifically to have "actually happened." Only those words of the prophets or of Jesus can be credited that can be proved historically to have been spoken by them. The Bible is judged and dissected, by both groups, by strictly rational means, with no appreciation for its community-creating power.

This rationalistic, strictly historical approach to the scriptures, then, has been carried even further by special-interest groups in our day, such as the liberationist theologians or the feminists, who lift out particular parts of the scriptures to support their various causes. For them, only that is true in the scriptures which emphasizes human freedom from oppression; or only that is true in the Bible which sets forth the equality of male and female. Either the rest is historically conditioned and distorted and can be safely cast aside, or the rest must be altered, as in the *Inclusive Language Lectionary,* to conform to the truth of the excerpted portions.

Third, the strictly scientific, historical, rationalistic approach to the Bible has had the effect of atomizing it. Each pericope must be understood for itself alone, in its own historical setting, or each narrative whole has solely its own context and meaning and there is nothing that necessarily holds the separate parts together. Above all, there is nothing that necessarily binds the Old and New Testaments. In both Testaments we are dealing with disparate groups, from many different times and places, who produced their own unique literature and pursued their own unique religious practices, and there is no thread of divine activity and purpose that ties the whole story together.

Fourth, and most seriously, because the Bible is approached from a historical, rationalistic viewpoint, it is emptied of its power now to create the church as one church, living from a common story, and disparate groups within Christianity seek other sources that will sustain and guide their fellowship. The Bible is made one authority alongside other authorities, or its word is, for all practical purposes, abandoned altogether. Separate communities retain the name "Christian," but their founding and sustaining base actually consists in something other than scripture—a common cause, an ideology, a liturgical routine, an ethic adopted from the culture, even simply a desire for status or sociability.

Many biblical scholars and theologians have become aware of these harmful and often unintended by-products of the historical-critical approach to the Bible, and many now are searching for a hermeneutic that will retain the beneficial results of critical scholarship while at the same time recovering the community-creating potential of the Bible's word for the church. Not many have discussed the deleterious effects, however, that historical criticism has had on preaching. What have been the effects on the pulpit of a purely rationalistic, scientific approach to the scriptures?

Certainly historical criticism has aided the preaching task, although it has also complicated it, and the average preacher now feels called to master a growing array of scholarly sciences. (Literary criticism and sociology are probably the latest additions to the list.) But most seriously, the historical and scientific approach to the Bible has tended to limit the Bible's word strictly to the human level, so that many preachers, in order to claim any truth for the Bible's message, have felt compelled to turn it into moralistic admonitions that are valued for their pragmatism, or into psychological and mental health dictums that are judged according to their coherence with those human sciences. More irresponsibly still, some preachers have even tried to show the agreement of the Bible with the latest sociological, economic, or political fad. The resulting sermons have carried little of the word of God's transforming and community-building power, and one minister's opinions, thus preached, have been viewed by the congregation as just as good as the next's.

Because critical work has tended to atomize the Bible, sermons based solely on such work and formed totally out of the critical commentaries have also atomized the proclamation of the gospel. Even when the scripture for the day is granted divine authority, sermons from an atomized Bible tend to proclaim isolated "spiritual truths." The "truth" is directed to one aspect of the Christian life, for the strengthening and guidance of the individual or of the group assembled for worship, but the "truth" bears little relation to a history-encompassing activity of God, and the worshiper is ministered to only for the moment. A different occasion will need a different sermon spoken to it. The worshiper has little sense of belonging to an ongoing history, shaped and moved forward by the word of God, that encompasses the totality of the congregation's life.

Recovering the One Story

The Bible is a multifaceted collection of books, assembled from many different times, places, and groups, representing thousands of different experiences and witnesses to God's revelation. Amid all its varying testimonies, only one thing holds the Bible together: the action of the living God, to which the whole Bible testifies. In many respects, the scriptures are not history books—although they do contain some very good history. Rather, the scriptures are confessions of faith. All their thousands of voices claim that the one true God, the Lord of Israel and the Father of Jesus Christ, has acted and spoken in their lives. God is the subject of the Bible and its one source of unity. The canon coheres as one, because it contains the some 2,150-years-long account of what God has said and done in human life.

Obviously, because God is the subject and chief actor in the Bible, a solely scientific and rationalistic approach to the Bible cannot fully recover its story. Historical criticism can aid in the task; it cannot complete it. There has to be some way of hearing the one story into which all the various parts fit, and of listening to it in such a way that its true subject is revealed.

So, first of all, is there a way of hearing the Bible as one story? I believe there is, and I think that the Bible itself furnishes that approach. The whole story hangs together as an account of the promises of God and of how he has kept those promises in the realm of human life.

The sacred story begins in history with the call of Abraham out of Mesopotamia, sometime—perhaps about 1750 B.C.—in the second millennium B.C. (Gen. 12:1–3). At that time, Abraham is given a fourfold promise: (1) God will make of his descendants a great nation; (2) to those descendants God will give a land of their own (12:7); (3) God will enter into a special relationship with Abraham and his descendants, in an everlasting covenant (Gen. 17:7—the Priestly version of the promise); (4) through Abraham and his descendants, God will bring his blessing on all the families of the earth (12:3).

The reason for that entrance of God into Semitic history is clearly set forth in the preface to the promise: namely, in Genesis 1–11, which is intended by the writers.to be the story of us all. ("Adam" in the Hebrew is the word for "humankind.") God made a good creation, overflowing with abundant life, but human beings, in their attempts to be their own gods and goddesses, have corrupted the creation and introduced sin and evil into the world. God intended for male and female to be joined together in the joyful marital unity of "one flesh" (2:24). Our sin has now disrupted that unity and brought the "battle of the sexes" (3:7, 16). God gave humankind the good gifts of beauty and fruitfulness in the surrounding world (2:9) and of creative and preservative work (2:15). Our rebellion against the Creator has now turned the gift of work into drudgery and the beauty of the world into ugliness and barrenness (3:17–19). God desired that we should live forever in an intimate, obedient, and eternal fellowship with him. Our disobedience has broken that divine-human relationship and brought upon us the sentence of death (3:8, 19, 22–23). We have lost the gift of abundant life, and there is no way we can recover it on our own (3:24).

As we have lived our lives in a fallen world, we have spread our sin to every corner of the universe, and the stories that follow in Genesis 4–11 graphically depict that spread. The story of Cain and Abel pictures the resulting hatred of brother for brother (4:1–16). The little portrayal of the rise of civilization in 4:17–24 brings with it Lamech's bigamy (4:19) and his terrible sword of vengeance, the symbolic depiction of human hatred for all humankind. In 6:1–4, even the heavenly realm is infected by our disobedience, until finally our wickedness is "great in the earth" and "every imagination of the thoughts of [our hearts is] only evil continually" (6:5).

At each juncture in the story, God's judgment grows ever more severe, to match the ever-spreading corruption caused by our rebellion against his rule (Gen. 4:11–12; 6:3; 6:7–7:24). But his judgment is always accompanied by an overriding mercy (3:21; 4:1, 15; 7:1, 16b; chs. 8–9). Yet, after the judgment of the flood, humankind has not improved (8:21; 9:20–27), and the primeval history ends with the final depiction of sin, in the story of the Tower of Babel (11:1–9). At the height of their creativity, in a cooperative endeavor, human beings determine to create for themselves their own security and fame (11:4). The resulting judgment is that all human community becomes impossible (11:7–9), and Genesis' introductory hamartiology ends with the earth cursed, human beings under the sentence of meaningless toil, strife, and death, and the relationship with God destroyed by sinful willfulness. Seemingly, that awful and realistic portrayal of what our lives and world are like is the final word in the story.

But no. God calls Abraham, and the promises he gives him are intended to overcome the effects of our cursed rebellion. We have lost our paradise, and so God will give Abraham and his descendants a new land, "flowing with milk and honey" (cf. Deut. 8:7–10). Human community has become impossible, and so God will make from Abraham a new people, and he will bestow their "name" on them

(Gen. 12:2). The relation with God has been broken, and so the Lord himself will reestablish it in an everlasting covenant, in which Abraham's descendants will be God's people and God will be their Lord, securing their life in the world of nations. And finally, the cursed state of the judged world will be reversed, and God will bring his blessing instead on all the families of the earth. In short, God calls Abraham and gives him promises, because God loves all people, and he sets out in Abraham's history to restore the good life to all that he intended for humanity in the beginning.

The sacred history records for us, then, in the rest of Genesis and the following five books of the Old Testament (Exodus through Joshua), the account of how God works to keep these promises to Abraham. In Genesis, we find all the difficulties connected with God's attempts to give Abraham descendants—the old age of Abraham and Sarah his wife, the sterility of Rebekah and Rachel, the lack of faith on the patriarchs' parts (e.g., 15:2–3; 16:1–6; 17:17–18), their conniving and their deception (25:26–34; chs. 27, 30), and the very real threats to their lives from those who hate them (27:41–45; 31:1–2; 32:6–8). All are to be understood in the light of God's promise of descendants, just as is the final story of Joseph and his brothers in Genesis 37–50. If Jacob and his family die from famine, what becomes of God's promise? And so Joseph, by the working of God, is sent ahead of his family into Egypt, in order to preserve Israel alive, in fulfillment of God's word (cf. Gen. 45:4–8; 50:20).

Israel, however, is now in Egypt and falls into slavery to Pharaoh, precisely because God continues to multiply Abraham's descendants (Exodus 1). How can God make them a nation and give them a land when they are captive in the brick factories of Egypt? The story of Moses and the exodus thus follows (Exodus 3–15), and God delivers his people, bringing them finally to Sinai, where he enters into the promised covenant with them (Exodus 19–40). Then through forty years, despite their murmuring and rebellion in the wilderness wanderings, God leads the Israelites through the terrors of the desert, finally bringing their descendants into the promised land in the time of Joshua. At the end of the Hexateuch, therefore, Joshua can affirm that "not one thing has failed of all the good things which the LORD your God promised concerning you; all have come to pass for you, not one of them has failed" (Josh. 23:14). This God of Israel is a promise-keeping God, whose mercy has ever overcome Israel's disobedience and whose power has preserved her life, in the face of every threat and obstacle to the fulfillment of his word.

Israel, however, is intended to be the means whereby God will bring his blessing on all the families of the earth, and her time in the promised land is now a test of whether she will serve God as that medium of blessing (Josh. 23:15–16; see also Ex. 19:4–6; Deut. 30:15–20). The remarkable fact about her account of her history is that she confesses that she never does so serve. The time of the Judges, when she is a loose federation of tribes, is a time of repeated apostasy. Her longing for a king to preserve her alive before the Philistine threat in the time of Samuel manifests her lack of trust in God's protection and rule over her (1 Samuel 8). Her first king, Saul, grievously fails to lead her in the way of obedience. But God, always merciful, always forgiving, always true to his promises, raises up for her a new king and even makes an addition to his promise: There will never be lacking an heir to sit upon the Davidic throne, and as long as a Davidic king rules, Israel will live in God's favor (2 Samuel 7).

The time of the monarchy, so vividly pictured in so many places in the books of Samuel and of Kings, is also the time of the early and of the writing prophets, however, and through all those stories we see an Israel stubbornly set against her God—breaking every commandment of God's covenant law, destroying the community he wishes to establish in her, spurning his mercy, killing his prophets, trusting everything and everyone but him. The results are the exiles of 722, 593, 587, and 582 b.c. The ten northern tribes are lost to Assyria; Judah (plus Benjamin) in the south is enslaved to Babylonia. Seemingly, God's promises have failed, and Israel's sacred history has come to an end. Her population has been greatly reduced, her land of milk and honey lost, and her Davidic king taken into exile. The covenant is broken by Israel's sin (Hos. 1:6, 9; Jer. 12:8; 31:32), and rather than a source of blessing in the earth, Israel has become, according to Jeremiah, a horror, a curse, and a hissing (Jer. 25:9, 18; 29:18). God's promises have apparently all been taken back, and the sacred history has come to a standstill. If God is the Lord of Israel's life, then she must suffer the results of her rebellion against him. And yet his judgment on her means that her sin has triumphed and God has been unable to keep his word.

Not so, therefore proclaims the prophet of the exile, Second Isaiah. "The grass withers, the flower fades; but the word of our God will stand for ever" (Isa. 40:8). The prophets all proclaim, in a multitude of ways, that God will yet redeem his people, buying them back out of slavery and restoring them to their land, multiplying their population like the sands of the seashore, entering once again into an everlasting covenant with them, restoring one David to rule over a new and prosperous united kingdom, and making them a source of blessing in the midst of the earth. It will be a totally new act of God, according to Second Isaiah (43:19), but it will at the same time gather up all of

God's past promises and bring them to fulfillment. God's word will not return to him void but will accomplish that which he has purposed, for this God of Israel is a promise-keeping God.

Some of the Israelites did return to Palestine in the time of Nehemiah and Ezra, after the freeing decree of Cyrus of Persia was issued in 538 B.C. But except for a brief period under the Maccabees in 166–143 B.C., Old Testament Israel never again was a nation but, rather, became just a tiny subprovince, first of the Persian Empire and then of the Ptolemies, Seleucids, and Romans. The way in which God was to fulfill his promises to her was not evident on the stage of world history but came in the form of the incarnation of all those words of God.

In his person the Son of God became what Israel was meant to be, and through him God gave to the world all that Israel was meant to give. Christ became, in his flesh broken and his blood shed, God's new covenant, binding his people to himself in a relationship that nothing can now destroy. Hailed as Davidic king when he rode into Jerusalem, Christ was crowned on the cross and became the Lord and raised on high to the right hand of God, to intercede and ensure God's favor forever toward his own. Once the stone that the builders rejected, Jesus Christ became the head of the corner of a new universal community of God, including now Jews and Greeks, slaves and free, male and female, from every race and clime. In fulfillment of the promise to Abraham, he is that descendant of the patriarch through whom God now turns every curse into blessing. In him, the battle of the sexes is stilled and husband and wife are again made one flesh; in him, daily work is given its meaning once more as a means of glorifying God; in him, brother is reconciled with brother and human hatred is forgiven and turned to love; in him, death is overcome and the restoration of all nature promised (Rom. 8:19–21). Indeed, in Jesus Christ, even the promised land—that place of "rest" in the Old Testament—is now made incarnate, and we journey not toward a geographical location but toward our promised rest in Christ (Hebrews 3–4; 12:1–2; Phil. 3:12–14). "All the promises of God find their Yes in him" (2 Cor. 1:20)—the promises of land, of descendants built into a great community, of covenant, of Davidic king, of blessing. The word of God, spoken into the sacred history in the Old Testament, finds its fulfillment in that Word made flesh, and all who trust the work of God in Jesus Christ are made heirs of the fulfillment, journeying now toward that assured time when the last enemy, death, has been destroyed, and God's kingdom has come on earth, even as it is in heaven.

The Bible's story is one story. It concerns the promises of God, and it is held together in its unity by the faithfulness of God to his promised word. We Christians not only inherit that story by being baptized into the body of Christ, the church, as adopted children of God and therefore as historical heirs of the promise (see Gal. 4:4–7), but, by the faith of the church, the story is made our history along every step of the way. The promises to Israel have become, through Christ, promises now made also to us, and so, by analogy and foreshadowing, every word to Israel is now the word of God to us. There we are, writ large, upon every page of the Old and New Testaments, with God at each turn pouring out that judgment that is alien to his love (Isa. 28:21) and his saving mercy upon us. We are set into the ongoing history of the work of God in the world, and it is that history that creates our life as a community of God's people. It brings us into covenant relation with the living God and thus tells us who we are. It gives us the reason for our existence as a united people and furnishes us the motive power to live in love with God and neighbor. It sets us on our pilgrimage toward the final triumph of God's rule, when the earth shall be full of the knowledge of God as the waters cover the seas.

Obviously, a strictly scientific, historical, rational approach to the scriptures cannot tell that story, because it cannot comprehend the work of the principal actor, God, in the drama. Historical criticism can aid mightily in illumining what human beings have said and done in reaction to God's working, but it finally cannot judge the truth or falsehood of the claims about God. Thus the simplest, most uneducated believer, reading or hearing the biblical story, may appropriate its meaning more fully and profoundly than the most learned biblical scholar who has no faith, a fact attested to—thank God—throughout the history of the church.

Preaching, then, has the task of using every scientific method at its disposal to get at the original meaning of a biblical text for its author, but that is not sufficient in itself. Finally the question must always be asked of every biblical passage: What is that God who created the world, who made a people for himself, and who now is moving on toward the goal of his kingdom—what is that God doing, according to the words of this particular biblical passage? Each part of the Bible is but an episode in the ongoing story of God's salvation of his world, and that dynamic whole informs every separate part. If the preacher approaches every text from such a faithful stance, perhaps the church may begin to recover its nature as one community of God and to reclaim its purpose and message of good news for the world.

CHAPTER 4

Basics of Sermon Preparation

When developing a sermon from the Old Testament, there is no substitute for a meticulous, reflective, theological study of the text. Here is where so many preachers go awry; they do not carefully study and reflect on the text from which they are going to preach. Most busy students or pastors will read through a biblical text in one English translation until they get a sermon idea. At that point the text and its context are left behind, and the preacher develops the idea into a supposedly "biblical" sermon. But the finished product may bear no relation to the meaning of the text and little relation to the biblical message as a whole. What are the methods one can use actually to uncover the meaning of a biblical passage and to relate it to the life of the congregation?

The Use of Rhetorical Analysis

The first step is to translate the text from the original Hebrew into rough English, or to read it in several responsible English translations and compare them (never use *The Living Bible!*), or to use an interlinear Hebrew-English Bible. There are some advantages to the last, because it preserves the Hebrew word order, which is important for meaning.

Second, write down a rough English translation of the text, preserving, insofar as possible, all the features of the Hebrew text—the word order, the conjunctions, those exclamations and repetitions that English translations tend to leave out. (I usually note these features by transliterations of some of the Hebrew, written above the line.) If the text is poetry, write it in poetic form, according to the placement of the lines in the Hebrew. Even if you are comparing English translations, write your version down on paper.

Third, do a rhetorical analysis of the text: that is, carefully note the patterns, emphases, and constructions of Hebrew speech in the text.

This is done in the following way:

1. Underline all imperative verbs. They are emphatic.

2. Underline repeated words and join them with a line. The Bible repeats for emphasis, and repeated words often reveal the key thought of a passage.

3. Put a dotted line under exclamations.

4. Circle the Hebrew word *ki* ("for," "because") when it begins a phrase. In such usage, the *ki* phrase gives the reason for the preceding statement and is often a key to the meaning of the passage.

5. Put a broken line under phrases such as "now therefore," "but I," "but you," "nevertheless," "therefore," "yet," "as for me," "but now." These often mark a change in thought.

6. Put a box around pronouns that are separate words in the Hebrew from their verbs. These are emphatic.

7. Carefully note:

    a. Parallelisms. They can repeat or enlarge on a thought.

    b. Questions.

    c. Contrasts in thought or scenes or characters.

    d. Changes in subject matter or speakers.

    e. Participial phrases that begin with "who" or "the one who" in the English. These are used for purposes of description, often hymnic description of God.

    f. Repetitions in thought. This is used for emphasis and can furnish a further key to the meaning of a passage.

    g. Triadic structures of verbs or other words. These are used for emphasis, with the climax often following on the third word.

    h. The beginning and ending of the passage. Often they are similar in thought or structure, giving boundaries to the passage.

Were we to follow such procedures using Jeremiah 2:4–13, Figure 1 shows what it would look like.

What can we learn from this analysis of the text?

From the repetitions

    The people have gone far away from Yahweh.

        Repetition of "me," vs. 5 (twice), 8 (twice), 13.

        The thought begins and ends the poem.

            v. 5: They went far away from me.

            v. 13: Me they have forsaken.

    They have not inquired of Yahweh and his will.

            vs. 6, 8: repetition of "did not say, 'Where is Yahweh'"

            v. 8: The priests have abandoned the torah.

    Instead they have followed after emptiness and that which is useless, vs. 5, 8, 11.

4. Hear the word of Yahweh house of Jacob,   {imperative}
    and all the families of the house of Israel!   {parallelism}

5. Thus says Yahweh:

    What did your fathers find in me? Wickedness?   {question}
    (For) they went far away from me,
    and they followed after emptiness,
    and they became empty.

6. And they did not say, "Where is Yahweh,   {question}
    the one who brought us up from the land of Egypt,
    the one who led us in the wilderness,   {participial phrases}
    in the land of desert and pit,
    in a land of dryness and deep darkness,   {parallelisms}
    in a land that no man passes through,
    (and no man dwells there)?

7. But I brought you to a garden-land   {contrast}
    to eat its fruit and its good.

    But you came and you defiled my land,   {contrast}
    and my heritage you made an abomination.   {parallelisms}

8. The priests did not say,   {parallelism}
    "Where is Yahweh?"   {question}
    and the handlers of the torah did not know me,
    and the shepherds rebelled against me,
    and the prophets prophesied by Baal,
    and they followed after that which is useless.

9. Therefore now I will go to court with you,
    oracle of Yahweh,   {parallelism}
    and with the children of your children I will go to court.

10. (For) pass over to the isles of the Mediterranean,
    and send to Kedar and consider well,   {triadic verbs}
    and see. Behold! Has there been anything like this?

11. Has a nation changed gods,
    and they are no gods?   {question}
    But my people changed its glory   {parallelism}
    for that which is useless.   {contrast}

12. Be astonished, heavens, at this!
    Be astounded! Be utterly dry!   {triadic imperative}
    Oracle of Yahweh.

13. (For) two evils my people have done.
    Me they have forsaken,
    a fountain of living waters,
    to dig for themselves cisterns,
    broken cisterns,
    that cannot hold waters.

Figure 1. Rhetorical analysis of Jeremiah 2:4–13.

The thought begins and ends the poem.
  v. 5: They have gone after emptiness.
  v. 13: They have dug broken cisterns that can hold no waters:
    that is, that are useless.
The meaning of this is spelled out in further detail:
  v. 8: The rulers (shepherds) have rebelled against Yahweh.
  v. 8: The prophets have prophesied by Baal.
  v. 11: This is an exchange of the glory of Yahweh for useless
    pagan gods. No other nation has ever done such a thing.
  v. 5: The Israelites themselves have therefore become empty
    and useless for Yahweh's purpose. They have become what
    they worship.
  vs. 11, 13: Israel has done this, even though she is Yahweh's
    covenant people. Repetition of "my people."
  v. 9: Therefore Yahweh will take her and her children to
    court.

From the imperatives
  All of Israel is to "hear" Yahweh's indictment against them, v. 4.
  The jury are the heavens, who examine the evidence against
    Israel, v. 10.
  The jury is to be shocked at such an appalling act on Israel's
    part, and is asked to judge her by drying up all rain and
    thus bringing drought and famine on the people, v. 12.

From the use of *ki*
  It begins those phrases in vs. 5 and 13 that summarize Israel's
    sin.
  It begins the sentence that explains why Yahweh is taking Israel
    to court, v. 10.

From the participial phrases
  Yahweh's past goodness to Israel is celebrated in hymnic fashion
    in v. 6, where the exodus and his constant leading through
    the terrors of the wilderness are mentioned.

From the contrasts and adversative phrases
  Yahweh's act of mercy in giving the promised land is contrasted
    in v. 7, by the use of adversative *waws*, with Israel's
    faithless defilement of the land by her idols.
  Israel's unfaithfulness is further contrasted with the faithfulness
    of other nations to their gods, in v. 11, again by the use of
    an adversative *waw*.

Obviously, by this simple exercise we are a long way toward uncovering the meaning of this poem. But the rhetorical analysis is completed by dividing the poem into strophes or stanzas.

Features that often mark the beginning of a strophe are: (1) an imperative; (2) an invocation; (3) an exclamation; (4) an interrogative; (5) a change of subject matter or speakers; (6) phrases such as "now therefore," "but I," "nevertheless," "therefore," "yet," "as for me/you," "if," "then." Strophes rarely begin with the particle *ki*, when it has the meaning of "for" or "because." Participial phrases beginning with "who" or "the one who" are not to be separated from their subject sentence.

Features that often mark the end of a strophe are: (1) a quotation; (2) a climax in thought; (3) the presence of a recurring refrain. The thought at the end of a poem may repeat that at the beginning, or the same thought may occur at the end of each strophe.

Strophes do not have to be of equal length, in terms of lines and half lines, although sometimes they are. Or the length of strophes may alternate in a regular pattern.

If we divide Jeremiah 2:4–13 into strophes on the basis of these criteria: Vs. 4 and 5a form the introduction. Vs. 5b–6 are strophe 1, which begins with a question. Vs. 7–8 are strophe 2, beginning with "But I." Vs. 9–11 are strophe 3, beginning with "Therefore." Vs. 12–13 are strophe 4, beginning with an imperative. Strophes 1, 2, and 3 have ten lines each. (The last line of v. 6 is omitted on this basis.) Strophe 4 has nine lines.

When we divide the poem into strophes, we then notice an amazing fact. Strophes 2, 3, and 4 all end with the thought of uselessness, while the same thought occurs at the beginning of strophe 1, in v. 5. Our previous analysis has noted the emphasis of the poem on emptiness or uselessness, but the strophic division highlights that feature. The principal theme is announced at the poem's beginning and then repeated in each of the strophes that follow. In short, this poem is primarily about the empty uselessness of the covenant people's life when they forsake the one true God, the Lord of Israel. That, then, would be the primary message of a sermon preached from this text, and surely it is a message relevant to the church in our day. But we have uncovered that principal thrust of the text without ever looking at a commentary and without imposing any extraneous thought or presupposition on the passage.

Not every passage in the Old Testament will yield so many clear results from rhetorical analysis. Nevertheless, it is an invaluable aid in studying any text. It lends itself best to Hebrew poetry, as found in the prophets or the psalms, and every biblical poem should be analyzed in the manner we have demonstrated. But prose passages are also illumined by careful analysis of the features we have mentioned. For example, the unspoken feelings of the characters in Genesis 22:1–14 are quickly illumined if one notices the constant repetition of "your son," "your only son," "his son"; "his father," "my father"; and "they went both of them together." Again, the meaning of a prose passage such as Deuteronomy 10:12–22 quickly becomes apparent if one notices its repetitions, imperatives, adversatives, *ki* phrases, parallelisms, and participial phrases. If a preacher studies a passage in such detail, it is very hard to miss its meaning. Above all, the message of the text shapes the thought of the preacher, rather than vice versa. It is out of such careful analysis of the text that all truly biblical sermons are born.

The Use of Form Criticism

Another helpful step in developing a sermon from a biblical text is to subject the chosen passage to form criticism: that is, to discover with what kind of literature one is dealing. We bring different expectations to different kinds of texts. If a story begins, "Once upon a time," we know it is a fairy tale, and we expect to read it as such. If a letter begins, "My dearest," we expect from it affection and intimacy. Expectation makes a lot of difference in the way we read a text, and so it is with the Bible.

The Old Testament is replete with various types of literature. In its prose passages, it has all kinds of sagas, legends, anecdotes, tales, fables, historical narratives, broken pieces of myths, reports, autobiographies, sayings, allegories, confessions, laws, records, lists, contracts, letters—the variety is almost endless. Many of these genres are easily recognizable, and the preacher will just bear in mind the type of literature with which he or she is dealing. Two facts need to be emphasized, however.

First, unless a text is clearly meant to be an artistic and imaginary construction, such as Jotham's fable in Judges 9:8–15 or Ezekiel's allegory in 17:22–24, the genre of a passage says nothing about its historicity. Form criticism deals with typical *form*, or structure, and the original situation in Israel's life in which that form was used. It makes no judgment about whether or not actual happenings lie behind the prose account. Thus, to say that Genesis is made up largely of sagas and legends is to say nothing about the historicity of Genesis. The Yahwist, Elohist, and Priestly writers and their redactors who shaped the stories of Genesis into coherent wholes and wove them all together had no intention of writing fiction. There is not one passage that they do not intend us to take seriously. But they chose types of literature that would not only tell what had happened in Israel's pilgrimage with God but would also allow the hearer and reader to feel and experience and enter into what had happened, so that the event continued to have an effect on each new generation. The sagas of Genesis get at our hearts as well as at our minds. They exercise a transforming influence on us.

Second, the preacher should be clear about the fact that there are no complete myths in the Bible. Mythological language is sometimes borrowed by the Old Testament framers. For example, there can be no doubt that the Priestly writers borrowed phrases and concepts from the Mesopotamian chaos dragon myth to portray the primeval state of creation, in Genesis 1:2–8 (cf. Ps. 74:13–14; 89:9–10; Isa. 51:9), just as Genesis 6:1–4 has mythological motifs lying behind it, and just as the story of Noah finds many parallels in the Sumerian myth of the Deluge. But myths, in form criticism, are stories of the gods—usually of conflicts between the gods—and their setting is timeless. The biblical stories, in contrast, deal with the one God, who is sovereign over all gods and need fight none of them, and every story about the one true God is set in the context of time. Mythical stories, in their timelessness, presuppose the cyclical nature of human time on earth. Biblical time, on the other hand, has a beginning and moves forward toward a goal, in a linear understanding of human history. Thus, while the Old Testament may borrow some of the mythological language of its day, it demythologizes the material and sets it in the historical context of the one God who is working out his purpose on earth. Far too many homileticians have spoken carelessly of the "myths" of the Bible, to the dismay of their congregations or the confusion of their readers.

We shall deal more fully in the next chapter with the way we use the various narrative portions of the Old Testament in preaching. At this point, we need to say more about the form criticism of the prophetic literature and of the psalms. When dealing with those books, the preacher should apply form criticism for several reasons.

First, when we read the prophetic literature, it is sometimes very difficult to tell where a passage begins and ends. This is also sometimes true in the psalms. For example, the refrain in Psalm 43:5 is found in Psalm 42, verses 5 and 11, and the two psalms were probably originally one. The lectionary may be no help with the prophetic literature, because it sometimes begins a stated reading in the middle of one pericope and ends in the middle of another. Texts for preaching should deal with complete units, or else the meaning of a passage is likely to be distorted or lost. It therefore is necessary for the preacher to know the basic form of various prophetic oracles.

Second, the genre of a passage determines its tone and often something of its meaning. For example, when a preacher reads Amos 5:2, he or she needs to know that the verse is a funeral dirge, uttered over one who is dead; Amos is prophesying that Israel is going to die! To give another example, if we are dealing with Isaiah 1:18–20 or 41:1–42:4 or Micah 6:1–5 or our passage of Jeremiah 2:4–13, it helps to know that such passages are set in the form of court cases. One then looks for possible indictments and sentences, plaintiffs and juries.

Third, because various types or genres of literature in the Old Testament have their own characteristic forms, one can sometimes note where the text has altered the traditional form for the purpose of emphasis or surprise. For example, Jeremiah 15:15–18 has the form of an individual lament, a type found frequently in the Psalter. Usually such laments ended with statements of joy and trust, signifying that the speaker believed God had heard his complaint and would come to his rescue. (See, for example, Jer. 20:7–13 or Ps. 6.) But that which follows Jeremiah 15:15–18, in verses 19–21, is not certainty and trust but rebuke from Yahweh and a conditional promise. The crisis in the prophet's faith is thereby highlighted.

Fourth, it is sometimes helpful in interpreting a passage to know the original situation-in-life *(Sitz-im-Leben)* in which the genre was used. For example, Psalm 17 can appear, on casual reading, to embody a terrible self-righteousness on the psalmist's part: "Thou wilt find no wickedness in me" (v. 3d). That does not seem to accord too well with the biblical requirement of humility and repentance before God. But if we know the situation-in-life of the psalmist, the meaning is illumined. Psalm 17 is probably the prayer of one falsely accused of a crime. The case has been too difficult for a local court to decide and therefore, in accordance with the law of Deuteronomy 17:8–13, it has been brought to the temple to be decided by the priest. In that setting, the accused adhered to very strict cultic rites. He went through a purification ceremony; he spent the night in self-examination (v. 3), and he was required to give an abjuration or protestation of his innocence. This last is taking place in verses 3–5 of this psalm. Thus the psalmist is not self-righteous at all but is stating that he is innocent of the charge against him, and he is sure that he will be judged innocent by the priest on the morrow (v. 15).

To give another example, it is very helpful to know that Psalm 24:7–10 is an entrance liturgy, used when the ark of the covenant was carried in procession to the temple. (The ark was viewed as the base of the invisible God's throne and was symbolic of his presence with his people; cf. 1 Sam. 4:4.) Thus the priests accompanying the ark cry out for the doors of the temple to be opened to allow the ark to enter, while the priests inside the temple doors ask the questions of verses 8a and 10a. With the pronouncement of the sacred name in verse 10b, the doors are flung wide.

We can by no means identify all the situations-in-life in which various genres were used, but the knowledge we do have of them is useful to the preacher.

Forms in the Prophetic Literature

The basic form first used by the prophets was that of the judgment speech to an individual (see 1 Kings 21:18–19; Amos 7:16–17), but this form that was expanded by the preexilic writing prophets into the judgment speech to the nation. (See Figure 2.)[1] The basic elements in a prophetic oracle are, in short:

The reason for the announcement
The messenger formula
The announcement

	Amos 4:1–2	Isaiah 8:6–8
Introduction	Hear this word, you cows of Bashan, who are in the mountain of Samaria,	
Accusation/ Situation	who oppress the poor, who crush the needy,	Because this people have refused the waters of Shiloah that flow gently,
Further development	who say to their husbands, "Bring, that we may drink!"	and melt in fear before Rezin and the son of Remaliah;
Messenger formula	The Lord GOD has sworn by his holiness	therefore, behold,
Announcement Intervention of God	that, behold, the days are coming upon you,	the Lord is bringing up against them the waters of the River, mighty and many, . . .
Results of the intervention	when they shall take you away with hooks, even the last of you with fishhooks.	and it will rise over all its channels . . . and pass on, reaching even to the neck.

Figure 2. Judgment speech to the nation.

In some passages, the order of these elements is reversed, as in Jeremiah 2:26–28, or one part is expanded and the other abbreviated, as in Jeremiah 2:1–13. Some have only the reason for the announcement (Jer. 2:20–25), some only the announcement (Jer. 13:12–14). Sometimes the messenger formula comes at the beginning or is lacking altogether or is repeated. By the time of Jeremiah and Ezekiel, the standard form was greatly loosened or expanded in any one of its parts. Nevertheless, when preaching from the prophets, the homiletician should try to mark off the passage in terms of these three basic elements, in order to determine its limits and analyze its contents.

Prophecies of salvation have essentially the same structure (see Jer. 35:18–19), although the description of the situation may describe at length God's gracious acts (see Isa. 9:2–7), and the announcement may be based not on human deserving but on God's grace (see Jer. 32:14–15).

Another prominent genre in the prophetic writings is that of the woe oracle. Its structure can be seen in Isaiah 5:8–10 and is as follows:

The exclamation "Woe!" or "Alas!", v. 8a

A participial phrase, designating those subject to the woe, v. 8a

A second participial phrase, describing their offense, v. 8bcde

Announcement of divine judgment, vs. 9–10

The woe oracle may have had its origin in the funeral ritual of mourning and lamentation and thus is an announcement of imminent death. Sometimes the announcement of judgment may not come until the end of a series of woes, as in Isaiah 5:11–25, where the announcement does not occur until verses 24–25. In preaching from such a passage, a homiletician could use the whole series or just one of the woes, followed by the announcement (e.g., v. 20 and vs. 24–25). In its function, the woe oracle is very similar to that of the dirge (see Amos 5:1–3). Both announce the sure death of the persons being judged.

One genre found frequently in Second Isaiah is the priestly oracle of salvation, which may have originated in the cult as the priest's response to an individual's lament. It has this structure, as seen in Isaiah 41:8–13:

A statement of God's past dealings with Israel, vs. 8–9.

"Fear not!" and a promise of God's intervention, v. 10.

A description of the results of God's actions, vs. 11–12.

An explanation of God's actions, v. 13.

A preacher might use just the oracle itself as the text for the sermon. However, Second Isaiah employs the form as an integral part of much longer poems. In the case of Isaiah 41:8–13, it forms the fourth strophe of a poem encompassing Isaiah 41:1 — 42:4, and the preacher would want to be careful to exegete the part in relation to its greater whole.

An exceedingly important genre in the prophetic writings is the legal procedure, which can be illustrated by Isaiah 1:18–20. It has this form:

Summons to court proceedings, v. 18a
The complainant presents his case, vs. 18b–19.
The judge decides, v. 20 ("since you refuse . . .").

Many passages in the prophetic books portray legal procedures and can be correctly interpreted only in that setting (see Hos. 4:1–10; Micah 6:1–5). If the preacher uses an interlinear Hebrew/English Bible, the appearance of the word *rib* (transliterated *rybh*=court case) in the Hebrew immediately alerts one to the presence of this form. The preacher should then look for possible judges, plaintiffs, defendants, and juries in the passage, as well as the sentence handed down and the words of the parties involved. For example, in Hosea 4:1–10, the Lord takes Israel to court (v. 1), but it is finally the priests who are judged (vs. 4–10).

Also important in the prophetic writings is the prophetic torah, in which the prophet exercises his function as one who teaches the people the way to walk, in the light of the past sacred history and God's dealings with the people. An example is found in Isaiah 1:10–17, which has:

An introduction, v. 10
A reproof, vs. 11–15b
An accusation, v. 15c ("your hands are full of blood")
Instruction, vs. 16–17

Such passages may serve as the basis for the instruction of a congregation, when the situation of the new Israel of the church is analogous to that of Israel in the Old Testament.

There are many other genres to be found in the prophetic books, but these are perhaps the most important for homiletical purposes.

Forms in the Psalms

Hermann Gunkel of Germany first classified the psalms by type, pointing out their typical structures and attempting to identify their original situation in the worship and communal life of Israel. Gunkel listed some seventeen different types or subtypes of psalms, but we shall discuss only the most important among those.

Probably the most easily identified psalm genre is that of the hymn, which is found in such great psalms as numbers 8, 19, 96, 98, 100, 103, and 145–150. The purpose of a hymn is to praise God, and it does so by giving a rather general description of his person and acts. Structures of hymns are rather simple, as can be seen in Psalm 98:

1. A call to sing, rejoice, praise, or bless (v. 1a).

2. A transitional device consisting of the word "for," meaning "because" *(ki)* (v. 1b). This is one of the most important words in the psalm, because it introduces the reason for the statement that precedes it. It thus gives the theological rationale for the praise and often points to the heart of a sermon on the psalm. Another type of transitional device is the participial phrase in the Hebrew, beginning with "who" or "the one who" in English translation (see Ps. 104:2–4). These further elaborate the description of God and thus again give the reason for praising him.

3. The body of the hymn, which tells further what God has done and therefore who he is (Ps. 98:2–3).

Sometimes there is a conclusion, sometimes not. Psalm 98 has no conclusion. Instead it repeats the hymnic form, with the call to praise (vs. 4–9a), followed by the transitional "for" (v. 9b), and the body (v. 9cd). On the other hand, a hymn can end with a petition, as in Psalm 19:14, or with a renewed call to praise, as in Psalm 103:20–22. All of the hymns of Psalms 146–150 begin and end with "Hallelujah!", which means "Praise the Lord!", and are thus known as Hallelujah psalms. (Cf. the beginning of Psalms 111–113.)

Hymns are found throughout the Bible. For example, Mary's Magnificat is a hymn (Luke 1:46–55), as is Zechariah's Song (Luke 1:68–79). The prophets frequently have snatches of hymns in their writings (see, e.g., Isa. 44:23–28), and the style of a hymn is a good one to emulate in those portions of sermons where the preacher wants to praise and expound on the nature of God.[2] Above all, however, when the preacher is preaching from a hymn text, the sermon should duplicate the function of the hymn: namely, to call forth praise of God because of who he is and what he has done.

As subcategories under hymns, Gunkel included songs of Zion, which praise the city where God dwells; enthronement hymns, which celebrate God's kingship; and communal thanksgivings.

If we are speaking of the thanksgiving song of the individual, a somewhat different form is involved, and this can be seen in Psalm 116. It includes:

A statement of or invitation to praise, v. 1a ("I love the LORD")

An account of the singer's experience, vs. 1b–4

A confession of faith in God as Savior or an instruction of others, vs. 5–11

A reference to a thank offering or payment of a vow, vs. 12–14 (this is not found in all thanksgivings)

A conclusion, with a confession to Yahweh and a renewed call to
praise, vs. 15–19

Thanksgivings differ from hymns in their praise of God by declaring
the *specific* acts whereby God has saved the singer. Thus, Claus
Westermann has given the titles of "declarative praise" to
thanksgivings and "descriptive praise" to hymns.

One of the important characteristics of thanksgiving psalms is their
public confession of God's acts of salvation. God was not properly
thanked unless others were told of what he had done. In fact, the
Hebrew word used to mean "to thank" has the basic meaning "to
confess." To thank God was to confess what he had done, in the
hearing of others, so that others too would praise and glorify God's
holy name and have their faith in him awakened. Thanksgiving was
testimonial in Israel; the saved person became a missionary. Obviously, that can also be the purpose of a sermon when it is using a
thanksgiving psalm.

The form most frequently used in the Psalter is that of the lament,
either of the individual or of the community, and the fact that laments
make up two thirds of the Psalter illumines an important aspect of
prayer that is missing from most of our worship. Our congregations
rarely have opportunity to bring their complaints before God. But
Israel did. When she suffered distress of any sort—war, famine,
drought, pestilence, captivity—the whole community gathered together in rituals of lamentation and repentance (see Psalm 79 for a
communal lament; cf., e.g., Judg. 20:23–28 or Joel 1:1—2:17 for
such occasions). Similarly, individuals in distress from sickness or
enemies or other trials brought their situation and petitions before
God. Both types of lament had the same form (see Psalm 22).

An invocation, vs. 1–5 (also in vs. 9–10)

A description of the sufferer's situation, vs. 6–8, 14–18

Petitions to God for help, vs. 19–21 (anticipated in v. 11)

Expressions of certainty that God would rescue, vs. 22–31

It is the last element in this form that is especially remarkable. Most
of the laments in the Psalter end with expressions of faith (see Ps.
13:5–6), and such expressions sometimes developed into independent
songs of trust (Psalms 11; 16; 27:1–6; 52; 131 may have had such
origin). The psalmists were sure that God would come to their aid;
they were sure, even though their situation of suffering had not
changed. Thus the singer of Psalm 4 could say (v. 8), "In peace I will
both lie down and sleep; for thou alone, O LORD, makest me dwell in
safety." Faith brings with it peace which the world can neither give
nor take away, and such psalmic expressions of faith can be powerful
instruments for the preacher who is dealing with the suffering of the
congregation.

Among the minor genres that Gunkel classified were songs of pilgrimage (see, e.g., Psalm 84), prophetic liturgies (see Psalms 75; 126), and Wisdom poems (see Psalms 1; 37; 49; 73; 112; 127; 128; 133). The last should be interpreted in the context of Wisdom theology (see chapter 9). Perhaps most important for our purposes, among the minor types, are the torah or entrance liturgies, represented in Psalms 15 and 24. Psalm 24:1–2, 7–10 testifies to the magnificent nature of the God we worship. Psalms 15 and 24:3–6 therefore represent priestly admonitions to self-examination before entering to worship such a God. One might say that they are the ancient equivalent of our fencing of the Lord's table. Taken as a whole, both psalms can be used in preaching to proclaim the necessity of worshiping the Lord in spirit and in truth.

The Conversations of the Text

With the Canon

After a preacher has thoroughly analyzed the chosen sermon text, a third indispensable step in developing a sermon is to set the text into conversation with the whole canon of the Bible. This is done for several reasons, which might all be summed up in the Reformation adage that the scriptures interpret the scriptures. It is really only in the light of the whole canon that any one text can be properly interpreted, and thus the text's conversation with the rest of the Bible is indispensable to the preacher.

When the sermon text is set in its canonical context, there may be several practical results: (1) The thought of the sermon text may be greatly enlarged or the text may be clarified. (2) The preacher may be able to see how the text has been used throughout the biblical history and thus trace its trajectory in that history. (3) The canonical context of the text may serve as a corrective of its thought. (4) The preacher may gain valuable suggestions about which New Testament text to pair with the Old.

Two tools are extremely helpful in this regard, a center-column cross-reference Bible and a complete concordance. Let us demonstrate, using our previously analyzed passage, Jeremiah 2:4–13.

Suppose we consider some of the cross-references that a center-column RSV lists for Jeremiah 2:4–13:

v. 5: Isaiah 5:4 and Micah 6:3 both have similar questions addressed to Israel by God, followed by a recounting of what God has done in the past for his people. In short, in these prophetic court cases, God finds his people's sin incomprehensible in the light of his past acts of mercy.

v. 6: Deuteronomy 32:10 also recounts God's care for his people in the wilderness and says that God has kept Israel "as the apple of his eye." God's loving defense of Israel has been as instinctive as a wink is, in defense of the pupil of the eye.

v. 7: The defilement of the land has involved, according to Psalm 106:38, even child sacrifice, in the time of Manasseh, shortly before Jeremiah's ministry.

v. 11: The cross-reference to Isaiah 37:19 shows clearly what Jeremiah means when he speaks of "no gods."

v. 13: Psalm 36:9 describes God in similar terms: "For with thee is the fountain of life; in thy light do we see light" (cf. Jeremiah 17:13).

Now suppose we use a concordance and look up some of the words found in the Jeremiah text. If we look up "living," Jeremiah 2:13, we find:

Ps. 42:2: "My soul thirsts for God, for the living God."

Zech. 14:8: "On that day living waters shall flow out from Jerusalem."

John 4:10–11: "Jesus answered her, 'If you knew the gift of God, and who it is that is saying to you, "Give me a drink," you would have asked him, and he would have given you living water.'"

John 7:38: "He who believes in me, as the scripture has said, 'Out of his heart shall flow rivers of living water.'"

Rev. 7:17: "For the Lamb in the midst of the throne will be their shepherd, and he will guide them to springs of living water; and God will wipe away every tear from their eyes."

The motif of God as the source of living water—that is, life—runs throughout the scriptures. Further, any one of the three New Testament passages listed, in their context, might possibly form the New Testament text to be paired with Jeremiah's oracle.

If we look up "worthless" (which we have translated "empty"), we find Hebrews 6:8: "But if it bears thorns and thistles, it is worthless and near to being cursed; its end is to be burned." As in the Jeremiah passage, the people of God are to be useful to his purpose.

If we look up "profit" (as in "do not profit," which we have translated "useless"), we find Mark 8:36: "For what does it profit a man, to gain the whole world and forfeit his life?"

Only following the true God brings the reward of life. Either the Hebrews or Mark text, in its context, might serve as a passage to pair with Jeremiah's oracle.

In such a manner, we use the scriptures themselves to broaden and clarify the thought of the text and to link it with similar passages and motifs in other parts of the Bible. And all of that becomes material that the preacher possibly may use in the sermon.

If the preacher is familiar with the whole of Jeremiah—and when preaching from a single text, one should familiarize oneself with the viewpoint of the whole book in which it is found—it is also helpful to note that Jeremiah 14:1–10 portrays a drought that has come upon Judah, in fulfillment of God's command to the heavens to be "utterly dry" in 2:12. Also, in Jeremiah 15:18, the persecuted and suffering prophet accuses God of being like "a deceitful brook, like waters that fail"—a vivid contrast, at the depths of Jeremiah's extremity, to his witness to God in 2:13 as the "fountain of living waters." Perhaps someone in the preacher's congregation can identify with such despair and thus be prompted to be open to Jeremiah's message. This brings us to the second conversation of the text.

With the Congregation

When developing sermons, preachers are to listen to their texts *on behalf of their congregations.* The preacher is the point at which text and congregation meet, and so the preacher must ask, "How will my people hear this biblical text? What is the message of God for them in this passage on this particular Sunday morning?" A preacher never hears a text for himself or herself alone, and therefore never simply gives his or her own individual testimony from the text. Indeed, the preacher never separates himself or herself from the congregation. People and pastor are bound up in the bundle of life together. And so the question finally is, "What is the message of God for his people, including me, on this Sunday morning? How do we hear this biblical passage?"

In order to answer those questions, the preacher must have a thorough knowledge of the situation, life, and thought of the congregation. In light of that knowledge, the preacher puts questions to the text, which might be grouped under four headings.

1. What would my people doubt to be true in this text? In relation to Jeremiah 2:4–13, they may doubt that God would ever take them to court: that is, judge them in any way. Or they may not believe that they have gone far away from God and are living lives that are empty and useless for God's purpose. Or they may not think that they are any worse than anyone else (with reference to 2:11). Or they may not see

how God has dealt mercifully with them in the past. If the congregation harbors any of these doubts or fits any of these descriptions, the preacher may have to deal in the sermon with such obstacles to the reception of the text's message.

2. What do my people need to know or to be reminded of from this text? Using the Jeremiah passage, the answer could be varied. The congregation needs to be reminded of God's past mercies shown to them in Jesus Christ, analogous to those mercies shown to Israel (Jer. 2:6). Or they need to be reminded that God has chosen them to be useful for his purpose (Jer. 2:5, 11). Or they need to know that their true glory consists in serving as instruments of God's purpose (Jer. 2:11). Or they need to hear that from God alone, who is "the fountain of living waters," life is given and has been offered to us in Jesus Christ (Jer. 2:13; John 4:10–11; 7:38). Perhaps the sermon will include a number of these points. Certainly they all come out of the text.

3. With what inner feelings, longings, thoughts, and desires of my people does this text connect? Here the preacher might decide that there is in the congregation a sense of meaninglessness and uselessness, of life lived for no good purpose. Or there may be among the people a thirst for communion with God, the fountain of waters, as also expressed in Psalm 42:1–2, which we noted in a cross-reference. Or the people may have a sense of weariness and disgust with the false teachers and gods and goddesses and idols that populate their lives. Or they may want God's reassurance of that living water, that eternal life, offered them in Christ. Certainly the Jeremiah text, paired with a New Testament passage, could speak to all these inner longings.

4. If this text is true, what kind of world do we live in? Or what if the text were not true, what would be the consequences? One can sometimes most vividly illumine the meaning of a text by spelling out its opposite.

By asking such questions of the passage under consideration, the preacher turns up lots of possible sermonic approaches and is then free to choose those that are most pertinent to the congregation's life. There is no doubt that the main thrust of the Jeremiah text is its message of the emptiness and uselessness of human life lived apart from trust in and obedience to the living God. But whether the preacher wants to approach that in the sermon as judgment laid upon the congregation, as in the original Jeremiah passage, or as good news offered by both the Jeremiah oracle and by the New Testament's witness to Christ, or as the answering mercy to the congregation's hunger for God and his living waters, is a decision that only a faithful pastor of a specific congregation can make.

How the pastor decides to approach and preach the text will also determine in large measure with which New Testament text the pastor will pair the Jeremiah oracle. If the pastor wants to speak in terms of judgment, Jeremiah might be paired with Mark 8:34–38 or Hebrews 6:1–8 or a text such as John 3:16–21. If, on the other hand, the approach will be largely in terms of good news, John 4:7–15 or 7:37–44 would serve well as a paired passage. Certainly Revelation 7:13–17 could be the New Testament pairing, if "living water" in the Jeremiah oracle were discussed in terms of eternal life. There are many possibilities for sermon development. These are just a few, by way of example.

The Pairing of Old and New Testament Texts

We do need to give some more general guidelines as to how one goes about choosing a New Testament text to pair with an Old. Some have argued that such pairing is unnecessary; it is sufficient to have only an Old Testament text. After all, goes the reasoning, the Old Testament is fully as much canonical revelation as is the New, and one can therefore allow the Old Testament to stand as word of God to the people in its own right. Indeed, runs the argument, if one always introduces a New Testament text into the sermon, the Old Testament word may be perceived as unnecessary or emptied of its own message or even have the New Testament word read back into it. I would not disagree with any of that, and the pairing of texts, improperly used, can so vitiate the message of the Old Testament that the congregation, like Marcion, regards it as heretical and unnecessary. For example, if one understands the Old Testament solely as law and the New Testament as gospel, or if one considers Israel's religion an early primitive form of faith beyond which we now have progressed in some upward-developing scheme of history, one has totally misunderstood the Book of the Old Covenant, will surely misinterpret it, and will in fact sink into a heretical approach to the Bible.

The fact is, however, that apart from the New Testament, the Old Testament does not belong to the Christian church and is not its book. The Old Testament is the word of God to Israel, and unless we Christians have some connection with Israel, the Old Testament is not spoken to us. But of course we do have such a connection. We are the wild branches grafted into the root of Israel (Rom. 11:17–24), the people who were once "no people," who have now been brought by the blood of Christ into the commonwealth of Israel (Eph. 2:11–22) —as Paul calls us, "the Israel of God" (Gal. 6:16), members now of God's covenant with his chosen people (1 Cor. 11:23–25), adopted as God's children and therefore heirs of the promises to Israel (Gal. 4:1–7). The only one who has made us one with Israel, however, is Jesus Christ, and so to hear the message of the Old Testament rightly, as members of God's covenant people, we must hear the Old Testament in Christ. The pairing of Old and New Testament texts acknowledges that fact.

Second, as we pointed out in chapter 3, the Bible's story is one story. The Old Testament does not end with the fulfillment of God's purposes, either of judgment or of salvation, but only with the promise of that fulfillment to come. Apart from the completion in the New Testament, we never know what happened to God's word. Did he keep his promises to judge and to save, or are those vows still left unfulfilled? Only by pairing texts can we hear the whole story. In implicit acknowledgment of that, preachers who preach only from an Old Testament text usually end their sermons by referring to the gospel in general terms. But the gospel is not given us in general. It is given to us in the specific acts and words recorded in the New Testament, and to preach the gospel, we need to be specific, telling concretely what God has said and done in fulfillment of his purpose.

Third, if we truly believe that Jesus Christ is the Word of God incarnate, the whole Old Testament history gathered up and brought to its completion, then our Lord serves as the final reinterpretation of a sacred history that is interpreted, and reinterpreted, and reinterpreted again throughout the Bible's story. Finally the Word becomes flesh, its full revelation accomplished, and we preach to our people not partial deeds but God's whole act of revealing his person and of reconciling the world to himself.

That is not to say, let it be emphasized, that only partial truth is given us in the Old Testament. All along the way of Israel's history, God speaks his word that is true—illumining, judging, saving, guiding his chosen people. And because we Christians are now also those people, those words are intended for us, and they work their effects on us as they worked on Israel. The Old Testament word may give us a new knowledge of God and communion with him that we have never known before; I know several people who have been converted to the Christian faith by the word of the Old Testament. The Old Testament may illumine a New Testament passage and bring it home to our hearts. It may strengthen us, enlighten us, guide us of itself. The Old Testament word carries the same power that works through the New Testament's revelation, and it is not contrary to or made unnecessary by the revelation in Jesus Christ. One becomes a better Christian by studying the Old Testament. But finally, once for all, God overcomes sin and death and reconciles the whole world to himself through the Old Testament's Word made flesh. God forbid that we do not see the whole history of God's work with his creation in the light of that final act. So we pair Old and New Testament texts.

There are multiple means for doing so. The preacher may want to work with a scheme of promise and fulfillment. When preaching from Jeremiah 2:4–13, for example, the preacher would want to ask how the judgment announced in that passage has been fulfilled. Certainly neither the Old Testament nor the New considers that the prophetic announcements of judgment are entirely fulfilled by the Assyrian and Babylonian exiles. Those announcements continue after 538 B.C. in the writings of the postexilic prophets (see, e.g., Mal. 3:1–5; 4:1–3; Joel 1:1—2:17), and when the New Testament recounts Israel's history, it omits any account of the exile (see the sermons in Acts). The preacher should therefore consider what the New Testament understands to be God's act of judgment, and certainly a passage such as John 3:19–21 gives an answer to that. Is that judgment then worked out in the emptiness and meaninglessness of our lives apart from Christ, or is the judgment reserved until the end of history? The New Testament contains both views, and the preacher will have to decide which text's message to use.

Old and New Testament texts may also be paired on the basis of analogy, and this is probably the most frequent method by which we relate the Old Testament to contemporary Christian life. The preacher asks if Israel's situation in relation to God, in the Jeremiah text, for example, is analogous to ours, and a New Testament text, such as one of those discovered in a cross-reference, is chosen that will illumine or support that fact.

Obviously, texts can also be paired on the basis of common motifs, and our concordance findings with regard to the terms "living water" or "worthless" or "profit" could be helpful here.

Texts can be paired simply on the basis of common thought, with the two Testaments mutually illumining each other. For example, any New Testament passage that sets forth what God has done for us in Christ could illumine Jeremiah's hymnic reference in 2:6 to God's past acts of mercy on Israel's behalf. The comparison is drawn then analogously: As God delivered Israel out of bondage in Egypt, for example, so too has he delivered us from our bondage to sin and death through the cross and the resurrection of Jesus Christ; and Jeremiah's word to us, the new Israel, is then delivered against the backdrop of that mercy.

Finally, there are occasions when Old and New Testament texts may contrast with one another, though this pairing device must be used cautiously, lest the Old Testament be presented as superseded by the New. For the most part, the two Testaments are in remarkable agreement, but one does occasionally find a text such as Genesis 4:7—an example that came up in one of my classes—where the preacher may be led astray theologically unless the New Testament is used as a corrective. Genesis 4:7 seems to contradict Paul's statement that we are slaves of sin (Rom. 6:17) and cannot overcome its power except through God's act in Jesus Christ. In fact, Genesis 4:7 contradicts much of the preaching of the prophets (see Hos. 5:4; Jer. 13:23), and it represents a text that needs badly to be put in canonical context. On the other hand, the Old Testament may occasionally correct the New. For example, 1 Timothy 2:11–14 falls short of a true understanding of Genesis 3, where Adam is equal transgressor with Eve and the domination of men over women is clearly understood as the result of sin. The New Testament itself also corrects 1 Timothy, both in the Gospels and in Paul, and the Timothy text sorely needs to be set in its canonical context.

Outlining the Sermon

Finally, let us say a few words about the necessity of outlining the thought of the *total* sermon before beginning to write it down. Some contemporary homileticians have objected to the practice of outlining because they want to avoid static and nonbiblical sermons, in which the preacher sets forth one point after another, often in relation to a theme divorced from the text. Certainly such sermons are to be avoided, but that should not prevent us from organizing our thought before we write down a sermon in full.

As we have seen, careful and responsible work with the biblical text yields many sermon possibilities. The preacher then has the task of sorting them out and of deciding which to use. Most important, the preacher must organize the whole into a logical, interesting, clear progression of thought *and* experience, that will engage the congregation's hearts and imaginations and minds and wills all the way through the sermon and bring them to the response desired to the word of God. Outlining the thought of the total sermon aids enormously in that task. If we set down our sermon in outline form, we can shape it creatively, eliminate any repetitions, and plan the introduction and illustrations. Above all, we know the conclusion toward which we are driving; we know how the sermon is going to end.

That knowledge prevents an enormous waste of time. Frequently, a preacher will have a good idea, an illustration or a point of entrance into the text, and will sit down and hurriedly begin to write out the result of such an inspiration. Two or three pages are hastily typed and then the preacher gets stuck—from failing to plan the total course of the sermon. The initial start is thrown in the wastebasket and the process starts over, perhaps to be repeated a second or third time.

Until we can jot down the total course of the sermon, or at least think it through in our minds, we should not attempt to shape it into spoken prose. Unified sermons and creative sermons spring from logically organized thought, and the product of that thought should be an outline, on paper or at least in the mind.

Once the outline is completed, the preacher can then bring all of his or her homiletical and rhetorical skills to shaping the words and phrases of the sermon manuscript, so that it announces that word of God that enters people's hearts and minds and wills and, by the inspiration of the Holy Spirit, works God's purpose in them.

CHAPTER 5

Preaching from the Narratives

After a preacher has analyzed a narrative text by rhetorical analysis and submitted it to form criticism, the preacher should picture the story in his or her own imagination. What are the scenes in the story? How are its episodes arranged? Who are the characters? What is told of their personalities and interactions, their conversations and responses? What are the details given? Is there a tension or problem in the story and how is it resolved? What is the course of the particular history recounted?

A preacher does not ask such questions in order to retell the whole biblical story in the sermon. That is seldom necessary, and sermons that are nothing but stories are usually not very effective; the Bible has already told the story probably far more skillfully than can the preacher. Rather, the preacher asks such questions in order to preserve the character of the biblical story as "happening." Far too many preachers extract general religious "principles" or "eternal or spiritual truths" out of biblical stories and thus deprive them of their character of being history in which the congregation is involved. By being analogous to our life, or by foreshadowing our situation with God, or by recounting promises whose fulfillment we have inherited, the Old Testament's narratives involve us in them, and the preacher must not deprive a congregation of that involvement. Otherwise the stories are likely to appear to a congregation as quaint but irrelevant fairy tales from a distant past. The task is to picture the Old Testament story in our mind's eye, and so the first question to ask of any narrative text is, What is going on in the story?

For example, suppose we are preaching from Deuteronomy 30:15–20: "See, I have set before you this day life and good, death and evil." According to this text, if Israel obeys the commandments of God by loving him and walking in his ways, she will have life in the promised land (see vs. 19–20).

The temptation of the preacher in using this text is to employ it in a moralistic fashion, to turn it into a legalistic exhortation to the congregation to choose the way of life and thus to live, apart from any reference to the history that is being worked out by God. And of course moralistic preachers have all sorts of ways they define the way of life: You must do such and such if you want to be a Christian.

But there is a story taking place in this text. Israel is under way, halfway between her redemption out of bondage in Egypt and her final inheritance of God's promised blessings in the settlement in the promised land. She has been redeemed, but she has not entered into her final fulfillment. She stands on the eastern side of the Jordan, looking over into the promised land. And Moses tells her here that only if she loves God with all her heart and soul and strength, only if she obeys him in a response of love to his love, will she finally enter into the fullness of abundant life. God wants life for his people, but he offers no cheap grace. They must love him in return as he has first loved them. They can still fail to inherit the final fruits of their redemption.

Having established what is happening in the story, the preacher then sets it in conversation with the rest of the canon, as we discussed in chapter 4. In relation to narrative texts, that also means inquiring after the outcome of the story. According to Deuteronomy 30:15–20, God spoke a word to his people there in the plains of Moab, through the preaching of Moses. What became of that word? Did it work its effects on the future, or was it allowed to fall aside, according to the rest of the canon? Obviously, the whole Deuteronomic history, of which Deuteronomy is the beginning, tells us that Israel did not love God in the obedience of faith, but rebelled against him and went after other gods. So the word was worked out, and Israel lost her good life in the land, as God had promised she would do.

What then? Was that the end of the story? Was God's purpose to give life to his people finally defeated? We have to ask what the outcome of the story was in the total canonical context. When we do that, we find God in his Son Jesus Christ once again redeeming the people of God out of slavery—the New Testament recapitulating the story of the Old Testament—and that immediately involves the Christian congregation in the conversation with the text. We, the new Israel in Christ in the church, have once more been delivered from bondage—this time from our bondage to sin and death—but, like Israel, we have not yet entered into our final fulfillment. We too are under way. "Not that I have already obtained," says Paul, ". . . but I press on" (Phil. 3:12). At that midpoint between our redemption and the final full inheritance of its fruits, we too are confronted with the words of the new Moses, if we pair the Deuteronomy text with Matthew 7:13–14. We too are asked to choose life or death:

> Enter by the narrow gate; for the gate is wide and the way is easy, that leads to destruction, and those who enter by it are many. For the gate is narrow and the way is hard, that leads to life, and those who find it are few.

Once again the call is made to respond in the obedience of faith. Once again God sets before us life and death, blessing and curse. And he wants so very much for us to choose life.

> One can almost hear the great voice, resonant with mercy, speaking out of the great heart of love: "O my people, choose life this day. O my people, choose life."[1]

By clinging to the narrative of the biblical history, by asking what is happening in it, and by inquiring what its outcome was in the total canonical context, we avoid turning the story into a timeless truth. We prevent the text from being moralistically applied to our lives, as some eternal legal principle. And we anchor the whole in the history which God in fact has brought about and in which we in fact now stand, as his new covenant people. We set our people in that real story, that great cosmic drama, that God is working out.

Those are the questions to ask of every narrative in the Old Testament: What is going on in it and what was its outcome? To give another example, Sunday school lessons often use the Joseph stories as moral lessons: As Joseph forgave his brothers, so should we; as Joseph learned humility, so should we. But that does not at all get at what is happening in the Joseph stories, as Genesis 45:4–8 and 50:19–20 so clearly tell us. God is at work in the Joseph stories, hidden behind all the hatred and deception of the brothers and behind all the temptations and imprisonment and successes of Joseph in Egypt. God is at work to keep his promise to make of Israel a great nation and a blessing in the midst of the earth. "You meant evil against me," Joseph tells his brothers; "but God meant it for good; to bring it about that many people should be kept alive, as they are today" (50:20). If we relate that to the whole canon, then, and see it as analogous to our lives as the new Israel in Christ, is that not the God we also see at work in the cross of Christ? We meant evil against our Lord at Golgotha, but God meant it for good, to bring it about that many should have life as at this day. And is that holy story, then, not our one true hope midst all the agonies and hatreds and wrongs of our present day?

Let us give one other example. Suppose we are preaching from the promise to Abraham, Genesis 12:3: "I will bless those who bless you, and him who curses you I will curse." Right there at the beginning of the story, we are told that our life or death depends on our attitude toward Abraham, but we are not to construct some sermon from that on anti-Semitism, for example. We do not turn the story into a statement of a general principle. Rather, we ask what is going on, and the answer clearly is that God is working out his purpose through Abraham and his descendants to bring blessing on all the families of the earth. It is no accident, therefore, that Paul, in Galatians 3:6–9 and Romans 4, deals with the outcome of the promise and shows that our life or death depends on our attitude toward that descendant of Abraham, Jesus Christ. We ask what is going on in the story and what its outcome was, and we show how we are involved in that which has taken place.

To be sure, there are often times when a preacher does not want to deal with the outcome of a particular Old Testament story in the total historical canonical context. Otherwise, the preacher could end up simply repeating every Sunday how the Old Testament has been fulfilled in the New. Rather, the preacher wants to remain within the confines of one Old Testament narrative and relate that to the congregation's life. This is done most frequently by the use of analogy, by drawing parallels between the relationship with God portrayed in the Old Testament story and our relationship with him.

For example, are we in the church not very much like Israel there at the foot of Mount Sinai, in Exodus 32, when she made the golden calf? We Christians too are a bunch of rescued refugees, delivered out of bondage, and we Christians too have entered into covenant with our Lord and promised, "All that the LORD has spoken we will do." But there is an awful lot of desert out there in our lives, and we need something or someone to get us through it. So we forget our God, as Israel forgot hers, and we ask some modern equivalent of Aaron to make us substitute gods to go before us.

> Faced with tension and anxiety in our daily round, unable to rest at night, we rely not on the peace and strength of our Lord but on the idols of tranquilizers and sleeping pills to keep us serene and relaxed and unafraid. And we demand that some doctor become Aaron for us and write us a prescription for Valium.
>
> Or confronted with the terrifying epidemic of AIDS, our society does not repent of sexual promiscuity or return to obedience to the commands of God for the use of our bodies. Instead it looks to substitute saviors—to condoms and education—to save us. And it requires that our research scientists play the role of Aaron and quickly find a vaccine that will protect us against the consequences of our disobedience.

Obviously, the preacher sets the stage for such parallels by describing Israel's situation in the Old Testament story. Or sometimes, just that of an individual is portrayed. For example, I wanted to pair the similar thought found in Genesis 28:15 and Philippians 1:6, and the point of my sermon was to assure the congregation that God would fulfill the purpose for which he originally called them. But that aim was accomplished by getting the congregation into the story taking place.

About three days out, at a place called Luz, Jacob makes his camp for the night. Propping his head upon a stone for a pillow, he falls into a guilty sleep, which is interrupted by a very strange dream. Jacob sees the angels, the messengers of God, ascending and descending a ramp that leads from heaven to earth, going about their business of carrying out God's orders on earth. . . . Jacob wakes with a shudder, and in shivering awe he comes to the realization that this is none other than the place where heaven and earth meet. This is the gate of heaven. The Lord has invaded my world, he realizes. I am not alone on this journey.

Somewhere on our journey through life, we all have had a similar experience—that heaven has invaded our ordinary realm, that we are not alone in our world, but that we are accompanied on our pilgrimage by a mysterious presence, whose name is Jesus Christ. Surely if ever heaven descended to this earth, it did so in that man of Nazareth, and now he walks the road with us, as we go on our common journeys.

Genesis 28:10–17 and Philippians 1:1–11 were the paired texts for the sermon, and since Jacob's dream in Genesis involves the meeting place of heaven and earth, the only proper New Testament parallel to that is the figure of Jesus Christ. The preacher should not allegorize Jacob's dream and try to apply his words to some contemporary place, such as a church building or a retreat site. Heaven and earth have met, for us, only in the person of our Lord. The analogies must be based upon that parallel.

In drawing such parallels, we must not think that the preacher then abandons the Old Testament text. No, the sermon remains with the story of Jacob, and it is out of his experience that the points of the sermon are formed. The sermon moves constantly back and forth between Jacob's experiences and those of the congregation. But the parallel serves to show how we are related to Jacob and finally anchors the message of the sermon in the Christian gospel.

The Text as Control of Imagination

When dealing with the narrative texts of the Old Testament, the preacher must let the chosen text act as the control of imagination. Because we are to picture the scenes and characters of biblical stories in our mind's eye, the vividness of those portrayals may cause our imaginations to run away with us. If that happens, we may very well distort the intention and message of the biblical text and end up preaching not the word of God but our own fanciful meditations. The latter very often are the stuff of so-called biblical novels, poems, and movies, but they bear little resemblance to the actual word of the Bible. They may sometimes result in good literature, such as Christopher Fry's imaginative biblical scenes in his play *A Sleep of Prisoners*, but they are not a substitute for the canonical word, and they are not to be preached as such. Rather, the Old Testament story itself gives the limits of what should and should not be included in the sermon.

For example, it is very easy to sentimentalize some Old Testament stories. Laban's famous covenant statement at Mizpah comes immediately to mind: "The LORD watch between you and me, when we are absent one from the other" (Gen. 31:49). Popular piety has lifted that from its context and turned it into a loving farewell, and sermons on the text may be tempted to do the same. But the actual story shows that Laban is saying, "Watch it, Jacob! The Lord is the guarantor of this covenant, and he will punish you if you break it." Similarly, who could not let imagination run rampant with regard to Jacob's distaste for Leah (Gen. 29:25), or the anguish of Moses' mother as she consigns him to the basket in the river (Ex. 2:3)? Who could not elaborate on the feelings of Elisha when Elijah is taken up (2 Kings 2) or on the love of Jonathan for David (1 Sam. 18:1–4)? But the stories themselves elaborate on none of these things, and neither must the sermons from them. The biblical text is the control for the preacher's imagination.

Similarly, many preachers inject their own imaginary psychological musings into the biblical stories, giving us long accounts of what Abraham thought and felt as he journeyed to Moriah to sacrifice Isaac (Gen. 22:1–19), or what Moses experienced as he encountered the burning bush (Ex. 3:1–6), or what Elijah feared as he fled from Jezebel (1 Kings 19:1–14). In all these instances, there is some indication in the texts of how the stories' characters reacted, but they are very limited indications, and the preacher should not go beyond them. The biblical texts tell us as much as we need to know to make their messages clear. When we go beyond their limits, we begin to distort their messages, usually exaggerating the human element in the stories that are intended to be principally about God and thus diluting or corrupting the primary thrust of the biblical word.

One of the marvelous characteristics of Old Testament stories is their realism about human beings, and that realism too should act as a control of the preacher's imagination. Like all great literature, the Old Testament's stories deal with the basics of human life. Genesis, for example, treats all the great themes of our existence—life and death, love and hate, sin and goodness, work and rest, slavery and freedom. Within those themes, all human relationships are portrayed—of husband with wife, brother with brother, parents with children, male with female, slave with free, relative with relation, citizen with foreigner. Second, however, human beings are portrayed in all their glory and misery—in faith and doubt, in decency and deceit, in courage and fear, in joy and anguish. There are no whitewashed saints in the Old Testament's narratives. (The only exception is David in Kings and Chronicles, but alongside these idealized portraits are left the vivid portrayals in 1–2 Samuel.) Even the greatest leaders are shown in their fallible human condition. Abraham is a liar, who would save his own neck. Jacob is a scoundrel from beginning to end. Moses is a murderer fleeing for his life, David an opportunist politician and a terrible father, with adultery and murder on his record. Solomon becomes a model of how not to be a king, Jeroboam the prototype of all idolators. Samuel raises sons who are crooks; Saul is consumed by hatred. One cannot idealize the human condition if one wishes to preach from the Old Testament's stories, and that realistic assessment of our human nature should act as a control on our sermons even if, unfortunately, it has not permeated much of our Sunday school material.

Very often the writers and compilers of the Old Testament insert interpretive guides into their stories. For example, at the beginning of the story of the flood in Genesis 6:5–8, we have the Yahwist's interpretation of how we are to understand the catastrophe that follows: It is the pouring out of God's grieving heart in reaction to the evil hearts of human beings. Or in Joshua 21:43–45, the Deuteronomic historians tell us what the Hexateuch has been about: It is the story of the fulfillment of God's promises to Abraham. Or in the seemingly totally secular story of David and Bathsheba, the writer tells us that God is not absent from this history and that everything that follows in David's life will be subject to the pleasure or displeasure of God (2 Sam. 11:27b). Indeed, in the books of Kings, the writers furnish us with a whole series of interpretive introductions to the histories of the kings (see 1 Kings 15:1–3; 22:51–52 for examples). Such guides to interpretation then also become controls for the preacher. The Bible's interpretation of its stories are part of the revelation given to us and should not be ignored in a sermon's hermeneutics.

Indeed, when preaching from the Old Testament's narratives, we must be willing to take them at face value and to accept the scripture's interpretation of the events it recounts to us. Some well-meaning commentators have attempted to "demythologize" the Old Testament. For example, they would maintain that the stories of the plagues in Exodus reflect natural hazards of life on the Nile: Every now and then Egypt does have a natural plague of locusts or of frogs, or the waters of the Nile become polluted and undrinkable. One commentator has even written that the plague on the domestic animals "may have been any one of a number of diseases, such as anthrax or foot-and-mouth disease."[2] The plague of darkness was a sandstorm.[3] The slaying of the Egyptian firstborn may have been due to infantile diarrhea.[4] By their reinterpretation of what the Bible says, such commentators lose the revelation given by the exodus stories—that God is Lord over nature and empire and the gods of Egypt.

Not only do some commentators engage in such demythologizing, but some will also go to great lengths to soften offensive details in the Old Testament's stories. To be sure, sometimes such attempts mirror the reaction of a congregation to an offending story, and so that reaction must be dealt with in the sermon. This is the beginning of a sermon on Genesis 22:1–19, the story of the sacrifice of Isaac:

> The scripture passage that we heard for our Old Testament lesson may seem like a monstrous story to us—that command from God to Abraham: "Take your son, your only son Isaac, whom you love, and go to the land of Moriah, and offer him there as a burnt offering upon one of the mountains of which I shall tell you." That seems like an awful and simply unbelievable command for any God of love to give.
>
> And so down through the years, Sunday school lessons and preachers and we ourselves have tried to soften the story. Abraham came from a pagan background in Mesopotamia, goes the reasoning, and so he just mistakenly believed that God wanted him to sacrifice Isaac. The great Danish theologian Kierkegaard even made up a series of fanciful endings to the story. Abraham killed himself instead of Isaac, imagined Kierkegaard. Or Abraham pretended that his actions were the result of temporary insanity. Indeed, even the wife of Luther once objected to the Genesis account. "Martin," she said to her husband, "I don't believe God would ask anyone to sacrifice his only son."
>
> But for all of our objections to the Bible's words, the story means for us to take it literally. "God tested Abraham, and said to him,

'Take your son, your only son Isaac whom you love, and sacrifice him in the land of Moriah.' "

Now why? Why would God demand such a thing?

When preaching from the narratives, we need to take them at face value, as they are intended to be taken. Only then will we be able to uncover the message or re-create the experience that any particular story wishes to convey. We may initially have to deal with congregational offense at the story. But our job is not to apologize for the scriptures. It is to preach them.

This also means that the task of the preacher, when dealing with Old Testament narrative, is not suddenly to turn into historical critic and try to preach "what really happened." In the first place, the historical reconstruction of Israel's history up until the time of the monarchy is being increasingly shown by scholars to be fraught with difficulty, and if the proclamation of the gospel is to wait on scholarly consensus, it may never take place. While the outline of Israel's history in John Bright's classic *A History of Israel*[5] can be accepted as reliable, Bright himself would be the first to acknowledge that preachers are not to preach his reconstruction of Israel's history but the Bible's interpretation of it. It is very likely, for example, that not all the forebears of what became the later twelve tribes of Israel were in Egypt at the time of the exodus. But both Old Testament (Deut. 26:5–9) and New (1 Cor. 10:1–4) see that redemptive event as constitutive of the life of all Israel, and the preacher's task is to understand why such an interpretation of the exodus is given and how it is in fact true. If the preacher can arrive at such understanding, he or she then may begin to grasp how the scriptures present the sacred history and why, for example, Paul can say that all baptized Christians die with Christ, even though we are years distant from the original event on Golgotha.

The preacher can also count it as a given that the biblical history, from the time of Abraham on, is based on actual history—no people can or ever would invent such a story of its repeated failure vis-à-vis its God, nor could it invent a life for itself so drastically different from that of its neighbors. Anyone who would deny the Old Testament story is confronted with the questions of where this unique covenant people came from, of what sustained its life, and of how it managed to survive the vicissitudes of its turbulent history, just as anyone who questions the New Testament's history has to answer the same questions about the church. The point is, however, that the Bible's history is told in such a way that it can repeatedly be the history of each succeeding generation of believers. It is told in those kinds of literature that can involve us and that can become the story of our lives also. Thus, to ask the question "What really happened?" and to try to preach the answer in a sermon is to tell the biblical story in a way that it does not wish to be told.

Conversely, when preaching from the narratives, the preacher should cling to the character of the biblical story as having taken place in a specific geographical place at a particular time in world history. One of the difficulties that many lay people have with the Bible is that they envision it as some sort of sacred object, containing magical stories from a never-never land that does not exist. The Bible then becomes a magical charm that the young bride bears down the aisle or that, carried in a pocket, deflects a bullet from a soldier's heart, but for them the stories in the Bible have nothing to do with this world or with actual everyday life. The Old Testament's concrete details of time, place, geography, and culture, if mentioned in the sermon, serve to anchor its stories firmly in history and to convey their this-worldly character. God has acted in the actual land of Palestine, in events related to actual travels and migrations of peoples and in relation to particular Mesopotamian and Egyptian empires, and sermons from the narratives of the Old Testament need to make that clear.

This further means that the preacher should never turn an Old Testament story into an allegory, in which the details in the story are made to stand for something else. For example, sermons have been preached in which the mark that God put on Cain (Gen. 4:15) has been interpreted as the sign of the cross; or the fact that Joseph was thrown into a pit (Gen. 37:24) has been made the symbol of our spiritual lostness—"All the world's in a well"; or the empty vessels of 2 Kings 4:3 have been interpreted as symbols of our emptiness that Christ can fill. Such allegorical interpretation removes the biblical narrative from history and thus deprives us of our participation in the one history that leads to our salvation.

To be sure, there are some symbolic passages in the Old Testament. For example, the figure of chaos, in Genesis 1:2, takes on a wide range of meanings: It is pathless waste through which the nations of the world wander in their affairs, without wisdom or guidance (Job 12:24); or the symbol of the powerlessness and delusion of those who worship false gods (Isa. 41:29; 44:9); or the figure of a life apart from truth and purpose (Isa. 45:19) that brings no result (Isa. 49:4); or the howling waste through which the Israelites wander for forty years in their desert years (Deut. 32:10). Careful exegesis of a chosen passage on the basis of the original Hebrew can uncover such meanings. Nevertheless, the principal questions to put to a narrative are: What is God doing in this story? What is going on? and What is the outcome of the action? In short, the preacher preaches the narrative, rather than the symbolic character of the text.

There is one section of the Old Testament, however, that is meant to be symbolic in its entirety.

The Special Character of Genesis 1–11

It is important for the homiletician to realize that the so-called primeval history in Genesis is not intended by its writers or compilers to be a history of the beginnings of the world. If we try to turn Adam and Eve into an original couple from whom the human race has sprung, then the most important date in history becomes the time of their disobedience in the Garden of Eden, and all sin becomes the inherited result of their fall, rather than our responsibility. Also, one is left with irrelevant questions such as "Where did Cain's wife come from?" (Gen. 4:17). No. The primeval stories in these eleven chapters are intended by the Bible itself to be the story of us all. This is a portrayal of the relation of every human being and community with God. As in Genesis 1, all are dependent for the order and structure of the world on God's faithfulness in holding back the chaos. All males and females have been created in the image of God and given dominion over the earth, under the lordship of God. Or as in Genesis 2, all are the careful creations of God the Potter, shaped in intimate fashion in his hands and sustained alive by his breath of life (cf. Job 10:8–10; Ps. 139:13; 104:29–30). All are the recipients of God's merciful gifts of beauty and food (Gen. 2:9), of meaningful work (2:15), and of loving human relationships (2:18–25). All are creatures subject to the guiding will of our Creator, who asks from us obedience (2:16–17). Spelled out in these first two chapters of Genesis are the mercy and intention of God for all human life.

By the same token, the stories that follow in Genesis 3–11 are portrayals of us all, and how well they capture our common nature! Like Eve, we are zealous to justify our religious practices, but we do it by setting up our own laws—God never said to Eve, "Do not *touch* the tree" (3:1–3). And our sin always looks like the right thing to do at the time, just as the fruit looks so desirable to Eve (3:6). But the sin is that our "right thing" disobeys God's command. And how like Adam we are in our complicity in sin; we just go along (3:6)! Or how accurately the story has captured our propensity to pass the buck when we are called to take responsibility for our actions (3:12–13).

Then, like Cain, how envious we become of God's grace poured out on someone else (4:4–5; cf. the older brother in the parable of the Prodigal Son). And like the tower builders in their cooperative enterprise in Genesis 11:1–9, how tempted we are to seek our own fame and security, rather than looking to God for the preservation of our life. Indeed, in the Babel story, we are portrayed at the height of our creativity, and there, when everything is going right, it says, we are most tempted to sin.

But most importantly, at every juncture we are responsible to our God for our actions (3:11, 13; 4:10; 6:6–8; 11:5–9). We bear the consequences of our disobedience of God's loving will. And yet God weeps over our unfaithfulness (6:6) and constantly, mercifully, works to overcome the effects of our sin.

There are no historical times and places in these stories of Genesis 1–11. They are the portrayal of every time and of every place and of every human being in relation to God, but they set the stage for everything that follows in the sacred history. They tell why God called Abraham and gave promises to him and why God made the people Israel. They explain why our Creator, through two thousand years of history, has struggled and wept, judged and forgiven, molded and guided a people chosen for himself. They illumine God's purpose in the world and the goal of all his activity—to make a new community for himself that knows how to live in obedience and faithfulness and justice under his guiding lordship, in an earth restored to its original good and abundance. Unless a congregation comes to understand these initial tales, they are very likely not fully to understand anything else in the Bible.

The preacher can preach from some of the magnificent details of these stories to portray our sinful life in relation to God and our distortion of his good intentions for us. Few congregations fail to respond to the pictures of themselves that these stories furnish.

On the other hand, these stories can also be used as texts for presentations of basic Christian doctrine. For example, Genesis 2:7 sets forth biblical anthropology in one brief statement: We are essentially flesh, sustained alive by the breath of God, a view that contrasts sharply with the Greek understanding of human beings as essentially soul incarnated in flesh. In the biblical view, then, when we die God withdraws his breath of life and we return to dead physical matter: "Dust thou art, and unto dust shalt thou return." Eternal life therefore must consist in the re-creation and resurrection of the body, which is an essential part of us.

To give another example for doctrinal preaching, in Genesis 1 we have the basic theological presentation of the Creator's relation with his creation. No doctrine has been more neglected by the pulpit in our time, and yet no doctrine is more important for the theological developments taking place in our society. Most of current feminist theology, modeled after Tillichian understandings, views God and the creation as one, with the life of the Deity permeating all things and persons. Thus, our milieu and we ourselves have come to be viewed by some as divine. God is pictured as giving birth to the world; some even understand the world as God's body. But in Genesis 1 and throughout the scriptures, the Creator is totally other, above and beyond all creation as its sovereign Lord. He works with his creation solely through the instruments of his Word (cf. John 1) and Spirit, and though creation should pass away, God never passes away (Isa. 51:6; Matt. 24:35; Ps. 90:1–2). He therefore is able to take those who love him into an eternal fellowship with himself. That is an indispensable basis for confidence and hope in an atomic age, when human beings are liable at any time to blow up their world.

To cite another example, the expression of biblical faith in Genesis 1:28 has often been blamed for the ecological crisis, since human beings are given "dominion" over the earth. It is therefore assumed that humans can do with the creation whatever they like. But a proper understanding of the image of God in Genesis 1:26–28 reveals us to be but mirrors of our Creator, reflecting in our created nature the One who has made us. Apart from God, we cannot be comprehended; our very beings point to our Sovereign; and in the whole of Genesis 1, we are totally dependent on God for the structure and order of our universe. Throughout the scriptures, then, we are never given absolute dominion over the earth but are always responsible to our Creator for the stewardship of his creation (see, e.g., Ps. 24:1; 100:3; Ezek. 33:23–29). When we violate God's will, we are cast off the land (Gen. 4:12; Jer. 7:8–15; Deut. 30:17–18; Luke 19:41–44). As Psalm 39:12 so beautifully expresses it, we are God's passing guests, sojourners in his world. The ecological crisis has come about, not because we have obeyed God's will but because we have disobeyed it.

These first eleven chapters of Genesis also paint the universal backdrop for the Bible's entire history of sin and redemption, and Israel and the church then come onstage only against that background.

Notably, however, even these theological bases of our faith are presented to us in the form of stories, and the preacher will have much more success in presenting doctrine from the pulpit if he or she preserves its narrative character, rather than turning it into an abstract presentation of general theological truth. These are the things God has done, Genesis 1–11 is saying to us, and these stories portray how we all have responded to his creating love.

The stories in Genesis 1–11 are also foundational for topical preaching. Consider some of the burning topics of our day that are touched on in the primeval history: the relation of male and female and the "battle of the sexes," God's intention for marriage, the good gifts of the body and of sex, daily work and rest, astrology, capital

punishment, science and religion, the sabbath, lying, beauty, temptation, and responsibility. In these stories, God's attitudes and intentions toward all these areas of human life are set forth. If the preacher
starts with Genesis and, as is fitting in all topical preaching, then
investigates how these subjects are treated throughout the canon, he
or she may cast the light of the word of God on some hotly debated
issues of our day. Moreover, the preacher will not be giving personal
opinion, which is powerless to effect change, but will be anchoring the
sermon in the word of God, which has the power to transform human
life and society.

More About Genesis 12–50

We have already said a good deal about how the rest of the stories in
Genesis are to be approached. The context of all of them is God's
promise to Abraham, and most of them deal with the fulfillment of the
promise of descendants, although Genesis 23, for example, shows how
Abraham acquires a foretaste of the fulfillment of the promise of land.
When the patriarch buys that field at Machpelah as a burial ground for
Sarah, he acquires a down payment on God's promise. The story could
be paralleled with the foretaste we have of the kingdom's messianic
banquet, which we know when we celebrate the Lord's Supper.

Many of these patriarchal stories form such foretastes or types of
that which is to follow. For example, circumcision in Genesis 17 is the
Old Testament type or parallel to our baptism, although 1 Peter
3:20–22 compares the story of Noah typologically with baptism—a
tricky parallelism, it might be said, since the earth is not washed clean
of sin by the flood in Noah's story; rather, the water of the flood is
judgment on the world, the water of baptism its salvation, and we have
one of those rare legitimate contrasts that the preacher can draw
between Old Testament and New.

Nowhere is typology more in evidence than in the story of the
sacrifice of Isaac, and it can profitably be paired with Mark 15:6–39,
for example.

> Surely here too in Mark we have the picture of a Father and a Son, a
> Son and a Father, going both of them together to Moriah. Later
> legend even has it that the place of Moriah became the site of the
> city of Jerusalem. But whether that is true or not, the Father and his
> beloved Son go up to Jerusalem together. "My Father and I are
> one," Jesus said. He makes his last journey in the company of God
> his Father. Father and Son, Son and Father—they go "both of them
> together."
> The Son Jesus trusts his Father with his life, just as Isaac trusted

Abraham. But there is no record of anything they said to one another on the journey—only that brief conversation in the garden, a little way from the hill of sacrifice: "My Father, if it be possible, let this cup pass from me." Apparently the answer Jesus received was the same one Abraham implied to Isaac: "The sacrifice must be carried out, my son."

Like Isaac, Jesus begins to carry the wood up the hill to the place of offering, until he is relieved of the burden by Simon of Cyrene. Like Isaac, Jesus is laid out upon the wood. And as the knife was raised over Isaac's breast, so the hammers are raised over the nails for Jesus.

But here our stories become very different, do they not? There is no rescue for Jesus—no last-minute voice from heaven to save him from the awful death, no substitutionary ram, no rescuing Elijah to take away the pain. . . .

Could it be that the Son of God had to be so cursed by his Father for a little while, because God really meant that promise to Abraham . . . to bring blessing on all the families of the earth?

This sermon used the two scripture texts typologically but then moved into a discussion of the fulfillment of the promise to Abraham.

There are multitudinous texts in the patriarchal stories that can be used of promise and fulfillment. For example, there is the marvelous story in Genesis 18:16–33 of Abraham's conversation with the Lord. Abraham knows that human beings should not question God, and he approaches his Lord in all humility: "Behold, I have taken upon myself to speak to the Lord, I who am but dust and ashes" (v. 27); we could profitably learn that attitude. Yet Abraham, in a boldness approaching that of the psalmists, demands justice from his God: "Shall not the Judge of all the earth do right?" (v. 25). That with which the Lord replies is incredible mercy instead: "For the sake of ten [righteous], I will not destroy [Sodom]." God will forgive beyond all requirements of justice, and, of course, the outcome is that for the sake of one righteous man named Jesus Christ, God will not destroy us either (Luke 23:1–25).

Sometimes Genesis texts have been used as hopeful promises for our future. For example, in the story of Joseph in Genesis 37, the brothers see their idle, pampered sibling approaching them across the field, and they say to one another, "Here comes this dreamer. Come now, let us kill him . . . , and we shall see what will become of his dreams" (vs. 19–20). In an inspired vision, the Southern Christian Leadership Conference inscribed those words of Joseph's brothers on a plaque for the wall of the motel in Memphis where Martin Luther King, Jr., was shot to death. That is a proclamation of confidence in God's future, for in Genesis, Joseph's dreams did indeed come true because they were given by God. If we dream God's dreams, we know they will come to pass.

Surely these Genesis stories vividly portray the unearned grace contained in God's promises to the patriarchal families. When Abraham and Sarah are told they will have a son, in fulfillment of the promise of descendants, two of the narrators tell us that Abraham and Sarah did not believe God's word. In Genesis 17 from the Priestly writers, Abraham falls on his face in worship, but he also laughs (v. 17), just as the Yahwist's tale in Genesis 18 records Sarah giggling at the door of her tent (v. 12); neither of them had great faith in God's promise of an heir.

So too do these Genesis stories record what it costs to be the elected people of God. Jacob wrestles with God and prevails and receives the blessing, because he persists in clinging to his mysterious assailant. But Jacob-become-Israel is also wounded in his encounter with the divine (Gen. 32:13–32); it costs Israel something to be the elected people of the Lord, just as it costs the church to be the heir of that gracious choosing.

Finally, the patriarchal stories also lay the groundwork for much of Christian doctrine. For example, in the Elohist's version of the promise of descendants to Abraham, in Genesis 15:1–5, the patriarch at first exhibits doubt much like ours. When God tells him that his "reward"—that is, his progeny—will be numerous, Abraham blasphemously contradicts his God with the statement that the son of his slave woman will be his heir; once again, Abraham does not deserve the promise. But then when God takes Abraham out in the night and shows him the innumerable stars and promises him, "So shall your descendants be," Abraham believes the Lord, and God "reckons it to him as righteousness" (v. 6). That is the Bible's first presentation of the doctrine of justification by faith—placed once again, it should be noted, in a narrative context. Faith, according to the story, consists in clinging to the promises of God, and that faith makes Abraham accounted righteous in the eyes of the Lord. The same God is at work in these stories as is at work in the New Testament's record, and these Old Testament narratives can be used vividly to witness to his nature.

Creating a People: Exodus–Joshua

No material in the scriptures is more suited to the education of a congregation about its nature and function as the people of God than are the narratives found in the books of Exodus through Joshua. In these stories, Israel is created, and because the church is the new

Israel in Jesus Christ, these stories are also the portrayal of our creation and life as the covenant people of God.

Our life as the church has its beginning in the mercy of God: "God shows his love for us in that while we were yet sinners Christ died for us" (Rom. 5:8). How the story of Israel in Egypt illumines the meaning of that! That disparate bunch of seminomadic wanderers knows nothing of the God of the patriarchs. They are far from being a united people of one race or clan or background (cf. Ex. 12:38), but they share the common condition of having fallen into slavery to Rameses II, and they groan under their bondage and cry out for help to some quarter. "And God heard their groaning, and God remembered his covenant with Abraham, with Isaac, and with Jacob. And God saw the people of Israel, and God knew their condition" (Ex. 2:24–25).

"God remembered." What a fantastic revelation that is to hear that God remembers us! You and I forget the names of people we have met several times over. A year's separation and someone, even a dearest friend, is out of sight, out of mind. Memories fade. Even our greatest heroes become nothing but nameless statues on a street corner. We human beings forget, but God remembers us. . . .

God sees our affliction also. . . . "If I say, let only darkness cover me," prays the psalmist, "even the darkness is not dark to thee; the night is bright as the day; for darkness is as light with thee." We are never hidden from God. He always sees us, hidden though we be in some dark valley of the shadow . . . and the look is one of un-dimmed mercy, the gaze that of a loving Father toward his child. God sees that you hurt, and he sees all your suffering.

But ours is not a Father who is a cool, detached observer of his children. You all know fathers who, when they get home from work, do not want to be bothered with their children. Just leave such fathers in peace with the evening paper or before the television set. Let someone else in the family deal with the hassle, the discipline, the crying. . . . But our heavenly Father is the one, above all human fathers, who is willing to be bothered. He is a God who refuses to shed his burden of troubled care. He is a God who hears our cry and who comes down, who stoops, and, yes, who shares our condition.

The God of the exodus and of the cross delivers us from our slavery, and it is that redemption alone that creates us a people. Very often we have nothing in common with one another except the fact that we have all been redeemed together, and so we are joined in a common memory and in a common worship of our Redeemer. But if that memory of our redemption fades in the church and we forget what

God has done for us, then, like Israel, we too cease to be a people (cf. Hos. 1:8–9; Ps. 106:21–23).

Unearned, undeserved, and long before we knew anything of him (a fact symbolized in the rite of infant baptism), the redemption price of our release out of bondage to sin and death was paid by our Redeemer God. But a Redeemer in the Bible's understanding is one who buys back a *family member* out of slavery (cf. Lev. 25:47–55), and so God, by redeeming Israel out of Egypt, adopts that people as his son (cf. Hos. 11:1; Jer. 31:20; Isa. 1:2; Ex. 4:22; Deut. 32:10). It is the same image that Paul uses in Galatians 4:4–7. By his redemption of us in Jesus Christ, God has adopted us as his sons and daughters, and only by receiving that redemption by faith can we claim to be God's children and name him "Father."

God's release of us out of slavery, however, is done for a purpose, and this too the story of Israel can make very clear to a congregation. Born a people solely by the mercy and love and power of God (cf. Ex. 14:13–14), Israel is brought to Sinai, the mount of covenant, to hear of her place in the purpose of God. Now she is called to respond to the prior actions of God; now she is asked to love the Lord in return for his love.

Israel's love for God can be manifested by obeying his commandments (Ex. 19:5), and in the exodus story such obedience will serve God's purpose. Israel will, by her obedience, become his "kingdom of priests and a holy nation" (19:6). That is, she will be set apart ("holy") to serve God's purpose alone, and she will become priests who mediate the knowledge and love of God to the rest of the world. This is exactly what the church also is called to be and do, according to 1 Peter 2:9–10. It uses the language of Exodus 19 to give us our purpose in the world.

> But you are a chosen race, a royal priesthood, a holy nation, God's own people, that you may declare the wonderful deeds of him who called you out of darkness into his marvelous light. Once you were no people but now you are God's people; once you had not received mercy but now you have received mercy.

We are to "declare the wonderful deeds" of God who has redeemed us and made us his people. There in a few brief words is the statement of the mission of the church—to witness in word and deed to the wonderful things that God has said and done. Everything else in the church's life is secondary to that purpose.

As Israel hears at Sinai, however, the people of God can fulfill that purpose only by obedience to God's commands, which are given to Israel in her covenant law and to us in the teachings of the New Testament. The mission of the church, its reason for being, depends on its obedience to its Lord. Exodus 19 and the stories that follow make this very clear.

Israel readily agrees in the exodus story to God's purpose for her life. "All that the Lord has spoken we will do," she glibly tells Moses. And do you remember how we, like Israel, made our covenant with our Lord and pledged to him our lives and love? How at our baptism or confirmation we were asked, "Do you confess Jesus Christ to be your Lord and Savior? . . . Do you intend to be Christ's faithful disciple, obeying his word, and showing his love, to your life's end?" And how to it all we replied, "I do; I promise; all that you have said, Lord, we will faithfully do; and wherever you may lead us, we will faithfully follow"? Do you remember?

Israel does not fully know the nature of this God to whom she so easily pledges her loyalty, however. Later, in the story of Joshua 24, that leader tries to warn his people against their easy fealty (see vs. 18–23).

The church needs to hear from such passages of the Old Testament the seriousness of its calling—of those gods that it must "put away" and of the one God to whom it owes its heart. The story of the God who descends to meet Israel at Sinai is an apt medium of that message.

In many ways, the exodus narratives are the founding documents of the people of God, portraying the nature of the God who enters into covenant with his chosen folk and the nature of the covenant responsibilities that Israel freely accepts as her own. But the Old Testament is always a realistic volume, and beginning in Exodus and filling the Hexateuch are also the unvarnished portrayals of our actions as God's covenant people: our immediate idolatry, practiced even before we get out of the church door, set forth so vividly in the story of the golden calf (Exodus 32); our despair and weariness with the church and its constant, sometimes petty demands upon us, mirrored in Moses' complaints in Numbers 11:10–15; our jealousies and spiteful criticisms of those called to lead us (Numbers 12); our fears before the obstacles and enemies that would turn us aside from God's goal for us (Numbers 13); and even our willingness to forget all about the sacred history and just return to our former bondage (Num. 14:1–10). How powerful this last text is, paired with Galatians 5:1: "Do not submit again to a yoke of slavery." In the stories of Israel, complaining and murmuring, repenting and forgetting, thirsting and hungering, worshiping and following the ark of the covenant through the wilderness (Num. 10:33; Josh. 3:3), we see our own pilgrimage, in all its glories and miseries, and the preacher is presented with countless texts that will portray a congregation to itself.

The stories of Balaam in Numbers 22–24 perhaps capture the very essence of Israel's life:

> Lo, a people dwelling alone,
> and not reckoning itself among the nations!
> 23:9

The covenant people are a unique folk, unlike any other in the world.

> The LORD their God is with them,
> and the shout of a king is among them.
> 23:21

Yet, in the Balaam stories, this people is confronted with its greatest danger thus far—that the evil of the pagan world around them, symbolized in Balaam's curse, will undo for them all that God has done. But this God of the Hexateuch's narratives cannot be turned aside from his promise and its fulfillment.

> Has he said, and will he not do it?
> Or has he spoken, and will he not fulfil it?
> 23:19

So it is that God leads this people every step of the way, always three days' journey ahead to seek out resting places for them (Num. 10:33), feeding them with manna and meat, clothing their backs and toughening their feet for the trek, disciplining them as a father would discipline a son (Deut. 8:1–5). When they rebel against God's leadership and reject the grace of his "daily bread," he brings his judgment upon the people in the form of fiery serpents. But God's mercy always overcomes his wrath, and the Israelites are healed by gazing on the bronze serpent lifted up (Num. 21:4–9)—a symbol that the Fourth Gospel then makes a type of Christ lifted up on the cross (John 3:14–15).

When God has had his fill of that stiff-necked people and would blot them out of his sight, he nevertheless heeds the voice of their mediator, Moses, and repents of his wrath (Deuteronomy 9–10).

Despite all our sin and our flight from God and our loss of a sense of his abiding presence, there pierces through our darkness and despair and terrible self-seeking the voice of the one who forgives and loves and wants only our abundant life, and who nevertheless accompanies us always along the way, even when we think him absent.

It is in God's "going with us . . . that we are distinct"—the church and Israel—"from all other people that are upon the face of the earth" (Ex. 33:16). That is the identifying mark of the people of God (cf. Josh. 3:10).

> And so we pray with Moses, "Lord, if thy presence will not go with us, do not carry us up from here" (Ex. 33:15). And his voice comes back in that promise of love that will not let us go, "Lo, I am with you always, to the close of the age" (Matt. 28:20).

The result is that Israel is given portions of the promised land, in fulfillment of God's promise to Abraham. In an exceedingly complex picture that parallels much of the Moses story (Joshua 2–5) and that describes central (Joshua 6–9), southern (Joshua 10), and northern (Joshua 11) defeats of the Canaanite population, the book of Joshua details the division of the promised land (Joshua 13–21), summing up its story in Joshua's final speech in chapter 23. The Lord has given Israel rest "from all their enemies round about" (v. 1). He has fought for his people and driven out their enemies before them (vs. 3, 9–10), although many Canaanites, with their gods and goddesses, still remain in the land as "a snare and a trap" for Israel (v. 13; see also vs. 7, 12, 16). In response to God's constant grace toward them, the Israelites are to "cleave" always to their one God (v. 8) in love (v. 11), following his commandments as those are now preserved in Deuteronomy (v. 6). God has kept his promises, and now Israel is to keep hers, made in her covenant with the Lord. Her time in the land is now a time of the testing of her faithfulness (vs. 14–16).

In Deuteronomy, Israel is also cautioned not to regard God's gift of the land as a reward of her faithfulness, for she has been constantly "a stubborn people" (see Deut. 9:4–6). The Old Testament repeatedly warns us against the temptation to regard our prosperity or success as a reward for our goodness. It also warns us against our propensity to claim our achievements as our own (see Deut. 8:17–18). The goods of this world are the gifts solely of God's mercy, unearned by our efforts and unmerited by our goodness (cf. Matt. 5:45). All that we are and have comes, undeserved, from God's hand, and he acts in faithfulness to his promises and in love toward us, for no other reason than that he is that kind of God. Israel—and we—therefore owe him our fiercest love and loyalty.

In Joshua 24, the whole story of God's graciousness is told once again, and those Semites who preceded Israel's crossing of the Jordan under Joshua, and who have dwelt previously in the land, are also brought into the covenant with Israel's God, forming now the entity of the twelve tribes of "all Israel." These newcomers too acknowledge that from God's grace alone they have their life and that therefore they, with all the chosen people, will love God in return for his love, by obeying his commandments for them and by putting aside every other loyalty. Israel now dwells as a gifted people, facing her greatest test.

In the World, but Not of It: Deuteronomy–2 Kings

One does not hear many sermons from this portion of the Old Testament. While Deuteronomy is increasingly being valued as a source of sermon texts,[6] and Joshua finds its place in the Hexateuchal story, the narratives concerning Israel's life as a loose federation of tribes (Judges) and then as a monarchy (Samuel–Kings) are often ignored by preachers.

The three-year ecumenical lectionary does list eighteen different passages from these books, and all of them deal with well-known figures. But one has the feeling when surveying the lectionary listings that the texts have been chosen only for their relation to the New Testament or for their so-called "spiritual" content. The rich tapestry of Israel's political life as a nation among other nations has been ignored.

To be sure, the only modern analogy to Israel, the covenant nation, is the Christian church, not the United States or any other national body. Nevertheless, Israel faces problems in her time as a federation and as a united and then divided monarchy that are crucial problems for the covenant people of God in any age.

The question that really dominates this whole section of the Old Testament is, How can the people of God be in the world but not of it? How can that covenant folk deal with all the threats and pressures and ambiguities of actual life in the ancient Near East and yet perfectly serve the one God to whom they have pledged their loyalty? Surely that is a question the church in the world faces every day. And within that comprehensive question, three lesser questions are raised.

The first question is, How can the people of God prosper their life or, indeed, who controls the sources of life? Human beings ultimately nourish and sustain their lives from the resources of the natural world around them. Food and clothing, fertility and the growth of crops and population, land and the acquisition of wealth based on ownership—these undergird human existence. The question that Israel faces, then, when she moves into Canaan is, Who can furnish her with the natural goods that will sustain and prosper her life? Israel has never been a settled people before, tilling and planting, husbanding and harvesting; nor has she previously known a God of the sown land. Her God has been a God of the desert, one who has come "from Sinai, and dawned from Seir upon" them (Deut. 33:2; see also Judg. 5:4–5). The temptation that therefore confronts her is to abandon her desert God and the past and to look to the deities of agricultural Palestine.

Around Israel, the Canaanites, still in the land, attempt to preserve the cycle of the seasons, call forth the fructifying rain, and ensure the fertility of life by sacrificing to the deities of nature, by acting out fertility in cultic prostitution, and by recounting the myths of El and Hadad, of Mot and Yam and Shemesh. For them, Ashtoreth is the genius of reproduction and fecundity, Baal the energizer of earth and sky. Israel's temptation is to construct a whole new culture on Canaanite models, in order to command the powers of Ashtoreth and Baal to come to her aid and to prosper her life.

It is a temptation that is not unknown in our day or, indeed, in any day. A number of modern theologies look to our harmony or oneness with the natural world for the sources of life. In the great Ground of Being, or in the Primal Matrix underlying all, or in some Great Goddess permeating the universe, or in a mystic world Soul or Spirit, or in Mother Earth, or even in Nature (with a capital *N*), such theologies find the fountainhead and energizer of existence. We "reclaim our true relationship with somatic reality, with body and earth, and with the Great Goddess that sustains our life in nature," writes Rosemary Ruether.[7] And a "new" faith and a "new" culture are posited on that basis, though it is actually a temptation that Israel knew some 3,200 years earlier.

Some, of course, in our rootless age, look to other sources—to pyramid or crystal power, magical or mystical Eastern rituals, astrological bodies, health foods and diets, exercise plans, ointments, herbal medicines, faith healers, bizarre gurus of every stripe—to preserve, sustain, enhance, and prosper their well-being and existence. A preacher might well ask where his or her congregation looks for its source of life.

Much of Deuteronomy is concerned with this question of whence comes life's energy. Its central passage of the Shemaʿ (Deut. 6:4–9) begins by emphasizing that the Lord of Israel is one (v. 4) and therefore is not to be equated with the diffuse *numina* that supposedly permeate the world or that inhabit Canaanite worship sites throughout the land. Its law of centrality (Deut. 12:5 et passim) demands that Israel seek her God only at that site where he shall "put his name": that is, in Jerusalem (cf. Acts 4:12). It constantly warns against the imitation of Canaanite worship practices (12:29–31) such as the eating of Canaanite totem animals (14:3–20), participation in cults of the dead (14:1–2), reliance on magical rites (22:9–11), soothsaying and divination (18:9–14), and masquerading known in the cult of Ashtoreth (22:5). Its stringent law of the *cherem*, the devotion of all prizes of war to the Lord (7:1–5, 25–26; 20:10–18; cf. Josh. 6:18—7:26; 1 Samuel 15), though impossible of implementation in Deuteronomy's time, has as its rationale the elimination of all things Canaanite. In Deuteronomy 7:5 and 12:3, Israel is commanded to break down all Canaanite altars and to do away with all cultic objects of the Canaanites and Phoenicians, lest her heart be lured away from the one God, to worship the deities of the cultivated land.

Similarly, there is constant emphasis in Deuteronomy on the fact that Israel has her land and all its fruitful goodness only from the hand of the Lord (8:7–20 et passim). In God alone are found the sources of life and of all material blessings (cf. 12:7; 15:6, 14; 16:10; 28:2–6), and therefore God alone can prosper life and sustain it, a fact reiterated in the teachings of our Lord (Matt. 6:25–33). It is no accident that Jesus Christ, in the Fourth Gospel, is the "life" (4:14; 11:25; 14:6), for as the revealer of the Father, he brings us into relationship with God, the one source of life.

In the books of Judges, Samuel, and Kings, too, there is constant attention to this question of whence comes life. The story of Gideon's fleece is a test of who controls nature's life-giving moisture (Judg. 6:36–40). The tales of the jar of meal and cruse of oil (1 Kings 17:8–16), of the empty vessels (2 Kings 4:1–7), of the poison pot (2 Kings 4:38–44), of the gift of a son (2 Kings 4:11–17), of the raising of the dead (1 Kings 17:17–24; 2 Kings 4:18–37), of the feeding of the multitude (2 Kings 4:42–44; cf. the feeding of the 5,000 in the New Testament), and of the cure of leprosy (2 Kings 5) emphasize again and again that the Lord of Israel controls the fountains of life and its sustenance.

Indeed, the Elijah cycle in 1 Kings 17–19 is framed around the gift of fructifying rain. At the beginning of the cycle, the word of the Lord brings the drought (1 Kings 17:1), which is ended by a deluge (1 Kings 18:41–46) only after Elijah has shown the four hundred prophets of Jezebel who worship Baal Hadad, lord of the storm and lightning, to have no power over fire and natural forces (1 Kings 18:20–40).

Such stories are indicative of the fight carried on by the early prophets against the Canaanization of Israel's society, a contest that continued into the time of the writing prophets. Israel's major sin in the times of Hosea and Jeremiah is still her idolatrous worship of foreign gods and goddesses of the natural world. In concert with that, Paul is still concerned, in Romans 1:22–25, with that idolatry that worships the creation rather than the Creator. This temptation to find the sources of life in the forces and processes of this world is a stumbling block to true faith in every age.

The second question raised in this portion of the Old Testament is, How are the people of God to defend their life? From the time of her deliverance out of Egypt until her entrance into the promised land, Israel's one source of defense has been her God. He has delivered her from the pursuing troops of the pharaoh, fought for her against the Amalekites (Ex. 17:8–16), Canaanites (Num. 21:1–3), and Amorites (Num. 21:21–32), turned aside the curse of Balaam (Numbers 22–24), defeated Midian (Numbers 31), Gilead (Numbers 32), and various populations of Canaan (Judg. 1:1—2:5), and settled her in the land. Repeatedly attacked by surrounding enemies, according to the book of Judges, Israel is just as repeatedly saved by God's gift to her of a charismatic leader, or judge, who rallies at least some of the free Israelite farmers to battle behind the all-powerful leadership of their defending God. With her settlement in the land, however, Israel has become a nation among other nations, and the question she faces is whether or not her Lord will continue to protect and defend her life against her enemies.

Israel lives in a precarious situation. Having settled into the hill country, in the midst of the Canaanites, on a strip of land that forms the international corridor of the world, Israel is faced on all sides by continual threats to her existence. Reuben and Gad front Moab and Ammon. The western half of the tribe of Manasseh has its northern border fringed with the fortified cities of the Canaanites. Most threatening of all, the Sea Peoples of the Aegean have invaded the Fertile Crescent.

We know that in the final decades of the thirteenth century B.C., the Philistines attempted to invade Egypt but were pushed back by the troops of Rameses III, to settle in five city-states along the coastal plain of Palestine. Each city, with the area it controlled, was ruled by a "lord" who, though politically independent, cooperated with the other lords in military matters. The Philistines constituted the most serious threat to Israel's existence in her early period as a tribal federation. Judges 13:1 and 14:4 show us Judah and Dan dominated by the Philistines for forty years and fighting for their very lives. In the time of Samuel, the central sanctuary of Israel at Shiloh was destroyed by the Philistines and the ark of the covenant was captured (1 Samuel 4–6).

The tribal federation was simply too weak to repel such a foe. It had no constancy of leadership, and often the judge who was called out to defend it was unknown even in his or her own tribe. Its troops were free farmers and traders, reluctant to leave their holdings to do battle (cf. Judg. 5:16–18) and inexperienced in the ways of warfare. As Judges states, "In those days there was no king in Israel; every man did what was right in his own eyes" (17:6; see also 18:1; 19:1; 21:25). The attempts to make first Gideon and then his son Abimelech king (Judg. 8:22—9:57) ended in idolatry and disaster, because God was the true king of Israel and its source of defense. Thus did Israel face the perennial question of how to be in the world but not of it. How do the people of God meet the historical threats to their existence and yet rely in faith solely on the protection of their God?

The Christian church is still struggling to answer that question. The query crops up in every debate over pacifism and militarism, over disarmament and nuclear deterrence, over civil disobedience and patriotism, even over whether or not a Christian should take any measures to resist evil (cf. Matt. 5:38–48). In our violent world, it is a burning question.

The difficulty of answering the question, however, is vividly illustrated in the stories of Saul in 1 Samuel. In some portions of that book, the anointing of Saul to the kingship is a gracious response by God to Israel's cries for help in the face of her Philistine foe (see 1 Sam. 9:15–16; cf. Ex. 3:7–8). But in other portions of 1 Samuel, the anointing of Saul is a rejection of the kingship of the Lord and an act of apostasy that manifests a lack of trust in God's defense of his people (see 1 Sam. 8:4–7). And the difficulty of answering the question about how to defend our life is poignantly illustrated in 1 Samuel 13's story of the rejection of Saul by God. The Israelites have been called out by Saul to do battle against the Philistines at Gilgal. Each time Israel went into battle, it was the legal responsibility of the priest to offer a sacrifice and to inquire of God as to the outcome of the fight. For seven days, in this story, the priest Samuel does not show up, and Saul's free-farmer troops begin to scatter to their homes. Saul, in desperation, offers the sacrifice in Samuel's stead. Immediately Samuel appears and announces God's judgment on Saul (1 Sam. 13:13–14).

How does one perfectly serve the Lord of history and yet meet the threats that history imposes upon us all? The Old Testament, in its realism, poses that difficult question by telling us the story of Saul—a story closer to Greek tragedy than any other narrative in the Bible. If we read the moving story of Saul's despair in 1 Samuel 28, when, with God turned against him, he seeks advice from the deceased Samuel through the medium of the witch of Endor, and then if we go further to read of Saul's courage in nevertheless going out to battle (1 Samuel 31), perhaps we will be prevented in our preaching from answering the question too simply and glibly. There is no one "right" course in Saul's story, no clear path of faith marked out. There are only the struggles of faith with fear, of sin-marred trust with history's awful necessities. Such struggles give the lie to all self-righteous groups who claim that their course alone serves the will of God.

The third question raised in the Deuteronomic narratives is, How is the people of God to govern its life? Or, perhaps better stated, What is the source of that people's ultimate authority?

Certainly the two parallel and tragic stories of the rejection of Saul (1 Sam. 13:1–15; 15:1–31) have lying behind them the prophetic protest against the absolutization of state power. It is because Saul takes it upon himself to defy the commandments of God that he is, in both stories, rejected as Israel's king, and this absolutization of his royal power is summarily condemned by Samuel, serving as a prophet:

> Because you have rejected the word of the LORD,
>   he has also rejected you from being king.
>
> 1 Sam. 15:23

There is never any doubt about it in the Old Testament: Israel's state is a theocracy over which the Lord rules as ultimate King, and therefore every human sovereign governs only under the divine authority, subject to the word of God. In Deuteronomy 17:14–20, God says that he will set up a king over the Israelites from among their number, but that ruler must write for himself a copy of the law of Deuteronomy and not turn aside from its commandments, "either to the right hand or to the left; so that he may continue long in his kingdom, he and his children, in Israel" (v. 20). In the Deuteronomic history in 1–2 Kings, then, every ruler of Israel, north and south, is judged according to whether or not he or she has kept the law of Deuteronomy, and principally whether or not he or she has obeyed Deuteronomy's law of centralization, which eliminated all foreign worship and centered the cult in Jerusalem. In the stories of Elijah and Elisha, those prophets are willing to bring down the entire Omri dynasty (see 1 Kings 19:15–18; 2 Kings 9) rather than allow Jezebel and Ahab to work their independent will by silencing the prophets (1 Kings 18:4) and by introducing foreign worship into Israel (1 Kings 18:20–46). Indeed, they will bring down that dynasty even over the issue of Naboth's little vineyard next to the royal palace (1 Kings 21), for the commandments of God cannot be limited in application only to the religious sphere. The will of the Lord is to be obeyed in every area of Israel's life.

Solomon, despite the Wisdom traditions that gathered about his name, is one of two models (Jeroboam I is the other) for the Deuteronomic historians of what a king should not be, for it was in Solomon's reign that state power reached its zenith. His was the time of bureaucracy, of international relations, of commerce. The splendor of his rule was magnified by the erection of magnificent buildings and garrison cities and storehouses. The old army of the people was replaced by mercenaries and the introduction of the war chariot. The land was divided into set districts under royal officials, for the purposes of taxation. Formerly free farmers were pressed into service as royal slaves in Solomon's construction projects, and the very temple itself, abounding in Canaanite images and constructed with Phoenician materials and labor, was Solomon's royal chapel. One wall surrounded temple and palace, and so God and the king now lived within the same wall, illumined by the same supernatural glory, and the king became the earthly representative of God, judging the people from his six-stepped throne and manifesting the infallible word of God (1 Kings 3–11). It is no accident that when Samuel protests against the introduction of a monarchy into Israel's life, the picture he draws of the kingship's evil effects is taken from the reign of Solomon (1 Sam. 8:11–18; cf. Deut. 17:16).

We in our time, of course, are not unfamiliar with the absolutization of state power. Every tyrant in history has attempted to usurp the throne of God and claim absolute power for himself. The divine right of kings, infallible emperors, and popes; the claims of Hitler or Sun Myung Moon to be the messiah; the ruthless authority of a Stalin or a Jim Jones or an Idi Amin or a Khomeini; indeed, even the scheme to hold church services in the White House and censor the sermons to be preached there—these arrogate to themselves the authority that belongs to God alone. So it is that the stories of the monarchy in the books of Samuel and Kings are peppered with figures of prophets, both named and unnamed—those mediators of the word of God that finally shapes all history. All human rule is provisional and transitory, because God's rule alone is absolute and eternal.

This question about ultimate authority has dozens of implications, of course, not only in the church-state realm but within the life of the church itself. It implies that no human program, not even a religious program, can be equated with the absolute will of God. It also implies that no human science can overrule the word of God, when that word is presented unambiguously in the Bible. There are some subjects about which the Bible leaves no doubt. And yet there are many attempts in our day to "correct" the scriptures on such subjects, with insights from psychology, medicine, sociology, even ethics and the pastoral disciplines. We know more today than those who wrote the scriptures, goes the reasoning, and therefore while the scriptures' insights may have been valid for their time, they are no longer valid for ours. The clear will of God is subjected to the wishes of society, and though the church formally declares that its one authority for faith and practice is the word of God, mediated to it through the Bible and illumined by the Holy Spirit, on many issues it denies that authority in practice.

The Old Testament does sanction the human government of society, however, just as does the New Testament (Rom. 13:1–7; Titus 3:1; 1 Peter 2:17; cf. Matt. 22:21), and that sanction in the Book of the Old Covenant is centered around the promise of God to David (2 Sam.

7:1–17). In that passage, which is basic to Old Testament messianic or royal theology, the Davidic throne is guaranteed forever. God will make David's name great (v. 9; cf. Gen. 12:2); he will adopt each Davidic heir to the throne as his son (v. 14; cf. Ps. 2:7; 89:26–27; Mark 1:11 and pars.); and though those heirs may sin and be judged, God will never remove his steadfast covenant love from them (v. 15; cf. Ps. 89:28–33). Israel's life under the Davidic heir will also be guaranteed forever (vs. 10–11, 24; cf. Isa. 55:3). That promise is the foundation of all messianic hope in the Old Testament. Israel looks always for its Davidic king, who will guarantee its life (cf. Isa. 11:1–9, 10; Jer. 23:5–6||33:14–16, 17; Ezek. 37:24–28). The judgment leveled against the monarchy in the time of Saul is superseded by God's sanction of the Davidic throne.

There is nevertheless always a tension connected with the Davidic government in the Old Testament. In 2 Samuel 7:8, David is not appointed "king" over the covenant people, but "prince" (so too in 1 Sam. 13:14; 25:30; 2 Sam. 5:2; 6:21; Ezek. 37:25)—the Lord remains the only "king" over his people. David therefore is subject to the covenant commandments. He becomes ruler over Judah (2 Sam. 2:4) and Israel (2 Sam. 5:1–3) only by covenanting with their representative elders, and he and his descendants are expected to keep the covenant commands. As in Psalm 132:12, the kingship is conditional. Thus Jeremiah, though he affirms the promise to David, nevertheless has no hesitancy in pronouncing God's destruction of the occupants of the Davidic throne (Jer. 22:1—23:8).

On the other hand, the royal prophetic oracle of 2 Samuel 23:5 speaks of God's "everlasting covenant" with David, "ordered in all things and secure," and the promise to David does guarantee his throne forever.

This tension created by the question of whether the Davidic reign is conditional or permanent is heightened by the Samuel stories of David himself. Though the Deuteronomic historian, in the books of Kings (and later the Chronicler) make David the model for kingship—the man after God's own heart (1 Kings 9:4; 11:4; 14:8)—the Deuteronomic historian nevertheless leaves virtually editorially untouched the Samuel stories about David, which picture David's violation of the basic covenant commands of the Decalogue. David covets the wife of Uriah, commits adultery with her, steals her from her faithful husband, and then is forced into the act of murder in order to hide his own sin (2 Samuel 11). He is ruthless in his politics, vacillating and unjust when dealing with his sons, arrogant in his wish to center the ark and the priesthood in his capital city and thus to give his rule religious sanction. He appoints his own sons as priests in his realm; he makes the high priesthood a dual office for the political purpose of holding northern and southern traditions together. And yet David is made the model for all kings who come after him.

In other words, David too is given the eternal promise and reigns only by the grace of that God who establishes the Davidic throne in spite of human sin. And the same pattern continues into the reign of Solomon, in the story of the successor to David's throne (2 Samuel 6—1 Kings 2). Amnon, Absalom, and Adonijah, in that story, all are rejected as heirs to the throne. Amnon cannot reign because of his unbridled sensuality in the rape of Tamar. Absalom is unacceptable because of his fratricide of Amnon and his attempt at usurpation of the reign. Adonijah too seeks the kingdom by his own power. But none can impose his ways or will upon the God who controls the throne. Solomon, whose name means "peace," is the beloved of the Lord (2 Sam. 12:25), and therefore Nathan the prophet and Bathsheba join forces to give the throne into the hands of Solomon. How ironic that is when we see the awful effects of Solomon's reign! And how ironic it is that Nathan and Bathsheba band together!

> Perhaps Nathan . . . can teach us modern-day Christians something, however, for Nathan is no ideologue, and he is not dedicated solely to some human purpose. Nathan obeys one voice and finds the guidance for his actions in society from one source: namely, from his Lord. . . .
>
> Nathan and all the other prophets in the Old Testament have something that we have lost in the church these days. They have freedom from the society around them. They are not blown about by all the winds of doctrine, as Paul would put it, because they do not follow the latest fad, they are not captive to special-interest groups, and they do not unquestioningly support the latest liberal or conservative pronouncement. They serve, instead, their living God —that God who is on the move toward the establishment of his kingdom on earth. They hear the voice of that God in the most intimate communion with him. . . . Like a faithful wife knowing the mind of her husband, or like an obedient child at the knee of its father, these prophets listen to God, as we are to listen to him through the word of scripture. And they hear, and do accordingly. And that gives them freedom from all the voices of this world and from every ideology that would capture them for its own selfish purposes.

Human wisdom might question the outcome of Nathan's actions, but human wisdom is folly with God, and God pursues his own purposes in the tangled affairs of this world. God puts up with the sin and degeneracy of the Davidic throne until finally, in the fullness of time, he can bring forth from its line that one King who perfectly keeps his covenant and who perfectly serves his word even unto death on a cross.

Human authority is subject always to the will of God, says the Old Testament (see, e.g., Isa. 40:22–24), but God graciously grants to human rulers and leaders their place in his history, despite their sinful and seemingly disastrous actions. The only fact that can keep the Christian from despairing of human rule is the knowledge finally demonstrated in Jesus Christ that, in reality, God rules. And the only loyalty that can free the Christian from slavery to the ways of this world is the joyful service of the Word of God that was finally made flesh in our Lord. The Word of God is ultimate authority. That is the message of Old and New Testaments.

CHAPTER 6

Preaching from the Law

Modern preachers sometimes ignore Old Testament law. Many believe that the law has little to do with the Christian faith. After all, goes the reasoning, Christianity is a religion not of law but of grace. We are justified, or made acceptable to God, not by fulfilling the law but only by faith, by trusting in God's work of mercy in Jesus Christ. The law of the Old Testament has therefore been superseded, it is held. While our Lord may have commended to us the two great commandments from the Old Testament—to love God and to love neighbor (Mark 12:28–31; Deut. 6:4; Lev. 19:18)—and while he may have looked with approval on the man who obeyed the Ten Commandments (Mark 10:17–21), all the rest of the laws in the Book of the Old Covenant may safely be ignored.

This attitude toward Old Testament law is often coupled with the mistaken belief that Old Testament religion is solely a religion of law. In such a stereotypical attitude that is shared by many lay people, the Old Testament as a whole is therefore seen as outdated and superficial and inconsequential for the church. Certainly everything that has been written in this book thus far contradicts such a stereotype.

Nevertheless, preachers neglect the legal portions of the Old Testament, and the material that is found in Exodus 19 through Numbers 10:10 and then in Deuteronomy is the least well known and certainly the most misunderstood portion of that Testament. But the irony is that many preachers frequently preach law. Much of American preaching takes the form of moralism. "We should," "we ought," "you need to," "you must"—these phrases pepper the sermons of the moralists, who Sunday after Sunday urge their people to adopt a particular course of action or belief. Law is laid on the congregation as the way to Christian faith and life, but much of it has little to do with biblical law or with the Bible's understanding of the place of law in the gospel. The biblical Christian faith is perverted, and such preaching profits the congregation nothing.

It is essential that Christian preachers and congregations have some understanding of Old Testament law, for law in the Old Testament, as in the New, is an essential part of the gospel and lays much of the basis for an understanding of the New Testament. In the covenant law is laid the foundation of the church and of God's lordship over it. In the priestly law is to be found part of the basis of the New Testament understanding of the atonement and of the sacrifice of Christ on the cross. In the Deuteronomic law are found the meaning and motive of the First Commandment, to love God with all our hearts and minds and strength. Thus to preach from the law is not an exercise that is sterile and outdated and lacking in spiritual insight, but a duty of the pulpit that is fundamental for understanding and living out the Christian faith.

Israel's Confession in the Law

To preach from Old Testament law, we must first understand it theologically, and to do that let us start very simply. If we ask after the origins of the law, the Old Testament maintains that its law has come from God and has been mediated to Israel through the person of Moses, either at Mount Sinai or subsequently during the trek through the wilderness. Deuteronomy, on the other hand, has a somewhat different view. It maintains that God gave all the laws to Moses at Mount Sinai, but, at the mountain, Moses passed on to the covenant people only the Ten Commandments. In Deuteronomy's setting, then, Israel is encamped on the plain of Moab on the eastern side of the Jordan, just before her entry into the promised land. Moses is old and about to die, but before his death he gives the rest of God's commandments to the people in order that they may know how to live as God's people in the promised land. Deuteronomy represents the whole counsel of God; therefore it is not to be added to or taken from (Deut. 4:2; 12:32), and Israel is not to turn aside from its commandments, either to the right or to the left (Deut. 5:32; 28:14).

In short, law, or *torah,* in the Old Testament represents God's teaching about how to live. The basic meaning of *torah* is "teaching" or "to point the finger": "This is the way. Walk in it."

The New Testament picks up the Old's understanding of Moses as the mediator of the law when it portrays Jesus as the new Moses on the new mount, giving the new law for the new people of God (Matthew 5–7; in Luke there is only a sermon on the plain, Luke 6:17). In view of Deuteronomy's injunctions not to add to or take from its law, we can imagine the shock Jesus caused among his hearers when he quoted a law from Deuteronomy—"You have heard that it was said to the men of old"—and then revised that law—"But I say to you . . ." (e.g., Matt. 5:33, 34).

The principal point is that the law has its origin in God's words through Moses, according to the Old Testament. Yet many of Israel's laws find close parallels in the law codes of other ancient Near Eastern societies. This is especially true of Israel's casuistic or case law—"If a person [does such and such], then [this is the law for that case]"—e.g., Exodus 22:1–2. It seems clear that Israel borrowed some of her laws. Israel's apodictic or incontestable law, on the other hand, finds few parallels in the surrounding cultures and represents the absolute commands given her by her sovereign Lord (see Ex. 23:16–19, e.g.). Thus, the Ten Commandments are apodictic laws. Nevertheless, Israel claims that all her laws come from God and have been mediated to her through Moses. Why does she make such a claim?

As is true in so much of the Old Testament, Israel is making a confession of faith about the nature of her life. By saying that the instructions for her life come from God alone, Israel is confessing that her society is different from that of other peoples. Her society is not formed and ordered solely on the basis of blood or soil or economic interest. She cannot be understood merely in sociological terms. She is not a people who lives according to the customs of human beings, or according to natural laws, or according to the dictates of human culture.

For example, there is no royal law in the Old Testament. The human king does not order society by his will but is subservient to the will and laws of God, as we saw in the preceding chapter. Or, to give another example, Israel's law subverts the natural acquisitiveness of human beings. Every seventh or sabbath year the land must lie fallow in recognition of God's ownership of the land and his will regarding it (Ex. 23:10–11). Every fiftieth or jubilee year, a parcel of land must be returned to its original owner, because it was the gift of God to that owner in fulfillment of the promise to Abraham (Lev. 25:13, 23). Israel is a people that is to live only by God's instructions.

> And the LORD said to Moses, "Say to the people of Israel, I am the LORD your God. You shall not do as they do in the land of Egypt, where you dwelt, and you shall not do as they do in the land of Canaan, to which I am bringing you. You shall not walk in their statutes. You shall do my ordinances and keep my statutes and walk in them. I am the LORD your God. You shall therefore keep my statutes and my ordinances, by doing which a man shall live: I am the LORD."
>
> Leviticus 18:1–5

Israel knows how to live and can have her life only if she stands in obedient relation with her Lord. If she loses that relation, chaos ensues in her society and she becomes "no people" (Hos. 1:8–9).

Certainly such an understanding of the life of the covenant people is indispensable also for the new Israel, the church, for Christians too are to live only by the will of God. We are not just to "do what comes naturally"; it is not natural to love our enemies or to pray for those who persecute us. We are not to do as the society around us does; it is the custom of our society to return evil for evil, to despise the poor and weak, to "look out for number one." But Jesus says, "A new commandment I give you, that you love one another as I have loved you." "Blessed are the poor." "The meek shall inherit the earth." "Whoever saves his life shall lose it."

Persons of biblical faith, according to both Testaments, have a revealed law given to them, a teaching from God that is different from the teachings of human beings and that gives God's instructions about how to order society and how to conduct and sustain one's life. Preaching from the law is aimed at producing a lifestyle different from that of the surrounding world.

The Law's Context of Grace

In order to avoid all legalism, however, we need to look at the context of the law. When we do that, it becomes clear that the Old Testament, at least up until the postexilic period of 538 B.C. and following, is not a legalistic book.

For example, in the introduction to the covenant at Mount Sinai, Exodus 19:4–6, God begins by saying, "You have seen what I did to the Egyptians, and how I bore you on eagles' wings and brought you to myself." God himself set up his relationship with his people and adopted them as his own before the law was even given! Consequently, the Ten Commandments in Exodus 20:1–17 and Deuteronomy 5:6–21 do not begin, as we usually begin them, with the command, "You shall have no other gods before me." Rather, they begin by remembering God's gracious action: "I am the LORD your God, who brought you out of the land of Egypt, out of the house of bondage." The implication is that *therefore* Israel is to have no other gods before him. Israel's obedience to the Ten Commandments is to be her response to God's redemptive action. Only because Israel has been redeemed is she given laws.

Further, when Israel breaks the commandments, she is not automatically cut off from her relationship with God. The law itself provides the means of forgiveness and atonement for Israel's sin (see Leviticus 16 on the day of atonement), a means furnished out of the mercy of

that God who continually forgives his sinful people. Israel's obedience
to the law is not the basis of her relationship with her Lord. Rather, as
in Genesis 15:6 and in the prophetic literature, Israel is joined to her
Lord by her trust in his gracious action toward her.

Indeed, for preexilic Israel, the gift of the law itself is further
evidence of that gracious action. After Israel is delivered from Egypt
and given a new life and made a people and set on a pilgrimage toward
the promised land, the place of rest, she has no idea how to order her
life or how to get along with this new God who has redeemed her and
given her "the glorious liberty of the children of God." But God does
not just leave her to her own devices, to stumble about in the
wilderness and order her community by trial and error. No. He
provides *torah* whereby Israel may know how to walk in the new life
that she has been given.

So it is too with the church. Jesus does not abandon us in our new
life as the children of God but also gives us instructions about how to
live and what to do and what it is that God desires from us as his
adopted covenant people. The commandments of our Lord and the
instructions of the apostles that frequent the New Testament are
merciful gifts of a loving God, who provides his continual guidance for
us.

In fact, Israel understood God's covenant commands as his continuing presence with her. In the law, God went with his people, walking
by their side and guiding them along the path of life (see Psalm 119).
So it is too with Jesus' commandments. By keeping his commandments, says the Fourth Gospel, we abide in our Lord. He walks with us
by means of his word (John 15:1–11) and directs us continually and
surely along the path of abundant life.

The law is therefore never understood by preexilic Israel as a
legalistic burden that she has to fulfill in order to be acceptable to her
God. Rather, the law is a gift of God's grace. It is sweeter than honey
and more to be desired than fine gold (Ps. 19:10). Or, in another figure
from the psalms, the law is God's stream of life-giving water that
enables us to bear our fruit in due season and prevents our life from
withering away (Ps. 1:2–3). God has redeemed us and made us his
own and given us the new life of the children of God. In his
instructions to us in his commandments, he cares for us and guides us
and walks continually by our side.

Why Israel Obeys the Law

It is abundantly clear, then, why we and Israel should want to obey
the commandments of God. First, apart from God's guidance of us in
his *torah* teachings, we do not know how to conduct ourselves in this

new life that God has given us. After all, Israel in the Old Testament and the church in the New have been delivered into an existence unknown to the rest of the world. We have become the redeemed, forgiven, adopted children of the one true God. How does a people or an individual act in such a relationship? Surely the world's wisdom is no help on the subject, because the world still lives in the darkness of its sin, separated from its Creator. God alone knows how we can live in the new life he himself has created. Apart from listening to his instruction, we inevitably will do the wrong and distort the nature of the new life that we have been given.

Second, we have entered into this new, redeemed life by confessing that God alone has saved us and has become our Lord. But if God is truly the Lord of our lives, how can we ignore the instructions he gives us? Either he is Ruler over us or he is not. Our attitude toward his commandments says what we believe about him. Our obedience is an integral part of our faith. "Faith apart from works is dead" (James 2:26).

Third, because God has redeemed us out of our bondage and given us a new life, our obedience to his commandments is our grateful response to his love shown toward us. In thankfulness for what God has done, we give back to him our loyalty.

Perhaps no book of the Bible makes this clearer than does the seventh century B.C. book of Deuteronomy. Over and over it recounts what God has done for Israel, retelling the sacred story from the time of the exodus on, of how God has created and cared for a people. Two verses sum up its teaching: "Keep silence and hear, O Israel: this day you have become the people of the LORD your God. You shall therefore obey the voice of the LORD your God, keeping his commandments and his statutes, which I command you this day" (27:9–10). This is a marvelous text for the celebration of the Lord's Supper.

It is a love that will not let us go, is it not?—the love that pursued Israel across forty years of murmuring and wandering in desert wastes, the love that fought and wept and pleaded with her through four centuries of turbulent monarchy, the love that could not be turned aside by bloody wars or unjust rulers or corrupt courts or scornful indifference and disbelief, the love that followed its straying children all the way from Palestine to Babylon and back again. And here now, this night at this table, that love pursues us also, and our Lord promises us, by this cup, the forgiveness of all we have done against him and welcomes us back into his fellowship as people of his covenant. . . .

Surely, then, our response to that love can only be the one given in our Old Testament lesson—that we therefore obey the voice of the Lord our God and keep his commandments and statutes. Surely our response, from grateful hearts, can only be those words said at the first covenant ceremony, "Oh, yes, all that the Lord has spoken to us, we will do." For you see, here at this table is manifested for us, in the bread and the wine, the love of God that finally pursued us all the way to a cross; the love that was willing to die for us rather than let us die; the love that was willing to accept the nails, the spear, the thirst, the darkness, that we might have the light of life. And so our text reads, "Therefore, you shall obey the voice of the Lord your God, keeping his commandments and his statutes."

And consider well, good Christians. Would this God of love give us directions that would not lead to life? Would he issue commands that had anything other than our good as their goal? Would he bid us follow him on a path that did not lead us into final joy? Oh, no, this God of ours would not do such things, for he has only our welfare at heart.

We respond in love to God's love toward us, and in the Bible's view we make that response by obediently following God's commandments. "If you love me, you will keep my commandments," Jesus taught (John 14:15); just as in Deuteronomy the central command is to love God with all our hearts and minds and strength (Deut. 6:4). The rest of Deuteronomy's commandments, then, are designed to show us how to love God in return for his love.

The Law as Guide to Love

How do we love God in response to his prior love? Deuteronomy spells it out. For example, we love God by showing the same mercy toward others in our society as God has shown toward us (see, e.g., Deut. 24:17–18). The ancient world, like our world, understood justice in terms of power. But God has shown in his actions toward Israel that he is the God who cares for the weak—who "executes justice for the fatherless and the widow, and loves the sojourner, giving him food and clothing" (10:18). Therefore Israel is to act in the same manner: "for you were sojourners in the land of Egypt" (10:19); "you shall remember that you were a slave in the land of Egypt, and the LORD your God redeemed you" (15:15).

This concern for the poor and helpless is a persistent note in Deuteronomy (14:28–29; 16:11, 14; 24:12–13, 14–15; 26:12–15), and thus we have the phenomenon of a society shaped by the mercy of God. That mercy is not limited to Israelites alone; there is consistent concern shown for the rights and food and faith of the alien, who had no power in Israel (1:16; 5:14 et passim). Indeed, the mercy extended to Israel in the exodus is even to be shown to animals, and the command to give rest to one's ox and ass is, in Deuteronomy's version of the Decalogue, based on the remembrance of the deliverance from Egypt (5:12–15).

Israelite society is to be permeated by a spirit of kindness and helpfulness toward one's neighbor. Therefore a neighbor is to be aided in recovering a lost animal or other property (Deut. 22:1–4). He is to be protected against injury that would cause strife between households (22:8). He is not to be subjected to usury (23:19) or deprived of the products of his labor (23:24–25). He is not to be held responsible for another's crime (24:16) or deprived of his means of livelihood (24:6). His inherited plot of land is his alone, and he is not to be cheated out of it (19:14). Even his dignity and truthfulness are to be honored and not demeaned (24:10–11).

Israel's society is to manifest the same righteousness and justice that God has manifested toward her. Thus the merchant is not to cheat his customers by the use of inaccurate weights and measures (Deut. 25:13–16). The courts of law are to follow "justice, and only justice" (16:20), and even the guilty cannot be given excessive or private punishment (25:1–3). Judges are not to show partiality, and they are not to take a bribe, "for a bribe blinds the eyes of the wise and subverts the cause of the righteous" (16:19).

But Deuteronomy goes beyond the bounds of legal justice and calls for the exercise of love within Israelite society. Relationships between human beings are characterized by devotion and love between master and slave (15:16), between husband and wife (21:15–16), between citizen and sojourner (10:19). In a world where slavery was the custom, no runaway foreign slave can be forced to return to his former master, and he is to be allowed to dwell in Israel in the place of his choosing (23:15–16) and not to be enslaved again. Hebrew slaves are to be released in the seventh year; God freed Israel from slavery in Egypt and therefore no Israelite is to be enslaved permanently, though he can sell himself for six years to pay off his debts (15:12–18). When such a Hebrew slave is released, he is to be given liberal gifts of meat and grain and wine (15:13–14) and released gladly, with gratitude for his six years of service (v. 18).

The poor are to be released from their debts every seventh year (15:2, 9), and those who lend to them are to pay no attention to the nearness of the year of release. They are to lend to the poor man whatever he may need (vs. 8–9), freely and ungrudgingly (v. 10), with a wide-open hand (v. 11). Such generosity is a matter of an open heart (v. 10), of a love manifested toward one's neighbor that flows forth in sharing.

"We love, because he first loved us" (1 John 4:19): No book of the Old Testament better expresses that spirit than does the book of Deuteronomy. Israel's response to the love of God must be heartfelt love within her society, manifested to every class and condition of person. Indeed, her humaneness is to spill over into her treatment of the world of nature (20:19–20; 22:6–7; 25:4); she acts out her love for God by responsibility for his world. In sole obedience to God's teaching, Israel acknowledges his loving sovereignty and gives back to him her total commitment of heart and soul and strength. That surely is the same love to which our Lord calls his church.[1]

To be sure, the commandments given to us in the New Testament are sometimes different from those given to Israel through Moses, but the reason for the commandments is the same: namely, God's mercy shown to us. And our response to the commandments is to be the same as that shown by Israel—grateful and obedient and loving response to what God has done for us.

In these understandings taken from Deuteronomy, we find the basis of all biblical ethics: We are to act toward God and other human beings and the world as God has acted toward us. As God had dealt with Israel in her history, she was to deal with others; as God has acted toward his church in Jesus Christ, we also are to act toward all around us. "Therefore be imitators of God, as beloved children. And walk in love, as Christ loved us and gave himself up for us" (Eph. 5:1–2).

When ethics are grounded on that base, other foundations are ruled out. Ethics are no longer a matter of just deserts: None of us deserved God's redemption of us in Jesus Christ, and therefore no Christian is to render to another person only what he or she deserves. Ethics also are no longer a matter simply of humanitarianism, of treating others kindly simply because they are human beings, for God's love and mercy extend far beyond human dispositions toward kindness. Ethics do not even have their basis only in the Golden Rule, for the second great commandment is set alongside the first, and obedience to both is a matter not of how we would like to be treated but of how God has treated us. Certainly, ethics are not dependent on the situation involved: Love toward another is not defined by the circumstances of some situation, but rather by the love that God has shown us in Jesus Christ. In short, ethics have an objective basis in the actions of God in history, and from his deeds the Christian is to take the pattern and motivation for all deeds.

The Law as Sanctifying

This imitation of the actions of God in the life of faith is also a leading motif in the sixth century B.C. priestly collection of laws that is known as the Holiness Code (Leviticus 17–26). Throughout that collection, there is the thought that Israel is to be God's holy people because the Lord is holy (19:2; 20:26; 21:6). God's holiness is that which makes him uniquely God; it is his qualitative otherness of moral purity and power and mercy that separates him from the profane world of sinful human beings and from the creaturely world of the creation. And Israel, as his covenant people, is to be like God in that separation from everything that is profane and impure, decaying and sinful, corrupted and dying.

Many areas of life are therefore dealt with in the Holiness Code, and all have as their object the sanctification of Israel's life, the permeation of her daily living with the purity and goodness of God in order that she may be a community fit for God's purposes and presence. God wants to sanctify his people, to make them good, and the way he does that is by giving guidance in his law. "Consecrate yourselves therefore, and be holy; for I am the LORD your God. Keep my statutes, and do them; I am the LORD who sanctify you" (Lev. 20:7–8). God sets before his people, in both Old and New Testaments, commandments that show us how to live a life of goodness—a life that will result in the maturation and purification of our characters; that will, in Paul's words, change us into the likeness of Jesus Christ "from one degree of glory to another" (2 Cor. 3:18).

That is not a goal that is sought after in our society. In modern America, who wants to be good anymore? We want to be free, self-fulfilled, integrated, successful, admired, even slim and beautiful —but good? No, that is not a sought-after character trait in our time. Despite the adulation we give to someone like Mother Teresa, few strive to be what an earlier society called a true man or woman of God—one in whom the Spirit of God shines forth in purity and integrity, one who is not just a decent person but a good person, who obviously lives in daily fellowship with God and obeys his commandments. God has too many demands that get in the way of our lifestyles, we think, and that contradict the easy immorality of our culture. So, while we will gratefully receive our redemption from our Lord, we often do not respond with gratitude for this gift by the obedience that leads to sanctification. Redeemed? Yes. Sanctified? No. Such is the spirit of our age.

God, however, has redeemed his people for a purpose, and so in the Holiness Code too, as in Deuteronomy, striving after holiness by way of obedience to God's commandments is the proper response to the redemptive action of the Lord (see Lev. 22:31–33).

God asks loving obedience in return for his love. He asked it at the very beginning, when he placed Adam in that garden, surrounded by gifts (Genesis 3). He asks it in his law and in every chapter of the scriptures that follow. "Take my yoke upon you, and learn from me" (Matt. 11:29). Taking that yoke is the way of abundant life, promise the scriptures. It is "for our good always," promises Deuteronomy. Out of his heart of overflowing love, God wishes us well. To trust this is so and therefore to accept God's guidance in his commandments is to love as he has first loved us.

The Distortion of the Law

These are the basic facts about the law and the commandments in the Old and New Testaments, but because this is the understanding of the law in most of the Bible, we need to ask why it is that Paul emphasizes justification by faith rather than by law, and why it is that Jesus attacks the practitioners of the law, the scribes and Pharisees.

The truth is that the nature and function of the law had come to be misunderstood in New Testament times and, in fact, ever since Israel had returned from Babylonian exile in the sixth and fifth centuries B.C.

As we have seen, the original understanding of the law presupposed that God had already entered into relation with his people. If God had not delivered Israel out of Egypt, there would have been no reason for the law. The law showed Israel how to live in her new life given her by God. It showed her how to respond to God's love and how to be a fit instrument of his redemption of all people. In short, the law was one evidence that Israel had been met by God and made his people.

If we ask, "Who was Israel?" the answer is that Israel was all those people who had been visited by God and who had experienced his presence. As we have seen before, Israel was the visited people (Ex. 33:12–16), and that visitation of his people by God was manifested in very concrete and material ways. God was present with Israel in her cult, the ark the symbol of his dwelling in her midst. When the ark was placed in the temple in Jerusalem, God resided in the midst of his chosen folk. But Israel also knew her God because he had done particular things in her history: He had delivered her out of Egypt, gone before her in the wilderness, established his covenant with her, given her the promised land, and founded her monarchy. Israel further, then, was made up of all those people who lived with the results of these actions of her present God. Israel was all those persons who were members of the covenant and who therefore lived as free men and women with their children in the promised land, under the rule of a Davidic king, and who worshiped in the temple on Zion. All those benefits were evidences of God's visitation of his people, and Israel was the people that enjoyed such benefits.

We must realize, however, that when Judah and Jerusalem were destroyed by the Babylonians in 587 B.C., these evidences of God's presence with and actions toward his people were wiped from the face of the earth in one great holocaust. The covenant was broken and covenant renewal ceremonies ended. Jerusalem with its temple was sacked and burned, the ark was lost, the Davidic king was taken in chains to Babylon, and Israel was deprived of her land and taken into exile. All evidences that the Lord had ever visited his people were destroyed except for one: Israel still had the law. That was the one gift of God that could be carried to Babylonia and back again; that was the one evidence left to Israel that she had ever been met by God.

When Nehemiah and Ezra returned to Judah with groups of exiles in the fifth century B.C. in order to restore the Jewish community, they found a diverse mixture of peoples living in that tiny subprovince of the Persian Empire. Many of the Jews inhabiting Judah had intermarried with surrounding peoples. Some of them spoke foreign tongues. The question was, Who in this diverse mixture of peoples is a member of Israel?

There was only one way to tell. The Israelite was the one who followed the law, because the law was the only remaining evidence of Israel's relation with the Lord. Obedience to the law became the criterion of who belonged to the people of God and who did not.

The Old Testament's original understanding of the law was therefore turned upside down. Israel was no longer defined by God's gracious actions, and a member of Israel was no longer one who had been redeemed by God, who enjoyed God's benefits, and who responded to that divine love by obedience and faith. An Israelite was now one who proved he or she was an Israelite by obedience to the law. A Jew was no longer made a member of the chosen people by God's act, but rather by his or her own act, and the law now replaced God's actions as the definition of the Israelite. Acceptance by God as a member of his people was no longer understood as a matter of faith in his activity. Instead, acceptance by God became a matter of works.

This was the position that Jesus attacked when he opposed the scribes and Pharisees and that Paul attacked when he inveighed against trust in the law. Both Jesus and Paul actually returned to the original understanding of the law, and both of them said that we are accepted by God and made members of his people not by our own inadequate works—we are always "unprofitable servants"; rather, we are made members of God's people simply by God's redemption of us and our trust in that redemption. Just as Deuteronomy had done, Jesus and Paul both called for our obedient response to God's deliverance of us (see Mark 12:29–31 and pars.; Rom. 12:1).

We love because he first loved us. We obey the commandments of our Lord, not in the effort to prove that we are his but because he has already made us his. We respond in obedience and thankfulness to God because he has already redeemed us.

Preaching from the Law

It is evident from the foregoing discussion that, when preaching from Old Testament law, one should keep several things in mind. First of all, many of the specific laws in the Old Testament cannot and should not be applied in their specificity to our society. After all, Israel's law was intended for people living in the ancient Near East between about 1200 and 350 B.C., and one cannot take God's instructions for that society and apply them willy-nilly to ours. The New Testament has made it quite clear that our Lord has fulfilled all the law and that we are delivered from many of the legal and cultic stipulations of the Book of the Old Covenant. In this respect, therefore, the lectionary is quite correct in citing only the Decalogue, the two great commandments from Deuteronomy and Leviticus, and largely narrative portions from Deuteronomy, along with the Aaronic blessing from Numbers 6 that is still used in our worship. Our Lord affirmed the continuing relevance of the Decalogue and of the two great commandments for our life (Mark 10:17–22 and pars.; 12:28–34 and pars; cf. Gal. 5:14), but most of Israel's cultic and societal laws are no longer applicable. We no longer have a sacrificial system of worship, or a court system like Israel's, or commerce or landholding or family life or warfare like hers, and she has laws regulating all those things. The specific laws simply do not apply.

Nevertheless, the *intention* of Israel's laws remains very pertinent to our lives as Christians, as I have tried to show. Israel's legal stipulations reveal much about God's basic desires for human life. For example, the ecumenical lectionary passage for the twenty-third Sunday in Pentecost, cycle A, from Exodus 22:21–27, calls for mercy toward the stranger, the poor, and the neighbor, and that demand is affirmed throughout the New Testament. Israel's laws reveal much about from what source the new Israel in Christ is to take the direction of its life, much about what it means to have a Lord, much about the manner in which we are to respond to his prior love toward us. We have shown these facts throughout this chapter, and the preacher should therefore use the law to instruct in these matters. That is one of the educational functions of the pulpit and the proper use of *torah* as teaching. Through such instruction, the people of God will come to have a better idea of who they are as God's covenant people and what they are to do in response to God's covenant mercy.

The preacher will also want to teach the congregation the Old Testament background and meaning of so much that has passed into Christian worship. A congregation needs to know what it means when the preacher pronounces the blessing or benediction upon them and says, "The LORD bless you and keep you: the LORD make his face to shine upon you, and be gracious to you: the LORD lift up his countenance upon you, and give you peace" (Num. 6:24–26). (A marvelous series of sermons could be preached on the benedictions in the Bible.) A congregation needs to know about the meaning and rituals of the Day of Atonement (Leviticus 16) and how those relate to the sacrifice of Christ on the cross. It needs to know the parallels and differences between Passover and the Lord's Supper. (There is a good deal of confusion in our time about the seder, which is often mistakenly identified with the eucharistic celebration.) It needs to hear about the Old Testament meaning of the covenant, and of covenant renewal ceremonies, and to realize that the Lord's Supper is also a covenant renewal. It needs to be taught about the responsibilities of the priesthood and how those relate to the priesthood of all believers. "You are to distinguish between the holy and the common, and between the unclean and the clean" (Lev. 10:10). Surely that commandment, if obeyed, could transform the life of a Christian community, as it lives in the midst of our society that is corrupt and degenerate in so many of its ways! It calls for the same pure goodness that Paul commanded of us (see Phil. 4:8).

Indeed, there is one way in which the specific laws in the Old Testament can legitimately be applied to the life of the Christian church: namely, if they are reflected and affirmed in the New Testament's teachings. The church is delivered from the necessity of obeying the law in order to gain its acceptance by God. We have seen that quite clearly. But the church shares with Israel the glad duty of responding to God's love by obedience to his directions in his commandments. Where Old Testament commandments are reaffirmed or deepened, as they often are by Jesus (cf. Matt. 5:17–48), they too serve as guides to the new life in Christ. For example, the Decalogue commands us to remember the sabbath day, to keep it holy (Ex. 20:8–10; cf. Deut. 5:12–14). In the Old Testament, that command is a gift of God's mercy. He not only gives to Israel work; he also gives her rest from work, along with all who come in contact with her and even those animals under her care. Meaningful labor and cessation from labor, in order to rest—both come from God's hand. We Christians no longer have a sabbath day; the day of resurrection, or

Sunday, has replaced it. But in his attitudes toward the sabbath day, Jesus affirmed the same mercy of God (Mark 2:23–28 and pars.): "The sabbath was made for man, not man for the sabbath." God wills for us the satisfaction of our physical needs, in the Markan story. The Letter to the Hebrews is even quite sure that rest from our labors and struggles is part of God's eschatological kingdom (Heb. 4:9), and insofar as the church has a foretaste of that kingdom, rest from labor is part of it (cf. Col. 2:17). God grants rest to his own; "he gives to his beloved sleep" (Ps. 127:2).

The pulpit should preach that merciful gift of God that is affirmed throughout the scriptures. The preacher should remember, however, not to turn the mercy into a legalistic command. The Fourth Commandment of the Decalogue is not a burden laid upon us, and it certainly is not an admonition to come to church every Sunday; other scripture passages call us to worship, but not this command in the Decalogue. God grants his beloved rest. That is purely mercy.

Perhaps this example of the sabbath illustrates the last point I would emphasize—that God's commandments in Old and New Testaments are gracious guidance for us in the way of abundant life. That cannot be emphasized too often. God wants abundant life for us. God loves us. He instructs us in order that we may fully live. He walks beside us, as he walked beside Israel, every step along the way, by means of his commandments. That can be applied to so many of the ethical issues in our society.

You see, when the Lord God created us, he wanted so much for us to understand, and so he gave us his word. "Beloved children," he said to us, "I want so much for you to live an abundant life, full of all the delights of my good earth, my gift to you. And so, please, please listen to me. There is a tree in the midst of the garden called disobedience. And if you eat of the fruit of that tree, the outcome of your eating will be death. For example, if you hate one another, you will destroy your community and nation and world. If you care only for yourself, you will disrupt your home and fail your children. If you despoil my good earth, you will end up with nothing but ugliness and want. And yes, if you do not properly use your bodies, and those of your spouse and neighbor, which I have created, you will surely die."

Can we be aware of the love in that statement—of the yearning of a God who wants so much for us to have life and have it more abundantly? "Oh that they had such a mind as this always," God cries out in Deuteronomy, "to fear me and to keep all my commandments, that it might go well with them and with their children for ever!" God forbids premarital, extramarital, promiscuous sexuality to us, because he wants it to go well with us and with our children forever. Is this not part of the message that we need to go out and tell to the church and the world in our troubled time—that God loves us, that he wants us to live, and so he has given us commandments about how to use our bodies?

The law and commandments, from Old Testament and New, are to be preached as merciful gifts given to us, out of the love of God.

CHAPTER 7

Preaching from the Prophets

Our understanding of the prophetic office and message influences the way we preach from the prophetic literature, and so it is necessary that we know what a prophet does before we can discuss how to preach from the Old Testament prophetic writings.

Certainly there are widespread misconceptions about the prophets' functions. Many clergy tend to view them simply as social reformers and preachers of ethics, who castigated their contemporaries for their failure to live up to proper ethical and moral standards. Thus, when modern preachers decry some practice in American society, they are often tempted self-righteously to believe that they are engaging in prophetic preaching. Or when church councils issue proclamations attacking particular government policies, they sometimes claim they are prophetic voices in the church. They may be. But the prophets of the Old Testament are not primarily social reformers, and their preaching is by no means limited to ethics, nor did they have some abstract standard of justice and morality by which they measured their society. The good for them was what God commanded, and it was good only because he commanded it. The prophets had no measure of righteousness outside of God himself.

Again, many persons believe that the prophets were little more than astute political observers, who were able to read the signs of the times and to foresee the inevitable consequences of individual and corporate actions. By such a definition, some statesmen in our day have been named prophets. But the prophets of the Old Testament are not political sages, advising and warning their compatriots on the basis of their own sagacity, and their message is not to be identified with political analysis and forecast.

In the minds of many lay people, of course, a prophet is one who foretells the future by some means. Thus, when popular psychics put out their annual forecasts of what is going to happen during the coming year, such forecasts are labeled "prophecy." The prophets of the Old Testament deal with the past and present almost as much as with the future, however, and predicting what is going to happen is not their sole or even primary function.

We use the word "prophet" carelessly. Persons in the church are often heard to say that Albert Schweitzer or Martin Luther King, Jr., was a prophet, but, when queried, they are not sure what they mean by that designation.

The Function of Prophets

What does a prophet do? If we may start with a rather general definition, an Old Testament prophet is one who illumines where and when and why God is at work in the world. For example, Amos 4:6–12 lists a whole series of natural and political events which God has brought about or in which he has been at work, just as Isaiah 10:5–6 maintains that God is at work in the ascendancy of the Assyrian Empire and its devastation of the nation Israel. According to Hosea 5:12 (cf. Isa. 28:13), God is also at work in the little judgments of every day, eating at Israel's internal supports like a moth and causing her self-dependencies to decay with dry rot. In Second Isaiah, the Creator God is the preserver of the round of nature (Isa. 40:26) and the Creator of the future, fulfilling all his promises (55:10–11). In Isaiah 57:15, he is the dweller with the contrite and humble, comforting and healing and restoring all those without a helper. The prophets of the Old Testament point to those events in which God is at work and tell why he is active in them. Thus, Jeremiah and Ezekiel can point to the destruction of Jerusalem and the exile of Judah in 587 B.C. and say they are events brought about by God because of Judah's sin, but they also can tell of that coming time when God will restore his people to their land, give them a future and a hope (Jer. 31:16–17), and cause them to live again (Ezek. 37:1–14).

Prophetic preaching therefore is preaching that illumines where God is at work in our world, whether in the realm of nature or of history. It therefore is very difficult for anyone in our time to function precisely as an Old Testament prophet functioned. They could be very specific. Isaiah could say God was at work in the attack of the Assyrian armies against Judah in 701 B.C., or Hosea could announce that God was *not* at work in the northern monarchy (8:4). They could put their finger on specific events and announce with great certainty the connection or absence of God. But the modern pulpit can no longer be that specific. We can say we believe God was at work defeating Hitler in World War II, but would any of us maintain that God was actively engaged in the firebombing of Dresden? We can believe that God is at work in the civil rights movement, but can we be sure that he sanctioned, much less caused, the Black Power movement, for example? Parishioners, in the depths of some tragedy, cry out, "How could God do this to me?" and we clergy must stammer and stutter or, better, remain silent, because we cannot be sure if God did it. We no longer can function as prophets, in the specific Old Testament sense of the word.

The reason is that the full Word of God has now been spoken and incarnated in Jesus Christ. The prophets of the Old Testament continually received new words from God, but now there is no new Word beyond that spoken in Christ Jesus. He has incarnated the whole Word of God in his life, death, and resurrection. The reconciliation between God and human beings has been effected; the kingdom of God has broken into time and space in the person of our Lord; eternal life under the reign of the Father has begun to become reality. There is nothing that need be added. Our preaching is prophecy, therefore, insofar as it points to God's work, only in a secondary sense. We explicate the meaning of the Word already spoken to us in Jesus Christ. We tell, on the basis of the scriptures' witness, where and why and how we see God at work in our time. But we do not receive words at odds with or in addition to that Word already spoken to us in our Lord.

Prophets in the Old Testament also mediated the will of God to Israel. They taught the *torah*. On the basis of the words given to them from God and in the light of Israel's sacred traditions, the prophets, along with the priests, taught their compatriots how to walk in their everyday lives (see Isa. 1:10–17 for an example). When the modern pulpit therefore spells out the manner of the Christian life on the basis of the full Word spoken in Jesus Christ, it is engaging in a prophetic function, just as was Jesus in the Sermon on the Mount or Paul in his instructions to his churches.

Prophets also represented Israel before God. We sometimes meet persons who think of the prophets as lonely martyr figures, who stood on God's side over against society, as they declared "to Judah her transgressions and to Israel her sins" (Micah 3:8); persecuted and rejected, the prophets represented God in the midst of a corrupt world and bore the consequences of that representation. Some modern ministers, ousted from their pulpits, have comforted themselves with that thought.

To be sure, the prophets were often persecuted (cf. Jeremiah 20) and some of them were killed (cf. 1 Kings 19:14; Matt. 5:12; Luke 13:34). True also, the prophet Jeremiah, in his call, was set against the whole land and its inhabitants (Jer. 1:18–19). We see the consequences of such prophetic isolation perhaps more clearly in

Jeremiah's book than in any other. "I sat alone, because thy hand was upon me," he complained to the Lord (Jer. 15:17; cf. 16:5–9).

The prophets of Israel never separated themselves from their sinful folk, however. They were not some sort of ancient beatniks, scorning and rejecting the establishment, nor were they revolutionaries, distancing themselves from society. Rather, they continually felt themselves bound up in the bundle of life with their fellow Israelites. Though set against his compatriots (see Jer. 9:1), Jeremiah weeps terribly over their fate, and that weeping is also the weeping of God. God loves his sinful folk, despite their rebellions against him, and the true prophets of God therefore love their people also. Like their Lord, the prophets cry out, "How can I give you up, O Ephraim! How can I hand you over, O Israel!" (Hos. 11:8).

The result is that one of the primary functions of the prophets is to intercede before God for the life of their people. The prophet Moses is portrayed at the beginning of Israel's history, exercising such intercession (so too Abraham in Gen. 20:17). He intercedes with God to turn aside his wrath over the golden calf (Ex. 32:11–14; Deut. 9:18–20) and over Israel's rebellion in the wilderness (Deut. 9:22–29), and many of the prophets who come after Moses follow in his footsteps. We think of Amos primarily as a prophet of stern justice, but when Amos is granted a vision of God's coming judgment on Israel's injustice, he begs that his people be spared.

> O Lord GOD, forgive, I beseech thee!
> How can Jacob stand?
> He is so small!
>
> Amos 7:2

Third Isaiah, after the return from exile, declares that he will never give the Lord rest; he will pound on the door in prayer, as it were, until God brings abundant life to Jerusalem and makes it a praise in the earth (Isa. 62:1). So insistent is Jeremiah in his pleading (cf. Jer. 11:14) that God must finally tell him to be silent and allow the judgment to come (7:16; cf. 15:1).

So deep is the prophets' identification with their sinful people that they suffer first in their own bodies and lives the destruction that is coming on their communities. Hosea must act out in his marriage with Gomer the separation of God from his whoring people (Hosea 1–3). Jeremiah is forbidden to marry, to go to a party, even to attend a funeral, because those are gifts of God's grace to Judah, and the Lord is withdrawing all means of grace (Jer. 16:5–9; note the marvelous view of a funeral: The ability to weep and mourn together is a gift of God's grace). Ezekiel must experience the horrors of siege, of exile, of captivity, by eating unclean food and thirsting for water and by being bound so he cannot move (Ezek 4:4–17). To show that the Lord's temple, "the delight of his eyes," will be destroyed in the fall of Jerusalem, Ezekiel must lose his own beloved wife (24:15–18). These prophets bear within themselves the burden of the word of God, and the judgment of that word on their people falls first on them. They are never separated from the society around them, and when their people are to be destroyed, their agonized cry is, "How long, O Lord?" (Isa. 6:11).

It is therefore no accident that the final picture of the true prophet in the Old Testament is that of a vicarious sufferer for both Israel and the nations. Moses had been the first vicarious sufferer for Israel's sin, dying outside of the promised land that his people might enter into it (Deut. 1:37; 3:26; 32:50–51 is an alternate priestly tradition, found also in Num. 20:12; 27:14). But the final prophet, the supreme prophet, is that Suffering Servant, by whose stripes all nations are healed and in whose death all righteousness is fulfilled for the peoples (Isa. 52:13—53:12).

That really is little different, however, from what Ezekiel had said a half century earlier. The true prophet, Ezekiel maintained, was one who had gone up into the breach and built up a wall for the house of Israel, that it might stand in battle in the day of the Lord (Ezek. 13:5; 22:30; cf. Ps. 106:23). Ezekiel was using military metaphors, and he saw God the Warrior turned enemy, attacking his people for their sins. The true prophet therefore, he said, is one who goes out on the front line, places his own body in the breach in the wall, and turns aside—by prayer and intercession and pleading and sacrifice—God's judgment on his people.

Is that not what the prophetic Word made flesh, Jesus Christ, did for us also? When the One came who fulfilled all the prophets, he went out there into no-man's-land, to the sinful breach in our wall, and he filled up the gap with his body and intercessions—"Father, forgive them; for they know not what they do" (Luke 23:34)—and he died to turn aside God's judgment on us and to give us eternal life.

Far from being a person who simply castigates society and individuals for their sins, a truly prophetic preacher is therefore one who goes out into the breach caused by our sinful rebellions against God and who, through prayer and preaching and love and sacrifice, builds up a wall for the new Israel, the church, that it may stand, and stand, and know salvation in the Day of the Lord (cf. Phil. 1:9–11).

The Prophetic Word

The prophets of the Old Testament function in their various roles on the basis of the revelation given to them by God at any particular time.

Over the years, the manner of that revelation changed. The early, nonwriting prophets, such as Elijah and Elisha and the other prophetic figures named and unnamed in the Samuel books and Kings, were recipients of the Spirit of God (cf. 1 Kings 22:1–23; 2 Kings 2:15). By the time of Amos, however, the emphasis shifted to revelation given by the word of God, and it is not until the time of Joel at the beginning of the fifth century B.C. that the Spirit occupies a central place again (Joel 2:28–29).

The word of God is the primary source of revelation for the writing prophets, but we have no idea how that word came to them. Isaiah says, "The LORD of hosts has sworn in my hearing" (Isa. 5:9), or "The LORD of hosts has revealed himself in my ears" (22:14), but we have little notion of what that means.

We can talk about the effects of the revelation on the prophets' lives. Ezekiel is sent into a seven-day stupor after the Lord calls him (Ezek. 3:15). Jeremiah hears sounds and sees sights of God's coming warfare against his people (Jer. 4:19–21). The author of Isaiah 21:3–4 is filled with anguish, so that his mind reels and horror appalls him. Isaiah feels that he is about to die (Isa. 6:5). The confrontation of the living God with these prophets has an overwhelming effect on them. They are set under a compulsion to speak the word, which they sometimes cannot resist (Jer. 20:9; but see 15:15–21), and they are sent to deliver that word to Israel, whether she hears or refuses to hear (Ezek. 3:11).

We can say with certainty, further, that the word of God is given to a prophet from outside of himself. The word is not the product of the prophet's thought, analysis, and musing. This is symbolized clearly by both Jeremiah and Ezekiel, who say that they have "eaten" the word (Jer. 15:16; Ezek. 3:1–3); the word has come from God and has been taken into their beings.

Apparently the prophets have no preparation for their calls. Amos disavows all connections with prophet tradition and guilds (Amos 7:14–15) and is seemingly jerked out of his former manner of life and sent on a mission for God. Ezekiel must be admonished, "Be not rebellious like that rebellious house; open your mouth, and eat what I give you" (Ezek. 2:8). Jeremiah tries to escape his calling by pleading that he is only a youth and does not know how to speak (Jer. 1:6; cf. Moses in Exodus 3 and 4). In fact, as Jeremiah's biography is revealed to us by his laments, sometimes called his "confessions," he seems almost totally unfit for his task. These prophets evidence no great personal faith or astute insight or prophetic training. They are simply set under a compulsion to speak the word of God, which takes their personalities and endowments into the divine service (cf. Acts 26:14).

The prophets are given the word in order to accomplish specific tasks. There is never any indication that the prophets' personal relations with God are the reasons for God's revelation to them, and such relations are not intended as models for the religious life. Rather, the prophets each are sent to reveal God's working in a specific situation in Israel's life or to give directions to her at a particular time in her history. We should therefore be very hesitant in our preaching to turn the prophetic message into timeless religious principles, which are then applied to our day and society. For example, the Lord, speaking through Isaiah of Jerusalem, urges King Ahaz of Judah to trust in the promise to David rather than in an international military alliance with Assyria (Isa. 7:1–9), but the modern preacher should not lift that text out of its historical context and use it as a timeless argument for pacifism or isolationism in our age.

The contemporary preacher also cannot legitimately identify the prophetic message with a particular ideology or social program in our time. This is a widespread practice of the American pulpit among both liberal and conservative church leaders, whose positions on any public issue can be fairly well predicted in terms of their ideologies. The claim, then, is that such positions are both Christian and prophetic. In truth, what they do is to freeze the free word of God into static propositions, and the lively oracles of God, which stood opposed to every human claim to absolute wisdom and power, have themselves been made the servant of absolutist pretensions.

There is nothing "frozen" about the prophetic word in the Bible. It moves and shifts and is reformulated with every restless, purposeful thrust of God forward toward the goal of his kingdom, and the prophets continually insist that knowledge of the purpose and will of God can be had only in the most intimate communion with him. Such communion is compared by Second Isaiah, for example, to that of expectant pupil with beloved teacher. "Morning by morning he wakens, he wakens my ear to hear as those who are taught," writes that prophet (Isa. 50:4). It therefore is very difficult for any preacher who does not himself or herself enjoy that intimate communion with God through the daily discipline of prayer and worship rightly to interpret the prophetic message, for he or she will not understand the context in which that message has been spoken. The prophets are totally dependent on God's lively, continuing revelation to them, in fellowship with them, and this is further emphasized by the fact that often the prophets had to wait for some time before they received God's word (cf. Jer. 42:7).

The specificity of the word spoken by God to the prophet concerning any particular event is further shown by the length of the prophets' ministries. By no means did all the prophets serve in that capacity all their lives. Amos was given a very short task to do. He went north, to the king's sanctuary at Bethel (Amos 7:12–13), he spoke the words God gave him to speak, and then he returned home to Tekoa to become a herdsman and dresser of sycamore trees again. God's revelations to Isaiah apparently took place in waves. He was given words to speak for a while and was then ordered to remain silent for a period (Isa. 8:16–17). Jeremiah, on the other hand, served as a prophet all his life long. Prophets were called in order to do a job for the Lord, and when the job was done the prophet received no further revelation and returned to his or her former occupation. Certainly the subsequent faith and life of an Amos, for example, were influenced by his brief prophetic ministry; but the fact that we hear nothing further of him testifies to the fact that his importance lay in the task he was called to do for God and not in his own personal experience.

This functional nature of the prophets' calling cannot be overemphasized, and the great stress that some interpreters have placed on the psychological adjustment of the prophets is misplaced. The Lord had very little interest in making his prophets "real persons," and the development of their individual personalities was never the goal of God's action. God asked of them obedience, faithfulness, courage, and sacrifice, but he never stopped to inquire if they were happy in their jobs. The prophets had little time in their work to keep pulling out their psychological roots for the purpose of self-examination. In the lives of the prophets, it was God's purposes and not those of human beings that were important. As in every other part of the Bible, the chief actor in the prophetic message is God. His doings, his purposes, his will hold the center of the stage, and only as the prophets serve his will and purpose do they possess any importance at all. That is something to remember in relation to the Christian ministry. It should also prompt us, in our sermons, to concentrate on the prophets' witnesses to God and not on their personalities, as is often the temptation, especially in preaching from Jeremiah.

As we pointed out in chapter 3, the prophetic word of God is an active, effective force that brings to pass that of which it speaks. Thus, when God speaks through Amos to say, "The end has come upon my people Israel" (Amos 8:2), that word is released into the northern kingdom's history and works its effects until the end does indeed come, in the fall of Israel to Assyria in 722 B.C.

Sometimes the word takes the form, in the prophetic books, of symbolic actions. Jeremiah wears a yoke, symbolic of the continuing captivity to Babylon (Jeremiah 28), or Ezekiel takes a brick and on it constructs a clay model of Jerusalem with siege works around it, symbolic of the siege of the city (Ezek. 4:1–2). Such instances are acted-out declarations of the word of God, and they too will affect the future until their messages come to pass. Whatever the manner in which the prophets release the word of God into time and space, it brings about a new situation.

It follows, therefore, that prophetic preaching is finally the proclamation of the active word of God from the scriptures—the release of that word into the life of a congregation to do its judging and saving work. God works his powerful will in the world through the instrument of his word, along with his Spirit, and that word will never return to God void, but will accomplish that which he purposes.

The Goal of the Prophets

Certainly the content of the prophetic messages can be understood properly only in the context of the Bible's one story. It is not surprising, therefore, that the prophets rehearse God's long history with his people.[1] The history has been evidence of God's mercy and love toward his elected people and of the divine purpose (Ex. 19:4–6) to which they have been called.

By way of response, Israel is asked to live as God's new community in justice and righteousness. She can live in such a manner by following God's covenant commandments, as they are delivered to her in the law and in the day-by-day *torah* instructions given by prophets and priests. Thus a multitude of ethical, economic, political, and cultic instructions for the life of the community are found in the prophetic writings. They deal with treatment of the poor, law courts, business dealings, prayer, government, international treaties, wealthy ostentation, family life and divorce, ritual fasts, tithing, sacrifices—in short, with almost every conceivable area of the community's life.

The prophets are not moralists or legalists, however, and they are not primarily preachers of the covenant law. Only twice in the prophetic writings do these men of God quote portions of Israel's basic law, the Decalogue (Hos. 4:2; Jer. 7:9). At the heart of the covenant relationship were the requirements of love and trust, and that which the prophets ask from Israel, above all else, is the devotion of her heart to God. "Circumcise yourselves to the LORD, remove the foreskin of your hearts," begs Jeremiah (4:4). "Get yourselves a new heart and a new spirit!" proclaims Ezekiel (18:31). All of the prophets echo that demand.[2] They ask from Israel, on God's behalf, that inner devotion that cleaves to God always and issues then in heartfelt love and obedience to his will. Whether the issue at hand be Israel's worship (Isa. 29:13–14) or means of government (Jer. 22:16) and defense (Isa. 31:1) or ethical practice within society, the prophets' call is for a love for God that eschews every other ultimate devotion and for a trust in his guidance and activity that dispels all reliance on or fear of human ways and powers.

In delivering such a call, the prophets emphasize various motifs. In Hosea and Jeremiah, the call is for love for God, like the love of a faithful wife for her husband (Hos. 6:4; Jer. 3:19) or the love of an obedient son for his father (Hos. 11:1–4; Jer. 3:19; cf. Mal. 1:6). At the same time, both prophets emphasize the necessity of *knowing* God (Hos. 4:1, 6; 5:4; 6:6; 13:4; Jer. 2:8; 4:22; 9:23–24; 31:34)—of intimately and interiorly knowing his character, because one has lived in personal relationship with him day by day. The result of such knowledge, then, is a saturation of oneself with the will of God, a delight in his purpose, and a willingness to be led by him in every area of life.

In Isaiah 1–39, the emphasis is on faith or trust. Ahaz of Judah is to trust God's promise to David in the face of the Syro-Ephraimitic threat (Isa. 7:9), just as Hezekiah is to trust the power and plan of God and not the horses and chariots of Egypt (31:1) or the shelter afforded by international military alliances (30:1–2). It is in "returning and rest" that Israel will be saved from Assyria and in "quietness and in trust" in the Holy One of Israel that her strength lies. God is the Lord of all nations and Assyria but an instrument in his hand. The cornerstone of the new Jerusalem, therefore, will be that congregation or that one who believes and who rests the future in God's plan (Isa. 28:16; cf. Rom. 9:30–33; 10:11; Mark 12:10; Acts 4:11; Eph. 2:20; 1 Peter 2:4–6).

In Second Isaiah, the prophet's call to Israel is to trust the future saving act of God that will bring her new life (Isa. 42:9; 43:19) and to wait for that action (40:27–31), just as, in Third Isaiah and Jeremiah and Ezekiel, all hope is to rest on God's coming salvation (Isaiah 60–62; Jer. 29:11; 32; Ezekiel 37). Similarly, in Habakkuk, the prophet relies, midst all the turmoil and terrors of life, on the promise that God's kingdom comes (Hab. 2:3), and it is that reliance that will enable Judah to deal justly in society (2:6–14) and that enables Habakkuk personally to sing his magnificent song of faith (3:17–19).

Proclaiming the Prophetic Message

These facts have decisive importance for preaching from the prophetic literature, because finally every sermon from that literature needs to be formed with the prophets' central call for love and trust in mind. Prophetic preaching deals with the hearts of the covenant people, and its goal is to awaken that faith in the congregation that will enable them to trust their Lord in all circumstances and to obey him with willing and grateful hearts. Prophetic preaching consists not in exhortation alone but, first of all, in that proclamation of God's gracious acts toward his covenant people that inspires them to respond to his love in reciprocal love, acted out in obedience.

Israel's failure to respond with such love and obedience is her sin, according to the prophets. Sin, in their writings, is not Israel's breaking of ethical and ritual rules or the violation of moral and religious norms, but the failure to love and trust her Lord. In every realm of her life, Israel rejects an intimate and faithful relationship with her God. In the light of all that the Lord has done for his people, that is almost incomprehensible.

> Have I been a wilderness to Israel,
>   or a land of thick darkness?
> Why then do my people say, "We are free,
>   we will come no more to thee"?
> Can a maiden forget her ornaments,
>   or a bride her attire?
> Yet my people have forgotten me
>   days without number.
>   Jeremiah 2:31–32[3]

As in Genesis 3 and throughout the Bible, sin in the prophets' views is real but finally inexplicable. Given all that God has done for her, why should Israel rebel against him? Given all that God has done in Jesus Christ in the history of the Christian church, why should we forget him days without number? The prophets recount Israel's past with God in order to reawaken her faith in her Lord, and we modern preachers tell "the old, old story" in order that faith may come by hearing (Rom. 10:17).

There is no denial in the Bible of the reality and power of sin, and those modern sects and success-preachers who would proclaim "'Peace, peace,' when there is no peace" with God (Jer. 6:14; 8:11) have nothing in common with the prophets. The latter know the awful, binding power of sin as it affects their people. Sin lames all power of self-assessment, so that Israel does not even see the evil she is doing (cf. Jer. 8:6–7), and part of the purpose of the prophets is to enable Israel to see, in order that she may repent, in order that she may turn around and walk her daily way in the opposite direction.

The prophets also find to their dismay, however, that sin holds their people captive and that Israel has no power within herself to repent and correct her ways (Hos. 5:4; Jer. 13:23). She is slave to sin and helpless to heed the call to repent (cf. Isa. 6:9–10; Rom. 6:17–22).

Israel is therefore one with all peoples and nations, joining with them in a common rebellion against the rule of the Lord over human life.

It is obvious therefore why moralistic preaching of itself cannot heal a people's life or effect their return to God. Sin "is written with a pen of iron; with a point of diamond it is engraved on the tablet" of our hearts (Jer. 17:1), and there is nothing we can do to expunge the writing. To be told by a preacher to turn from evil and do the good by our own power is to be assigned an impossible task. Sin is one slave master from which persons cannot escape on their own.

Sinful rejection of the lordship of God also bears with it consequences, however. God will not put up with rebellion against his rule or overlook rejection of his love (cf. Jer. 7:16–20). He is not mocked (Gal. 6:7), and he will not countenance wrong (Hab. 1:13). He declares to Israel:

> What is in your mind shall never happen—the thought, "Let us be like the nations." . . . As I live, says the Lord GOD, surely with a mighty hand and an outstretched arm, and with wrath poured out, I will be king over you.
>
> Ezekiel 20:32–33

God will be king over Israel, over his church, over his world—if not in love, then in wrath. The result is that the preexilic prophets announce God's warfare against his covenant people. An unrepentant people can no longer be forgiven their sins. Sin must finally be done to death (cf. Amos 7:1; 8:1–2). In the Lord's own fearful words:

> My heritage has become to me
>   like a lion in the forest,
> she has lifted up her voice against me;
>   therefore I hate her.
>
> Jeremiah 12:8

The divine hatred of sin can get rid of it only by destroying it. So we read the awful repetition in Ezekiel (vs. 5–7):

> Disaster after disaster! Behold, it *comes.* An end has *come,* the end has *come;* it has awakened against you. Behold, it *comes.* Your doom has *come* to you, O inhabitant of the land; the time has *come* (emphasis added).

Perhaps we modern preachers have never made such a message clear to our congregations—that God is not mocked and that we too therefore daily suffer under the wrath of a sovereign Lord. The breakdown of our communities, our darkness, pain, and strife, our warfare, our hatreds, our destruction, and our death are not just the automatic effects of our blind wrongdoings but are in fact God actively giving us up to our sins, returning them upon our own heads, as the Old Testament puts it, or subjecting us to the fire of his very real judgments. Our people do not believe that God does anything any more (cf. the same attitude in Zeph. 1:12), and so they do not believe there is actual, active judgment from God when we reject his fellowship. We are very much like the people in Jeremiah's time (Jer. 7:8–11). We believe we can break the commandments and go and stand before God in his house, which is called by his name, and say, " 'We are delivered!'—only to go on doing all these abominations." We have turned the place of worship into a "den of robbers" (cf. Mark 11:17 and pars.), where we think to hide and be safe from the consequences of our sins. We have little of the prophetic sense of God's active work of judgment, of God's purification and discipline and crucifixion of his people. Surely part of the task of prophetic preaching is to announce that "strange deed" and "alien work" of God's judgment (Isa. 28:21)—"strange" because we believe ourselves exempt and "alien" because God's nature is love that always desires that we live and not die (cf. Ezek. 18:32).

On the other hand, some preachers are prone to make the opposite error: They equate prophetic preaching *only* with judgmental preaching, and they fail to realize that the prophets all also proclaim salvation. God is not mocked, but he also is not defeated by Israel's rebellion against him. At the beginning of her history, God made a promise to Israel that he would be her God, make her a great nation, give her a land of her own, and bring blessing on all the families of the earth through her (Gen. 12:1–7). God never forgets his promises, nor does he leave them unfulfilled. The grass and flower that are human life and achievements wither and fade, but the word of our God stands forever (Isa. 40:8). On the other side of the judgment announced by the prophets, therefore, which finds its first fulfillments in the fall of the northern kingdom to Assyria in 722 B.C. and in the Babylonian exile of 593–538 B.C., and even in the midst of those judgments, these messengers from God foresee God's promises brought to abundant fruition. God cannot forget this covenant people whom he has chosen for himself any more than he can forget his church (Isa. 49:15). He has them graven on the palms of his hands (49:16), and though they have run away from him, God cannot give them up (Hos. 11:8–9). Though the sacred history seems at an end, the prophets nevertheless announce that new act of God in the future (Isa. 43:18–19; cf. 48:6; 54:4; 65:17) that will gather up all his past words and bring them to completion. There is no direct line in the Old Testament between God's promises of salvation and their fulfillment. The sacred history is marred and broken by Israel's disobedience and God's radical judgment upon it. There is nevertheless the silver cord of God's love for his own that binds the whole together, and that cord is never broken and that love never at an end.

So it is that the prophets announce to a people without a land that "houses and fields and vineyards shall again be bought" in Palestine (Jer. 32:15). To a decimated, struggling, impoverished population they promise offspring as numerous as the stars (Isa. 54:2–3) and the treasures of heaven and earth (Hag. 2:6–9). To a people that has become "no people," without king or independent government, they promise a ruler over a united kingdom who will feed his sheep like a good shepherd (Ezekiel 34; 37:24–28; Jer. 23:5). For exiles without a place to worship, they envision a glorious new temple (Zech. 4:7–10; Ezekiel 40–48). To a people cut off from God, they promise a new and unbreakable covenant (Jer. 31:31–34), with God's sanctuary set in the midst of them forevermore (Ezek. 37:26–28).

More, the prophets proclaim the transformation of Israel's hearts and wills, with their faithfulness the cornerstone of a new people of God (Isa. 28:16), so that they do no wrong and utter no deceit and God himself rejoices over them (Zeph. 3:11–17), as they find their sole refuge in him and look to him for all righteousness (Jer. 23:6). Such a renewed and transformed people will become God's promised blessing in the midst of the earth (Isa. 19:24–25), that light to the nations (Isa. 49:6) to whose brightness all peoples will stream (Isa. 60:1–2; 2:2) because the nations have perceived that God is in the midst of them (Zech. 8:20–23). Then the knowledge of God will cover the earth as the waters cover the sea (Isa. 11:9; Hab. 2:14), nations will learn war no more (Isa. 2:4), and none shall be afraid (Micah 4:4), for all will have become "holy to the LORD" and God will be all in all (Zech. 14:20–21).

In short, beyond God's alien work of warfare against his people, he promises the warfare ended, our iniquity pardoned, and the full covering over of all our sins—the divine voice proclaiming, "Comfort, comfort my people" (Isa. 40:1–2). Perhaps in our time of homelessness and hopelessness and helplessness, which so many in our congregations know and which we experience as a people who have lost our way, we need most of all to hear these prophetic oracles of salvation. Announcing them is also part of the work of prophetic preaching.

We must realize, however, that all these hopeful proclamations by the prophets are promises for the future, and we need to ask, therefore, What became of these ancient words? To answer that question for a congregation, the preacher must pair prophetic oracle with New Testament passage, and it is to that necessary art we now turn.

The Lectionary and the Pairing of Texts

Those preachers who follow, or at least consult, the three-year ecumenical lectionary have much of the work of pairing Old and New Testament texts already done for them. Throughout that lectionary and in accordance with New Testament understanding, Jesus is understood as the fulfillment of many of the prophetic promises. For example, on the second Sunday of Advent in Year A, he is understood as the promised shoot of Jesse, who will also rule the Gentiles, and Isaiah 11:1–10 is matched with Romans 15:4–13 and Matthew 3:1–12. Or on the fourth Sunday in that season, Christ is Immanuel, promised in Isaiah 7:10–14, and Romans 1:1–7 and Matthew 1:18–25 are used. Dozens of examples could be given.

This is a method of pairing texts that is often neglected in our preaching, because its primary concern is with identifying who Jesus is, and we preachers sometimes think that our congregations already know Jesus' identity. But a lot is at stake in that identification. It has to do with much more than simply acknowledging with our lips that Jesus is the Messiah or Immanuel or the Son of God. It concerns whether or not God is faithful to his promises and therefore whether we can trust the further promises God in Christ has made to us. It reveals the working of God in our world over centuries of history and sets us in that ongoing action as recipients of its grace. It illumines the breaking into time and space of God's new promised age, with all its powers of forgiveness and healing and victory over sin and death. For example, consider the old age and the new in Isaiah 35:1–10, which is a stated Old Testament lesson for Advent:

The old age is like a desert, says the prophet Isaiah in our Old Testament lesson. It is the age of desolation, of thirst, of wandering aimlessly through the wilderness of life. Or in the words of T. S. Eliot, the old age is a wasteland:

A heap of broken images, where the sun beats,
And the dead tree gives no shelter, the cricket no relief,
And the dry stone no sound of water.[4]

The old age is a time of despair, of no hope in the world—where generation after generation of young men go to war's bloody graves, with no good result from their sacrifice; the time when the strong strut ruthlessly through the earth and the weak have no helper; the age when violence rules a city's streets and the dark is a place of terror; the age when hatreds fester in our living rooms and families fall apart.

The old age is a time without God, when fulfillment lies only in ourselves; a time when pride drives us to a life of constant competition with our fellows; a time when there is no ultimate meaning to all that we are doing, and work after all is just a way to make a buck.

The ruler of the old age is the specter death, and all through the course of it, he inexorably claims his victims, putting an end to every dream, every joy, every lovely human relationship. Yes, I think we know the old age, because you and I are living in it. Scholars sometimes call it B.C.E.—before the common era—but it is all too common in our lives now, is it not? And so our forebears in the faith gave it another title. They said it was B.C.—before Christ—before Christmas ever came.

And the glad news of the Christian gospel is that there is also an A.D.—anno domini, the year of our Lord—the new age of Jesus Christ. It is the breaking in of this new age that we celebrate at Christmas.

What are the characteristics of this totally new time? It is, said the prophet Isaiah, peering into God's future, no longer a time of desert, of aimless wandering through the wilderness. No, the new age that God has planned is like a time of well-watered abundance, a time when flowers bloom in the crannies of human lives and bent souls are straightened and given some majesty. It is a time when sorrow and sighing have been done away, and joyful song has broken the stillness. It is a time when the powers of death no longer reign on the earth, and human beings are ransomed from the evil forces that hold them captive—from fear, from sin, from anxiety and weakness, from meaningless wandering through their days.

Indeed, proclaimed the prophet Isaiah, when the new age comes, the eyes of the blind shall be opened and the ears of the deaf unstopped; the lame man shall leap like a deer and the tongue of the dumb sing for joy. Human life, with all its still, sad song of sorrow, will be transformed into praise and joy, wholeness and health.

Significantly, then, some lectionaries pair Isaiah 35:1–10 with Matthew 11:2–15, and the preacher has the magnificent opportunity of explaining how the new age has begun in Christ, hidden and yet wondrously present for all those who trust him. The pairing of texts on the basis of promise and fulfillment allows us once again to tell the "old, old story" that is ever new.

Contrary to some published opinion, however, the ecumenical lectionary by no means relates Old Testament to New only on the basis of promise-fulfillment. It also picks up motifs common to both Testaments. For example, for the twentieth Sunday in Pentecost A, Isaiah's parable of the vineyard (Isa. 5:1–7) is coupled with Jesus' parable of the vineyard in Matthew 21:33–43. Thus, the warning to the vineyard of Israel is paralleled by that to the vineyard of the church. Again, the blind and deaf servant Israel, of Isaiah 42:14–21, is compared with the church that was once in darkness, in Ephesians 5:8–14 (Lent 3A), and Jesus' healing of that blindness is set forth by using the story of the man born blind, in John 9:1–41, for the gospel lesson.

Frequently the lectionary relates texts on the basis of common themes, as is true in the pairing of Isaiah 6:1–13 and Luke 5:1–11; of Jeremiah 1:1–10 and Luke 4:21–32; or of the joining of Ezekiel 37:1–14, Romans 8:6–11, and John 11:1–53; or of Malachi 4:1–2a, 2 Thessalonians 3:6–13, and Luke 21:5–19.

Sometimes one can work a contrast between the Old Testament and New Testament stated readings. For example, on the fourth Sunday in Lent of Year A, Hosea 5:15—6:6 is the stated reading, with its condemnation of Israel for her transitory love for God. Romans 8:1–10, then, is the epistle lesson, announcing that there is no condemnation in Christ. The textural pairings found in the ecumenical lectionary are powerful tools to aid in the development of sermons.

There are times, however, when the preacher may want to use a stated Old Testament text but then pair it with a different New Testament reading. For example, in several lectionaries Isaiah 52:7–10 is the assigned Old Testament reading for Christmas Day in Years B or C. Its beginning is familiar to all of us.

> How beautiful upon the mountains
>   are the feet of him who brings good tidings,
> who publishes peace, who brings good tidings of good,
>   who publishes salvation,
>   who says to Zion, "Your God reigns."

The lectionary may pair this with Hebrews 1:1–12, but one could take the central announcement of the Isaiah text—"Your God reigns"—and pair it with John 18:33—19:22 instead, to proclaim the reign of Christ from the cross.

Non-Lectionary Texts from the Prophets

There are also times when the preacher will want to use prophetic material that is not listed in a lectionary. If we survey the list of stated texts in the ecumenical lectionary, we find serious omissions in its employment of the prophets' messages; a three-year lectionary cannot include everything. By far, the Isaiah corpus receives the most attention. Here are the number of times prophetic texts are cited for the Old Testament readings:

Isaiah 1–39	17	Daniel	3	Micah	2
Isaiah 40–55	20	Hosea	4	Habakkuk	1
Isaiah 56–66	16	Joel	2	Zephaniah	4
Jeremiah	19	Amos	6	Zechariah	2
Ezekiel	9	Jonah	2	Malachi	3

Obadiah, Nahum, and Haggai are not cited at all and have become almost nonentities in the church; this is true also of the other minor prophets, with the exception of Amos and Hosea. Nor has the Common Lectionary remedied the situation. The result has been an incomplete presentation of the canonical revelation and a neglect of exceedingly fruitful preaching materials.

For example, Zechariah 8:1–8 presents the most startling new picture of the kingdom of God come on earth:

What is the kingdom of God, according to the prophet Zechariah? It is a public park! It is a park where old people are no longer cold and lonely and ill and senile, but participants in a community. It is a public park where the elderly can sit together and bask in the sun and talk and laugh over the good old days, in full vigor and clear mind and satisfaction of life.

The kingdom of God is a public park, where little children can run and play in its squares, in safety and fun and delight. It is a place where no pervert is waiting to lure them away with offers of candy, where no drug pusher is lurking to tempt the older children to try one of his brightly colored pills. It is a place where no child is abused or unwanted or malnourished, and where there is not even a bully among the group, shoving and taunting the littler ones until they break into tears. The kingdom of God, says Zechariah, is a public park, where the streets are safe for children.[5]

To give another example from the same prophet, Zechariah 2:1–5 lends itself beautifully to a sermon on the church as the new Zion of God. The text itself gives the outline of the sermon, when paired with 1 Corinthians 3:10–23:

1. The church, the new Jerusalem, is to have no walls, no manmade limits on its population or membership (Zech. 2:4). We cannot be satisfied with the dimensions of the old Jerusalem, of the church as it is or used to be.

2. But the church does have a cornerstone and a foundation, whose name is Jesus Christ (1 Cor. 3:11), and our membership is founded on him.

3. The church's only defense is her God (Zech. 2:5). She is not to rely on earthly power and politics.

4. The church's one glory is the presence of God in Christ in her

midst (Zech. 2:5). Her glory does not come from her learning or architecture or clergy or programs.

5. On these facts, build up the church.

The forgotten book of Nahum also bears a powerful message. The book is a prediction and a celebration of the fall of the Assyrian capital of Nineveh in 612 B.C. War-horses charge in this book, and war chariots rumble through the streets. Swords flash and spears glitter, and soldiers stumble over heaps of corpses. As a result, Nahum is never used in the church. All scripture is inspired by God—but maybe with the exception of Nahum, we think. However, Nahum is first of all a book about God, and the whole is to be interpreted in the light of its opening poem, Nahum 1:1–8. If we pair that with Romans 2:4–11, Nahum's message is the same as Paul's: "There will be tribulation and distress for every human being who does evil" (Rom. 2:9). And so nations still totter and disappear, as did Assyria, and warfare still engulfs the earth. Tanks rumble, and missiles flash, and soldiers stumble over heaps of corpses. Societies disintegrate, and families split, and we cannot get to sleep at night. For a jealous God, an avenging God, is the Lord of the church, who by no means clears the guilty.

But in the midst of the bloodshed, Nahum offers its word of grace: This avenging God is also "slow to anger."

How true that is to our experience of him! Think how long he put up with the follies and foibles and lack of faith of his people Israel! Then think how long he has put up with our equal shortcomings and sins! He has even been slow to threaten us: He has let us ignore the book of Nahum for years! He has let us wander on our merry way and never shown us the disaster staring us in the face. He has let us play at being our own gods and goddesses, as if we were children out-of-doors, engaged in charades, and he has been very hesitant to put an end to our game by telling us that the night is coming. Slow to threaten, slow even to show displeasure, has been this patient, long-suffering God of ours.

And then, when he has finally threatened us, how slow he has been to carry out the threat. . . . The nuclear missiles have not yet loosed their warheads, God's sun still shines on us, and you and I still draw those breaths of life with which a gracious God fills our lungs. Yes, God is slow, very slow, to carry out his threat of death.

Yet, "Do you not know," asks Paul in our New Testament lesson, "that God's kindness is meant to lead you to repentance?"

Nahum 1:1–8, paired with Romans 2:4–11, is a call to repentance—a call that the church of our day needs very much to hear.

Obadiah too is a neglected book, with its pronouncement of judgment on Edom for its violence against Judah at the time of the fall of Jerusalem to the Babylonians in 587 B.C. In the scriptures, Edom becomes a prophetic type for all those opposing God, and its downfall was understood by the prophets as an indispensable part of the messianic age (cf. Isa. 34:5–6; 63:1–6). Thus, Obadiah too may serve as a call to repentance. The book centers primarily, however, on Edom's violation of its brotherly covenant with Judah and is a testimony to how seriously God takes human covenants, founded in natural relationships. He is the Guardian of those human bonds—of parents with children, husbands with wives, siblings with siblings—just as he is the Guardian of the bonds between kings or judges or princes and their people. The sanctity of human and societal relationships is the primary emphasis of the book. One might pair its message with Matthew 5:21–32.

As for Haggai, its primary message is contained in 1:8: "Go up to the hills and bring wood and build the house, that I may take pleasure in it and that I may appear in my glory, says the LORD." The date is 520 B.C., Judah is in desperate straits as a tiny subprovince of the Persian Empire, and God's temple lies in ruins. Thus, this book has to do with building the temple and, by analogy, with building up the church. As in our day, there are those in Haggai's time who despair over the inglorious sanctuary they are able to provide for God. They criticize her tiny proportions and weep over her insignificant place in their society. But Haggai is a book of great expectations, founded on the presence and power and purpose of God: "Work, for I am with you, says the LORD of hosts, according to the promise that I made you when you came out of Egypt. My Spirit abides among you; fear not" (Hag. 2:4–5). Where God is present and at work, the future is full of promise, and "no eye has seen, nor ear heard, nor the heart of man conceived, what God has prepared for those who love him" (1 Cor. 2:9). Haggai serves as a call to show forth our love for God by building up his church, in anticipation of his glorious future.[6]

The list of prophetic texts not found in the lectionary but that certainly should be preached is almost endless. Consider these further examples:

From Isaiah

1:10–17   "Even though you make many prayers, I will not listen; your hands are full of blood": the relation of our worship to our life's practices

2:6–22   "The Lord alone will be exalted in that day": God's judgment on all sinful pride and glory at the end of history; the Christian hope

3:16—4:1   A scathing attack on high fashion and conspicuous consumption

14:4–21   A taunt song, the finest passage ever written about the result of national pride that ignores the sovereignty of God

28:14–22   The promised cornerstone of the new people of God, applied by the New Testament to Christ

32:1–8   The messianic king, "the shadow of a mighty rock within a weary land"

40:21–31   "But they who wait for the LORD shall renew their strength": the call to wait in faith for the action of the incomparable God

57:14–21   "I dwell in the high and holy place, and also with him who is of a contrite and humble spirit": God's forgiving advent to those who will receive him

63:1–6   "Mine eyes have seen the glory of the coming of the Lord": God's defeat of his enemies and his salvation of his people

From Jeremiah

2:4–13   God "the fountain of living waters": see the discussion of this text in the section on rhetorical analysis in chapter 3

4:23–26   The end of the world, the reversal of creation

5:1–9   Jeremiah searches Jerusalem for one righteous person, but finds that rich and poor alike are equally guilty: "None is righteous, no, not one" (Rom. 3:10)

8:18–9:1   "Is there no balm in Gilead?"

11:18–20   Jeremiah's earliest "confession," in which he shows us how to deal with our hatreds

I used this last text in a chapel meditation and paired it with Romans 12:14–21:

> "Let me see thy vengeance upon them, O Lord." There! the hatred is expressed, in all its reality, all its anger, all its justified claim. But the hatred is expressed to God and turned over to his hands. That is the one avenue of retaliation the wrongfully injured Christian has. And if you believe this God of ours acts in the world, then you know God will set things right. "Vengeance is mine. I will repay," says the Lord. If the cause is just, God will hear it and act. If it springs from our own illusion, God will take care of that too. But there it rests. The case is in his hands. The hatred has been turned over to him. And we no longer find it festering within us or affecting our daily life . . . . We can get on with our business of trying to lead faithful

lives. Indeed, we may even find ourselves so able once again to forgive and love our enemies, that the burning coals of repentance are heaped on them too, and their evil is replaced by good.

Also from Jeremiah

17:1–4	Sin is written with a point of diamond upon our hearts and cannot be erased by human means
18:1–12	God the Potter can remake the flawed vessels of our lives
20:14–18	"Cursed be the day on which I was born!": a text that can allow the preacher to get into the hearts and minds of all those who see no further point in living
32:1–3, 6–17, 25–30, 36–41	Jeremiah's proclamation of hope for the future when Jerusalem was under siege by the Babylonians in 588 B.C.

In a sermon entitled "The Purchase of Hope" I paired this text with Romans 8:18–25, 38–39.

A second word from God is given to the prophet according to our scripture reading, and that is the strange command, Get witnesses and buy a field. Buy that family field that has fallen to you by right of inheritance, in your hometown of Anathoth, just three and one-half miles north-northeast of besieged Jerusalem. Get witnesses and buy the field. Buy it now, Jeremiah. Now, when everything looks hopeless; when fields and farms aren't worth a penny. Pay ninety dollars for it—not a lot of money, but surely an exorbitant sum when the Babylonians are banging at the gate. Purchase a field: when there seems to be no hope because the world is crumbling around us, and the only thing worth doing seems to be to survive by any means here and now, and never mind the consequences; when our terrible, weak, blind human failures have gotten us into this mess, and we can no longer stand to analyze the guilty past or to look forward to the awful future that we have determined for ourselves.

Jeremiah becomes convinced that this command, too, is the word of God, because he is given the reason for it: "For thus says the LORD of hosts, the God of Israel: Houses and fields and vineyards shall again be bought in this land."

That is the second fact about which Jeremiah can say, "I am sure"—that when our sin has overcome us and everything is hopeless on this human scene, God still has a plan for the future. Think of it! When everything lovely and gracious and pure in our world seems to fall victim to corruption and evil; when no good work seems to endure, and no project of love seems to bear lasting fruit; when every single act we do is tainted by selfishness—God has a plan.

When we stand beside the grave of a loved one, and all the pain floods over us; when we realize that we can never more say what we wanted to say and can never more do what we wanted to do for that dead one—God has a plan.

When the meek, the peacemakers, the pure in heart, get trampled into the dirt; when the weak are constantly sacrificed on the altars of powers, and the tongues of the proud and mighty strut through the earth—God has a plan.

When there seems to lie ahead of us nothing but a crucifixion; when the Gethsemane of prayer is darkened by the shadow of a looming Golgotha; when we would rather do any other thing than obey the will of the Father, and we cry out to him to remove this cup from us—God has a plan.

And it is a plan of love to save us and our world, despite the fact that we deserve nothing but God's condemnation of death. . . . And he talked already about the plan to his prophet Jeremiah.

From Ezekiel

36:22–32	"A new heart I will give you, and a new spirit I will put within you": God's promised transformation of his covenant people, begun with Christ's Spirit poured into our hearts
43:1–9	The return of the glory of the Lord to the new temple, to dwell in the midst of his people (recall that Jesus replaces the temple, in John's Gospel, and that we have beheld his glory as of the only Son from the Father)
47:1–12	The river of life that flows out from God (cf. Rev. 22:1–5)

From Amos

8:11–14	The famine of the word of God, when a faithless society shall search for the word of God and find it withdrawn from them; imagine what it would mean if there were no word!

From Habakkuk

3:17–19	One of the most magnificent songs of faith ever sung in the midst of adversity

From Zechariah

4:1–14	"Not by might, nor by power, but by my Spirit, says the LORD of hosts": one of the most frequently preached texts of the past generation, but now largely ignored by the pulpit
6:9–15	The empty crown: a compelling symbolic action, in which Zechariah deposits the crown of the awaited Messiah in the temple, where it remains "until he comes whose right it is" (Ezek. 21:27); there the crown rests, unused, unclaimed, until God keeps his word to his prophet
8:20–23	"Let us go with you, for we have heard that God is with you": how the world will be converted

From Malachi

1:6–14	Weary and indifferent worship that despises and dishonors God
2:13–16	The marriage covenant and divorce
2:17	Our "newspeak" language, in which good is called evil and evil is called good
3:7–12	Our robbery of God, applied here to tithes; but we can rob God by distortion of doctrine, by neglect of worship, by moral disobedience, by failure to evangelize, by social injustice
3:13–15	"It is vain to serve God": times when there are no rewards for the righteous, but only for the wicked

This is just a minuscule sampling of the non-lectionary texts from the prophetic literature that could be preached, but perhaps this list will provide the reader with some preaching possibilities or, better, prompt the reader to study the prophets in a systematic and thorough way. Biblical sermons grow out of such study, and the church then begins to hear the word of God in its magnificent fullness.

Linking Text and Congregation

When a prophetic text is proclaimed for a modern congregation, the most frequent assumption should be that the ancient words, spoken to Israel, are the word of God now spoken to us, through Christ. Because the prophetic literature deals so often with national and international affairs, however, the preacher must keep very clearly in mind just who is addressed by the text. The modern equivalent of Israel is not the

United States of America, and American citizens, as a group, are not the covenant people of God. The United States is a pluralistic union, made up of persons of varying faiths and unfaiths, and there is no way in which it can be called God's chosen nation. Civil religion has tried to arrogate the title to our country. Abraham Lincoln called America God's "almost chosen people." But the parallel to the Israel of the Old Testament is not our nation but the church of Jesus Christ.

When a prophetic promise or word for the future is proclaimed from the pulpit, that promise is therefore directed to the church. For example, if the text is Amos 3:2, it is to be applied to the congregation. Similarly, all those words of judgment that the prophets level against their disobedient, distrustful people are now words leveled against the church, just as all the prophetic promises of hope and salvation are also promises for the church. The church is the heir of the total prophetic message, not just of its hopeful parts, and that fact gives enormous force to the prophetic proclamation in our day.

It may be that the church has already inherited the effects of some prophetic words of judgment, and the sermon needs to point that out. For example, we repeatedly have to ask if God does not reject our worship, as he rejected Israel's, according to Malachi 2:13–16, because of the violation of our marriage covenants. Or we repeatedly have to ask, on the basis of Hosea 4:1–10, if our land is full of "swearing, lying, killing, stealing, and committing adultery" because the priesthood of all believers has forgotten the teaching *(torah)* of God and not taught it to the world.

Why is it that when you and I stand up to preach or teach before any Christian gathering, we have to assume that there is only the most minimal knowledge of the Bible among our listeners? Why is it that there is no knowledge of the scriptures abroad in the land? Certainly part of the answer is that our society is no longer religious. Schoolchildren no longer use McGuffey's Readers, which assumed and plainly stated that God created them and all the world. Things religious now are strictly separated from the rest of life, and culture no longer supports our faith. But ours is not the first time in which the Christian church has been surrounded by a pagan society. So why is it that there is such ignorance of the Bible in our land? Despite all of our church school curricula, our abundance of books and media and communication technology, why is it that the average person knows almost nothing of the Bible's story? Is it because you and I, as "a kingdom of priests" who are supposed to mediate the knowledge of God, have rejected the source of that knowledge? Is it because we have not done a very good job of teaching the holy scriptures?

Frequently, of course, the church has already inherited the effects of the prophetic words of salvation, through their fulfillment in Jesus Christ, as amply demonstrated in the preceding discussion. The preacher therefore has to ask how God's redemption of us in Christ affects the judgment announced by the prophets. Does it do away with it? Israel too was a covenant people that had already been redeemed by her deliverance out of Egypt and her election by God's grace. So is it possible to be redeemed by the cross and resurrection of Christ and yet lose one's final salvation? (See Matt. 7:13–14; 22:1–14; 25; 1 Cor. 9:24–27; Phil. 3:2–16.) Must not the church, like Israel, respond to the grace and love of God? The tendency of our time is to believe that God only forgives. But does not our faithless age need a sober assessment, aided by the prophets, of the responsibilities of faith in a sovereign Lord?

We have previously noted that the preacher cannot lift a prophetic text out of its historical context and apply it, without further ado, to a modern congregation. The Old Testament must be left its historical integrity. The words of the prophets are God's words directed to specific situations in Israel's life, and the preacher must make that clear, spelling out their context in Israel's society and time.

The words of the prophets, then, become God's word to us very often on the basis of analogy. Our relation to God is analogous to Israel's relation to him in the text, or our historical situation is analogous to Israel's situation in the Old Testament history.

For example, in Isaiah 7:1–17, King Ahaz of Judah is promised that God will defeat the armies of Syria and Ephraim, if Ahaz trusts the promise of God to David. As a sign that the promise will be kept, God says, "Behold, a young woman shall conceive and bear a son, and shall call his name Immanuel" (v. 14). An analogy to our situation could be drawn in this fashion, pairing the text with the Christmas lesson of Luke 2:1–20:

> Like Ahaz in the days of Isaiah, we are given nothing more than a babe, and apparently our whole future depends on whether or not we believe the promise connected with that child.[7]

God's sign in Isaiah 7:14 is analogous to the sign of Luke 2:12 and finds its ultimate fulfillment in it. God offers to us the same invitation to faith that he offered Ahaz, and on this basis our relation to him is analogous to Israel's in Isaiah's time.

One also finds situations in Israel's society analogous to ours. For example, Amos 8:11–14, with its picture of Israel running to and fro, seeking the word of the Lord in vain, could remind one of the frantic search in our society for meaning and authoritative guide.

In drawing such analogies, the preacher must be careful not to allegorize the text, of course. Sometimes there are symbolic figures used by the prophets. For example, "wilderness" and "exile" in Second Isaiah finally symbolize life apart from God, for that prophet. But where the prophetic text is not employing such an imaginative figure, the actual historical situation must be dealt with and its circumstances compared to the circumstances of the preacher's congregation. Cling to the history! is a good watchword in preaching from the prophets. Yet never leave the prophetic word in the past. Address it to the contemporary covenant people of God, as a word spoken in a history that is also theirs. As Paul Scherer once remarked, "God didn't stop speaking when his book went to press." His word continues to speak out of Israel's life to that of the new Israel, the church, who is repeating Israel's pilgrimage.

Finally, it should also be said that there are some passages in the prophets that address nations other than Israel. God's oracle to Cyrus of Persia, in Isaiah 45:1–7, or the oracles to the nations found in so many of the prophetic books (Amos 1:3—2:3; Ezekiel 25–32, et al.), or the court cases that God carries on with the nations in Isaiah 41:1—42:4 illustrate the point. These are words addressed not to the covenant people Israel but to those outside of the covenant—to the *goyim*—and, as such, they may indeed apply to the United States and to every other secular or pluralistic country. Their main import is that God is Lord over all nations; that he both plants them and plucks them up, builds them and breaks them down (Jer. 1:10). He uses the nations and rulers of foreign countries in the achievement of his purposes (Isa. 10:5–6; Hab. 1:5–11; Jer. 34:1–3, et al.), but if in their pride the nations exceed their commission, they too will be destroyed (Isa. 10:12–19), just as they are held accountable for their sins against humanity (Hab. 2:6–20). The God of the Bible is Lord over all peoples (cf. Amos 9:7–9), and their final fate is in his hands.

We do not learn that from Assyria or Egypt or Babylonia, however, but only through the mediation of Israel; to show that he is universal God, the Lord reveals himself through one people. Nevertheless, the preacher can use the prophetic messages directed to the *goyim* to address the affairs of both the United States and other countries. Because we are U.S. citizens, the prophetic messages to the nations come to us as warnings. If we are faith-filled members of the covenant people, they come to us as comfort. Our destiny lies not in the hands of the rulers of this world but in the powerful and loving grasp of the Lord of hosts. In our day of national and international turmoil, we need also to preach that word.

CHAPTER 8

Preaching
from the Psalms

One of the disciplines that I often assign to students in homiletics classes is to read two psalms every day. Certainly the exercise improves their rhetorical skills and teaches them the use of figurative language. Who can improve on the psalmists' speech when they cry out to God? "Thou hast taken me up and thrown me away" (Ps. 102:10). "Put thou my tears in thy bottle!" (Ps. 56:8). Who can better describe the proud, arrogant, and prosperous secularist than does Psalm 73? "They have no pangs; their bodies are sound and sleek . . . pride is their necklace; violence covers them as a garment . . . they set their mouths against the heavens, and their tongue struts through the earth" (vs. 4, 6, 9; cf. Ps. 10). Where is there a better description of a false friend than in Psalm 55:21, or of the transitory nature of human life than in Psalm 39:4–6 (cf. Ps. 90)? The psalms speak the language of great literature.

Far more than that, the psalms speak the language of faith, and those who immerse themselves in the psalms receive a theological education, an insight into the ways of God unequaled in any other written collection. In the Psalter, Israel gathers up her whole history with her Lord and turns it into praise and prayer. But this is no history past for the Psalter's singers. This is the bedrock of their present faith. The God whom the psalmists meet in present experience and whose coming they await in the future is the God Israel has known all her life long.

What a God he is! "Most high over all the earth . . . exalted far above all gods" (Ps. 97:9), utterly holy (99:3, 9), unlike any human (50:21), there are none to compare to him, nor are there any works like his (86:8). If one wants to tell of God's relation to his creation, then the psalms furnish the words:

> Of old thou didst lay the foundation of the earth,
> and the heavens are the work of thy hands.

They will perish, but thou dost endure;
   they will all wear out like a garment.
Thou changest them like raiment, and they pass away;
   but thou art the same, and thy years have no end.
                            Psalm 102:25–27

This is the God who owns the cosmos and all that is in it (Ps. 50:10–11). In wisdom he has made all things (104:24). He sustains all creatures and determines their life and death (104:28–30). Therefore all creation utters its praise to its Lord (148).

This God of Israel not only rules the natural world, however, he also is Lord over the nations (Ps. 33:10–11). His will be the final outcome of human history: "All the kings of the earth shall praise thee, O LORD" (138:4). In the meantime, God will work his sovereign justice in the earth (34:15–18). How great is the mercy of this righteous judge (103:13–14)! In such a Lord, all people may find their forgiveness (65:2–3). In the fellowship of such a God, there are refuge and delight (36:7–9). Indeed, this God of Israel is the source of abundant life (16:11). From him finally will come that kingdom of heaven for which all peoples yearn (85:10–13).

Obviously, every preacher would like his or her congregation to share, from experience, in the psalmists' relation to God. That is the purpose of preaching from the Psalter—to so instruct a congregation in the life of faith, set forth in these songs, that such a life becomes the congregation's life; to let the words of the psalms so inspire and work among the gathered people that Israel's stance before God becomes the congregation's stance, Israel's depth of devotion becomes their devotion, Israel's heartfelt response to God's deeds becomes their response.

The Psalms in the Church

Certainly from the beginning the Psalter has been an integral part of the church's life of worship, a practice taken over from the Jews.[1] We are told that before Jesus and his disciples went out from the last supper, they sang a psalm hymn together (Matt. 26:30). When Paul and Silas were imprisoned at Philippi, they filled the midnight hour with praying and singing hymns to God, while the other prisoners listened (Acts 16:25). It was the custom, when the early Christians gathered in homes to worship, to sing "psalms and hymns and spiritual songs, singing and making melody to the Lord with all [their] heart" (Eph. 5:19).

The church was following the example of its Lord, for Jesus used the Psalter more than any other book of the Old Testament. When he taught, he frequently quoted from the psalms. For example, "Blessed are the meek, for they shall inherit the earth" is taken from Psalm 37:11 (cf. Matt. 7:23 with Ps. 6:8; Matt. 21:16 with Ps. 8:1–2; John 6:31 with Ps. 78:24; John 13:18 with Ps. 41:9). Jesus confounded his opponents with quotations from the psalms; Mark 12:36, for example, is taken from Psalm 110:1 (cf. Mark 12:10 with Ps. 118:22–23). And when our Lord reached the climax of his life, he prayed in the words of the Psalter (cf. John 12:27 with Ps. 6:3). His cry from the cross (Mark 15:34) is the first line of Psalm 22; his final prayer in Luke 23:46 is the fifth verse of Psalm 31.

The church has sung and still sings its praises and petitions by means of the psalms. In the Reformed churches of the sixteenth and seventeenth centuries, the Psalter was the only hymnbook known apart from a few paraphrases of other scriptures, and of course we still employ free translation of the psalms set to folk tunes by Martin Luther ("A Mighty Fortress Is Our God" based on Psalm 46) and songs from the Genevan Psalter ("All People That on Earth Do Dwell" from Psalm 100).

Responsive readings have now replaced the singing of many of the psalms, and yet a glance at the scripture index at the back of many hymnbooks will show how many of our hymns are based on psalms. Isaac Watts is famous for his use of them: "Jesus Shall Reign Where'er the Sun" (Psalm 72); "The Heavens Declare Thy Glory, Lord" (Psalm 19); "Bless, O My Soul! the Living God" (Psalm 103); "Before Jehovah's Awful Throne" (Psalm 100); "O God, Our Help in Ages Past" (Psalm 90); "Joy to the World" (Psalm 98). Every Christian has heard or knows "Lift Up Your Heads, Ye Mighty Gates" (Psalm 24); "The King of Love My Shepherd Is" (Psalm 23); "Glorious Things of Thee Are Spoken" (Psalm 87); "Immortal, Invisible, God Only Wise" (Ps. 90:1–4). The list could be multiplied many times. In addition, there are hundreds of choir anthems that are based on the psalms, such as, "How Lovely Is Thy Dwelling Place" (Psalm 84), translated from Brahms' Requiem.

When one considers the church's rich musical employment of the psalms and adds to that the use of the Psalter in other parts of the liturgy, it is clear that the preacher has ample opportunity to connect a sermon on a psalm with the life of the congregation. We can preach on a psalm that forms the basis of a hymn, or call to worship, or assurance of pardon, or responsive reading and thereby enrich the congregation's experience and understanding of both its God and its worship of him.

The Origin of the Psalter

Popular piety imagines that each psalm was written by a lonely individual, wandering a hillside and voicing his or her prayer to God. While we do hear individual voices in some of the psalms, most of them originated in Israel's community life and certainly all of them have been shaped over the years by that community's use of them. For example, some of the laments describe multiple experiences of suffering that are not likely to have happened to one individual. Israel has collected together in the laments multiple experiences that can then be voiced by individuals at prayer with their God. The psalms are the worshipbook of Israel, for use by all sorts and conditions of human beings, in all sorts of settings and situations. In the Psalter, individuals speak, but always at the same time out of the worship tradition of the covenant community.

That has implications for our use of the psalms in preaching. The psalms belong to Israel, and unless we have something to do with Israel, the Psalter cannot be our book. Certainly many of the psalms speak to the general condition of humanity. Pictured in their realistic words are our experiences of pain and joy, of good fellowship and loneliness, of death and the recovery from grave illness, of prosperity and want. We find writ large on the Psalter's pages our pride and our humility, our deceit and our honesty, our loves and our hatreds. But the Psalter is not a humanistic book. Every experience and condition of humankind is set in relation to the God of Israel; therein lies the Psalter's greatness. Just as Paul's letters have endured because they place every area of the church's life in the context of God's act in Jesus Christ, so too have the psalms endured because they frame every experience and condition of human beings with a testimony to the person and work of the God of Israel (59:5; 69:6; 72:18). God's choice of Israel (33:12; 69:33; 135:4); his friendship toward her (25:14) in his covenant (50:5; 74:20; 111:5); his covenant law delivered to Israel (25:10; 50:16; 103:18); his choice of Zion for his dwelling;[2] his promise to David; and his constant, never-failing steadfast love and loyalty to his people—these are the presuppositions of the psalms. The God to whom the psalms give testimony is the Holy One of Israel,[3] her Shepherd,[4] the Mighty One of Jacob,[5] the God of Jacob,[6] the Father of the adopted David,[7] the God of Israel's salvation,[8] her Rock,[9] and her King,[10] enthroned on her praises.[11] Therefore no psalm can properly be understood outside of God's relation with his elected people.

For example, some have thought to interpret Psalm 8 as a product of natural religion. But the singer of that song does not know God from looking at the heavens; the singer knows God from a received creation tradition that has been handed down in the cult. The psalmist spells out that tradition, known also to us from Genesis 1, in verses 5–6, and Psalm 8 can only properly be interpreted in the context of the creation theology of Israel.

Or consider the great communal lament of Psalm 44. It is precisely because the psalmists know the story of Israel's salvation in the past that her present situation of defeat and deportation is a problem for their faith (see vs. 1 and 9). The context for understanding the psalm is clearly Israel's history.

In the magnificent song of Psalm 73, it is because the psalmist has inherited Israel's Wisdom tradition, which says that God is good to the upright (v. 1), that his own pain and suffering over against the prosperity of the wicked are inexplicable. The whole psalm, then, is a reformulation of Israel's Wisdom theology. The singer begins with the Wisdom doctrine that God is "good" to the upright; he ends with the realization that the only "good" is to be near God (v. 28).

Even those psalms that have affinities with extra-Israelite literature of the ancient Near East, such as Psalm 29 or 82 or 104, or that seem to testify to universal religious experience, anchor themselves in the traditions of Israel and are to be understood as witnesses to her particular God, who has a particular history and character. The psalms must be understood in the context of God's relation with Israel in order to be properly interpreted.

By the mercies of that God, however, the Christian church has been grafted into Israel by Jesus Christ (Rom. 11:17–24; Eph. 2:11–22), and the Psalter has become our book of worship also. Its vision of the Holy One of Israel and its response to that vision can now be held out before a Christian congregation as their goal also, as they grow up into the measure of the fullness of the stature of their Lord.

Difficulties in Preaching from the Psalms

There are difficulties connected with preaching from the psalms, just as there are difficulties in preaching from any portion of the scriptures. The Psalter comes to us from different times and cultures, and its language is not ours. That is true of even the most familiar psalm. For example, every Christian knows Psalm 23 and can probably recite it from memory, and every congregation receives a feeling of comfort and assurance from the use of that song of trust. But what does the Twenty-third Psalm mean by verse 5? Commentators differ on their interpretation, but if the shepherd image is carried through, the picture is one of the shepherd driving out the snakes from the pasture and clearing it of thorns before letting the sheep into it to graze. Then, when the sheep return to the fold at night, any cuts or bruises they have received are anointed with medicinal healing oil. And they are given a special fermented brew to drink that was thought to have reinvigorating powers. (The Hebrew may be read, "My cup is intoxicating.") Thus, verse 5 of Psalm 23 deals with God's protection of his people from enemies, with his binding up of our wounds, and with his revitalization of our energies. But this is put in figures of speech that are strange to us and that have to be explained.

Similarly, most congregations are familiar with the opening lines of Psalm 46, having heard them often in calls to worship, but they are totally ignorant of the reference to the waters of chaos in verses 2 and 3, and when they hear verses 4 through 9, they have little idea of the psalm's meaning, until they finally hear again the familiar lines of verses 10 and 11. Psalm 46 is, however, a marvelous expression of faith, and every preacher will want to elucidate it for his or her congregation.

To cite an extreme example, Psalm 60 has the lines, "Moab is my washbasin; upon Edom I cast my shoe" (v. 8). That is meaningless to us unless we know that casting a shoe over a piece of property signified ownership of it (cf. Ruth 4:7). God is stating in this psalm that Edom belongs to him.

Israel's language, customs, traditions, and worship practices are mirrored in the psalms, and to preach from the psalms means making their original meanings clear. That in turn implies careful exegesis of these ancient songs on the preacher's part.

Imprecations in the Psalms

The psalms also express thoughts that seem to us less than Christian. We print verses 1 through 6 of the lovely exilic Psalm 137 among our responsive readings, but we omit verses 7 through 9 and the terrible imprecations against Babylon, with which the psalm closes: "Happy shall he be who takes your little ones and dashes them against the rock!" (v. 9). This verse conjures up for many of us the same atrocities committed by the Nazis during World War II, and no Christian should ever utter such thoughts. But the psalms, and especially the lament psalms, have many such imprecatory sentiments. Psalm 35:4–6 is one example among many. What are we to make of such destructive wishes for the psalmists' enemies?

Certainly we are to follow the command of our Lord to love our enemies and to pray for those who persecute us (Matt. 5:43–44). But even seemingly non-Christian portions of the Psalter can teach a Christian congregation something about the life of faith. First, such passages in the psalms make it clear that there are enemies of the faithful life, as Jesus makes clear in his commandments to us. There are those who are not on the side of God but on the side of evil, and they are roundly condemned by the psalmists. Especially do the psalms mention over and over those who bend the truth and speak deceitfully.

> Help, LORD; for there is no longer any that is godly:
>> for the faithful have vanished from among the sons of men.
> Every one utters lies to his neighbor;
>> with flattering lips and a double heart they speak.
>
> Psalm 12:1–2[12]

Surely, in a society such as ours, where "newspeak" has become the habit of the tongue, where many government pronouncements can no longer be believed, and where most journalists (pollsters have put the figure at 90 percent) have no relation to and therefore no understanding of the church, that is a prayer that is proper to every Christian, just as are the psalmists' prayers against those "whose portion in life is of the world" (17:14), or those who hate the Lord's discipline and ignore his word (50:17), or those who practice "oppression and fraud" in the marketplace (55:11). The preacher has in the Psalter a powerful tool against social injustice.

Second, the preacher must remember that these are prayers uttered *to God.* These psalmists do not take vengeance into their own hands. They may hate the Lord's enemies and their own enemies, but they do not settle scores by themselves. They bring their complaints and hatreds before God and turn them over to him. In God's court, good and evil are finally judged; with his wrath or his mercy, society and individuals are finally treated; and those are facts that can empty every believer's heart of hatred and give satisfaction and peace of mind.

Third, the church can learn from the psalmists that it is proper to pray for the destruction of the enemies of God. We finally desire that the kingdom of God will come on earth, do we not? But that means that God will put down every opposition to his rule, and the church should pray earnestly for the elimination of such opposition. One of the reasons we accept evil with such indifference in our society is because we do not sincerely pray for God to eliminate it. But should the church not petition God for an end to pornography, child abuse, adultery, murder? Should it not want the disappearance of the ruthless landlord, the unjust employer, the thief preying on the poor, the drug dealer, the arrogant rich? The psalmists want the elimination of the wicked with all their hearts, and we can learn from that opposition to evil. The psalmists know that "the eyes of the Lord are toward the righteous, and his . . . face . . . is against evildoers" (34:15–16). In our society, so much of which believes that God no longer judges anybody, these lively prayers can give us a new understanding of God's character. By the same token, these prayers can also lead us to ask for God's destruction of the evil within *ourselves* and *our* lives, and that too is a prayer needed on the lips of every Christian.

The Royal Psalms

Another difficulty in preaching from the Psalter comes from the presence in it of a large group of royal psalms, which were originally written for occasions connected with the Davidic kingship: the coronation or accession to the throne (Psalms 2; 110) or the anniversary of that accession (Psalms 21; 72; 101); the celebration of the founding of the Davidic dynasty (Psalm 132); prayers recited by the king (Ps. 144:1–11) or by a choir as the king set out to battle (Psalm 20); a song of thanksgiving recited by the king when he returned from battle (Psalm 18); the celebration of the marriage of a Davidic king (Psalm 45). Within these royal psalms are found oracles uttered by court prophets (Psalm 110; probably 18:7–15), just as prophetic oracles are also contained within other types of psalms (e.g., Ps. 95:7d–11 and the theophanic descriptions of God found in 77:16–20 or in 97:2–5 probably originated with prophets; cf. Hab. 3:1–15). Since we no longer have a king or are familiar with monarchical rule, what are we to do with this type of psalm?

The New Testament gives a partial answer. It uses some of these psalms in connection with the life of that final heir of David, Jesus Christ. For example, Psalm 110 is used in the New Testament more than any other psalm. Jesus quotes it in his disputes with the scribes (Mark 12:36 and pars.). Principally, however, the language of verse 1 is used to set forth the resurrection and ascension of Jesus Christ to the right hand of God,[13] where he will reign until God puts all his enemies under his feet (1 Cor. 15:25; Heb. 1:10, 12–13). From this royal psalm we get the language of the Apostles' Creed: "And sitteth on the right hand of God." In other words, the New Testament understands Jesus Christ as the Davidic Messiah, now raised on high to share in God's rule.

The letter to the Hebrews, on the other hand, uses verse 4 of Psalm 110 to apply to our Lord. Jesus Christ is now the high priest forever (Heb. 7:21) "after the order of Melchizedek" (Heb. 5:6, 10; 6:20; 7:11, 17), inheriting the title as the final heir of David and as the final high priest who makes satisfaction for sins once for all. Melchizedek was the ancient Jebusite priest-king of Salem, or Jerusalem, and after David conquered Jerusalem and made it his capital, the title was taken into Yahwism and applied to the Davidic line—that line, says the New Testament, that Christ has now completed and fulfilled.

Psalm 2:7, which speaks of the adoption of the Davidic ruler as the son of God, is used of Jesus at his baptism (Mark 1:11 and pars.; cf. Heb. 1:5; 5:5) and at his transfiguration (Mark 9:7 and pars; cf. 2 Peter 1:17). The voice of God identifies Jesus as God's Son, the final heir of the throne of David, the Messiah. In Revelation 19:15, then, the word of God incarnate is that Son who will rule the nations (Ps. 110:2) in the end time, as King of kings and Lord of lords.

In similar fashion, Hebrews 1:8–9 draws on Psalm 45:6–7; Luke 1:32 and Acts 2:30 quote Psalm 132:11; and Luke 1:69 quotes Psalm 132:17, all to show that Jesus is the final heir of the throne of David, fulfilling God's promise to that ruler (2 Samuel 7).

The preacher thus is instructed by the scriptures themselves to read these royal psalms in the light of God's work with the Davidic house. We do not read Christ back into these psalms, for they did not originally apply to Christ. They were, rather, idealized pictures of the office of the Davidic kings of Judah. Their original authors knew nothing of the man from Nazareth to come. They did, however, know what the ideal king would be like: He would manifest the justice and righteousness of God (Ps. 72:1–2), he would defend the cause of the poor and give deliverance to the needy (72:4), he would have dominion over all the earth and conquer all his foes (72:9–11), his reign would bring peace and fullness of life (72:6–7, 16), and he would reign eternally as a source of blessing forever (72:5, 17). To those inspired hopes God spoke his "yes" in Jesus Christ, and by recounting that holy history and showing how God fulfilled it, the preacher can testify to the faithfulness of God to his promise to David and proclaim that we now live in the time of a reign that will endure, until every knee bows and every tongue confesses that Jesus Christ is Lord of lords and King of kings.

Such a message can give a congregation great comfort and hope. For example, the following are excerpts from a sermon based on Psalm 2 and Philippians 4:4–7, preached on the Sunday of Christ the King.

I never before really heard what this psalm is saying. It pictures in its first three verses the chaos in our world. . . . In fact, this psalm pictures sinful human beings in deliberate rebellion against the Lord and against his Messiah. . . . But then, in an absolutely startling phrase, this psalm portrays God's reaction to such sinful defiance of him: "He who sits in the heavens laughs." God, in response to all the trouble we know in our time, sits back and laughs!

That is offensive, isn't it? . . . After all, we Christians have been scurrying around the world in this jet age, trying to put out the fires—in the Middle East and Central America and South Africa and Asia. We all are desperately busy as Christians, trying to contain nuclear wars and accidents, and terrorists and drug runners, not to mention hunger and organized crime, the breakup of homes and the breakdown of public education. And that God should laugh at all of that is shocking. . . .

What sort of laughter is this deep rumble in the heavens, and what should we anxious and busy Christians hear it to mean?

Certainly this laughter of God's is the laughter of one who sees things in their proper perspective. . . . He laughs at petty human beings, who think they can live without him. To be sure, he knows the suffering the rulers of this world can inflict on helpless human beings. And he knows the chaos we can wreak by trying to be our own gods and goddesses. But God sees it all in proper perspective. He overlooks all the span of time—and sees proud rulers forgotten in death. He peers into all human endeavors—and sees that only faith, hope, and love endure. He measures all the might the scoffers wield—and knows that one little word will fell them. . . .

And for all our troubles, we can laugh too, if we see things the way God sees them. . . .

But God also sits in the heavens and laughs at his enemies, because he holds all power. . . .

In the words of our psalm, Jesus was the king God set on Zion, his holy hill. . . . But then, what a mockery Herod and Pilate and the rest of them tried to make of that Son and his kingship. Jesus was kissed, to be sure, but by a traitor to betray him to the mob. . . . He was set up on a hill, but nailed to a cross. . . . And Jesus possessed the earth, but only in the form of a borrowed grave in a hillside. Thus did the powers of this world think to do away with God's purpose and with his laughter.

But then there came Easter morn, and the empty tomb, and the power of God's enemies broken. . . . And on that morning, God laughed in triumph in heaven, while the morning stars sang together for joy, and that laughter echoed forth to earth, and human beings began to join in it. . . .

But there is a final reason why God sits in heaven and laughs, and that is because he is good. God laughs with the wholesome merriment of goodness. . . .

Our utopias are pretty joyless, aren't they?—the cold gray totalitarianisms erected by petty tyrants; the tinseled, neon-lit boulevards to nowhere laid out by the rich; the daily routine of boredom and quiet desperation lived out by so many of our people . . . contrast those with the pictures of the kingdom of God that you find in the scriptures. . . . In Jesus' teachings, the kingdom is a wedding feast, or a party held for a returning prodigal, and there is neither suffering there, nor crying, nor pain anymore. For God is in the midst of it, and God is the God of good laughter. . . .

Now none of these are reasons for us Christians to cease our activities in this world of evil. There are lots of fires to be put out on earth. There are lots of battles to be fought with wrong and injustice and pride. There is a lot of suffering still to come and a lot of pain to be borne. . . . But knowing that God is the God of such laughter— such perspective, such power, such joyful victory—perhaps all of us here can be just a little less anxious in our busy battles. "Have no anxiety about anything," Paul writes to us, "but in everything by prayer and supplication with thanksgiving let your requests be made known to God"—to God, who sits in the heavens and laughs, and who can give you laughter also.

Approaching a Psalm for Preaching

When beginning exegetical work on a psalm, nothing is more important than that rhetorical criticism we discussed in chapter 4. Form criticism is important for analyzing the overall structure of the song, for determining its mood and purpose, and for possibly gaining some insight into its original use. Form criticism will reveal traditional structures, but rhetorical analysis uncovers the uniqueness of any particular psalm.

For example, Psalm 98 is clearly a hymn, with the hymn's traditional form twice repeated (imperative call to praise, vs. 1a, 4–9a; transitional device, vs. 1b, 9b; and body, vs. 1c–3, 9b–d). But a rhetorical analysis of the psalm reveals its inner thought. The Lord's salvation dominates verses 1 through 3, with the word occurring in verses 1, 2, and at the end of 3. (The RSV translates the word with "victory.") That salvation is equivalent to the "wonderful deeds" of verse 1b (RSV: "marvelous things") and to God's "righteousness," verse 2b (RSV: "vindication"). More, that salvation has taken place because the Lord has "remembered" his covenant with Israel and faithfully saved her, in fulfillment of his covenant relationship (v. 3). God alone has done the deed (v. 1c), rescuing Israel in some crisis. His rescue of her, in faithful fulfillment of his covenant, is God's "righteousness." But that rescue is not for Israel's sake alone. The Lord's salvation of Israel is revelation and testimony to all the nations of the earth that Yahweh alone is God. Such is the thought of the first strophe.

The second strophe, verses 4 through 6, building on the first, can therefore call "all the earth" to shout joyfully to the Lord, and that summons brackets this strophe, verses 4 and 6. All peoples are to shout, to sing (vs. 4, 5; the thought is repeated from v. 1), and to play the lyre, trumpet, and ram's horn (vs. 5–6) in joyful celebration of their king, Yahweh, who rules them all. His kingship forms the climax of the second strophe.

Not only peoples are to praise the king, but also all nature—the sea and every creature in it, the world with all its life forms (v. 7). The streams or rivers are to clap their hands and the mountains join in the song before the Lord (vs. 8–9a). The transitional "for" then spells out the final reason for such universal praise (v. 9b). The Lord, the King, who saved Israel, the Lord who faithfully keeps his covenant, comes to judge the entire earth and to make its life whole and upright again. He will judge the world with "righteousness" (v. 9c); that is, he will save it as he saved Israel (v. 2), restoring to it that good and equitable life that he intended for it in the beginning (vs. 9b–d). The universe thus waits for its Lord, not in fear but in praise, because he will keep his covenant with it also, faithfully fulfilling his good purpose for his creation when his kingdom comes.

The psalm has moved from the thought of God's salvation of Israel to that of his salvation of all creation, and of course that is the reason Israel was created in the first place—to be the medium of God's blessing on all that he has made. The repetitions and structures of this psalm, uncovered by rhetorical analysis, allow the preacher to trace its inner thought and movement.

Having discovered the intricacies of the thought in a psalm, however, probably the worst thing a preacher can do in the sermon is simply to describe the thought and experience of the psalmist, as objects "out there" to be considered by the congregation. Such sermons contain phrases such as "the psalmist feels," "the psalmist learns," "the psalmist realizes." The experience of the singer with God remains an event unconnected with the life of the listening congregation, an experience that happened to someone long ago but that has not happened to them. The point of a sermon from the psalms is so to appropriate the language of the psalm for the congregation that what happened long ago for the psalmist happens in the immediate now for the congregation. Israel's experience with its God becomes their experience. The psalmist's journey in the relation with God becomes their journey.

This means that exegetical and commentary work with a psalm to uncover its meaning does not suffice. A preacher may have a very clear idea, after doing exegesis, of what a psalm text meant originally, but the principal questions to be answered by the preacher are: What does this text mean for my people? How is it the mirror of their life? Where are they in this psalm's words, and how can I show them that is their position? And then how can I lead them through the experience of all that the psalmist has experienced, that they may grow in the faith and knowledge of their Lord? The way the preacher answers those questions in shaping a sermon will determine whether or not the word of God in the psalm comes home to the hearts of the congregation. Achieving such a goal requires the greatest skill on the preacher's part in maintaining the original meaning of the psalm, while at the same time making it the congregation's own. Let us therefore examine some psalms with such a goal in mind. For reasons of space, we will just try to suggest various points that could be made.

A Song of Trust: Psalm 131

The collection of Psalms 120–134 contains some of the loveliest songs in the Psalter, and certainly little Psalm 131 is one of the most beautiful. Probably the work of an individual, but later used in the congregation, it comes to us without indication of date or original situation. Though brief, it divides into three strophes, one to each verse.

Total humility and dependence on God dominate this psalmist's attitude and life, and, perhaps because the psalmist has achieved that life stance, he or she can pray to God in the most natural and forthright manner. It is when we do not know God, isn't it, that our prayers become pompous and homiletical, burdening him with things he already knows and directing him about what he should do?

> O Lord, my heart is not haughty,
>   and my eyes are not lifted up,
> and I have not walked in things great and impossible for me.
> (My translation)

Our life with God is not a standing still, but a walking day by day. We move ever along the path of life, always toward a goal. And this psalmist has learned to walk that path in total dependence on God.

What brings us to such a trusting, humble reliance on our Lord? Is it that we have learned we are not the rulers of the universe and cannot be, as Adam and Eve tried to be, our own gods? Is it that we have found that our ambition brought us to an empty success and that, after all, life without God is futile and ends in a grave? Or is it that we have been battered by some pain or loss, or have been overwhelmed by the world's needs and violence, and cannot find any rational meaning in suffering and pain and death? Whatever the psalmist went through, he is one with us in perplexity or weariness or suffering but has not ended up in despair. He has learned to trust his life and situation totally to the hands of a loving Lord. Like Paul, with his thorn in the flesh, this psalmist has learned "my grace is sufficient for you" (2 Cor. 12:1–10 might be paired with this psalm). The psalmist has renounced all pride which would separate him from God and which would wrest the direction and meaning of his life out of God's gracious grasp. Self-will is gone. God's companionship alone remains.

Faith like that is not achieved by easy and effortless religiosity. The Christian life is not a placid float on a carelessly constructed raft of belief down the stream of grace.

> But I have calmed and quieted myself
> like a weaned child upon his mother,
> like a weaned child is my inner self.
>   (My translation)

The psalmist has arrived at his stance of trust by deliberate effort, and behind his peace of mind and soul lies a determined struggle of will. "I have calmed and quieted myself." The Christian struggles with self-will, disciplining his or her spirit with worship and prayer and study of the scriptures, deciding each day afresh to rely on God for direction and purpose, deliberately choosing to obey God's commandments and to walk in his way until, with Paul, the Christian can say, "I have learned, in whatever state I am, to be content." (Phil. 4:8–13 is another possible New Testament pairing.)

Ultimately it is God who furnishes the motivation and power for that struggle. Like a child suckling at its mother's breast, or like a child weaned and sitting quietly on its mother's lap (the Hebrew can have either meaning), we finally draw our power to live the Christian life of trust from God, who provides his grace for us in word and sacrament. Like a mother comforting and giving security and life to a child, God surrounds us with his sustaining security. "My power is made perfect in [your] weakness," he tells us (2 Cor. 12:9). "I can do all things in him who strengthens me," writes Paul (Phil. 4:13). From God's sustaining grace flows the life of humble faith, that gives us peace and comfort, security, and strength to walk through this perplexing and violent world.

So to all people we can say, Rely on the Lord. Seek his grace; trust his action in your life, now and forever.

> Wait, O Israel, upon the Lord
> from this time and to everlasting.
>   (My translation)

For the Lord will satisfy our needs, and his grace will be sufficient in any situation that lies ahead. He will act. He will sustain us. He will provide. Wait for his action, like a weaned child, in patience and calmness and trust.

A Song of Zion: Psalm 48

It may seem impossible to preach from a psalm of Zion such as this, because it is connected so closely to Jerusalem of old. But the church has for years been given the title of "Zion." (See the hymn "O Zion, Haste, Thy Mission High Fulfilling.") It is on the basis of that analogy that this psalm can be used in the church.

The psalm divides into five strophes: verses 1–2, 3–6, 7–8, 9–11, and 12–14. Originally it may have been used during one of Israel's yearly festivals—perhaps the Feast of Tabernacles—and it was sung either during or just preceding a cultic procession around Jerusalem (v. 12).

In the first two verses, Mount Zion is described as the "holy mountain, beautiful in elevation . . . the joy of all the earth,"[14] and as the pilgrims to the holy city circle her in cultic procession, they fix in their hearts her towers and ramparts and the extent of her citadels (v. 13).

While the song concerns Jerusalem, its focus is on God and the hymnic praise of him as the great King (cf. Matt. 5:35). Jerusalem stands unassailed and fair, because her God is in her midst. Her great King has turned aside every attack against her. While the depiction of battle in verses 4 through 8 is vivid in its details, it probably is a summary of God's repeated protections of the capital throughout Israel's history. God has fought for his people with supernatural means (v. 7),[15] throwing the enemy into panic and confusion (v. 6),[16] so that they are routed in fear. The ark of the covenant is closely linked to such presence of the Lord in battle[17] and may have been carried in the festal procession connected with this psalm.

Israel here praises her God by recounting what he has done, and what he has done is testimony to his might, his love, his victory, his faithfulness to his covenant with his elected people (vs. 9–11). Israel has a God who has never deserted her, who has steadfastly preserved her against all her foes, and who will lead her all her life long (so v. 14). "This is God"—Yahweh Sebaoth—(v. 5) who has done all these things, "our God for ever and ever" (v. 14). That is the story Israel has to tell.

Does the Christian church not have the same story to tell—the story of how God has been her "sure defense" (v. 3) in every trial, of how her life has been preserved in the face of every foe—the ringing affirmation that the very gates of hell cannot prevail against her, because her great King Christ, the Son of God, is in the midst of her? (Matt. 16:13–20 could be paired with this psalm.)

The church, like the people of Israel, tells who her God is by recounting what he has done. And what a story it is: of Paul afflicted, perplexed, persecuted, but never crushed, despairing, or forsaken (2 Cor. 4:7–8); of Peter denying his Lord at cock's crow and then forgiven and made a rock; of a great crowd of witnesses of saints and martyrs sustained "in spite of dungeon, fire, and sword"; of Augustine, Luther, Calvin, Knox, Wesley, Bonhoeffer, and King; of missionaries and circuit riders; of evangelists, preachers, Sunday school teachers; of countless faithful souls, who have run their course and finished their race and kept their faith, all in the power of Christ, and who therefore have been able to proclaim, "This is God!"

Israel praises Zion in this psalm not because Jerusalem is an architectural wonder, not because the sight of her is lovely, not because they want to impress the home folks with their travels, but because Jerusalem preserved is testimony to the covenant love and faithfulness of her Lord. Jerusalem is "beautiful in elevation . . . the joy of all the earth" (v. 2) because her existence in the midst of the earth, despite all vicissitudes (even to the present day), witnesses to that great King who rules over all peoples.

Psalm 48 forms finally a challenge to the Christian church, for it puts two questions to us. First, is the church still the "joy of all the earth," a city set on a hill that cannot be hid, the glad home of every restless pilgrim? Or has she abandoned her task of being a beacon light to the world and moved down into the valley of the shadow and become lost in the darkness of the society around her? (Matt. 5:14–16 is a possible pairing.) Is the church a source of "joy" or has she become instead a cause for complaint, for scorn, for indifference, her voice a cacophony of confused pronouncements and competing one-issue ideologies? Second, is the church still "the city of our God"? Is Christ our glory, our sole defense, the church's one foundation? (1 Cor. 3:10–15 might be another possible pairing.) Or has the church become, rather, a bureaucracy, a social club, a political lobby, or a tool for humanistic activism, giving little thought to the commandments of her Lord and his rule over her life as King?

Israel remained the people of God only as she clung to the story of what he had done in her life. So too the church will remain the church "beautiful," "joy of all the earth," only as she remembers and clings to the most important story, which forms her glory and foundation—of how we were captive to sin, and Jesus Christ set us free; of how death had the last word in our lives, until God raised up his Son; of how we had no hope, until Christ gave us the promise of the kingdom; of how we were like sheep without a shepherd, until our Lord gathered us into one flock and gave us his commandments; of how we found ourselves impotent to obey, until he empowered us with his Spirit; of how we despaired over our world and its tribulations, until Christ overcame it and poured into our hearts a peace which the world can neither give nor take away.

"This is God"—the Father of our Lord Jesus Christ—who has done all these things. He is our God. And so we sing:

> Glorious things of thee are spoken,
> Zion, city of our God;
> He whose word cannot be broken
> Formed thee for his own abode:
> On the Rock of Ages founded,
> What can shake thy sure repose?
> With salvation's walls surrounded,
> Thou mayst smile at all thy foes.

We sing because our King, the Son of God, is in the midst of us. And if we tell of him to all the world, it too will be able to sing.

The Thanksgiving Song of an Individual: Psalm 32

Thanksgiving songs praise the Lord for some *specific* act of deliverance, and this psalm praises God for his forgiveness. Because of this, Psalm 32 has sometimes been classed among the penitential psalms, a subcategory under the laments. But this is properly a thanksgiving. It does not lament over sin; it recounts how God has forgiven it and praises God for that act.

The repetitions of key words are especially noteworthy. The psalm is divided into six strophes of two full lines each: verses 1–2, 3–4, 5, 6–7, 8–9, and 10–11. In the first strophe, the three principal words for sin are used—"rebellion" (RSV: "transgression"), "iniquity," and "sin"—and these are repeated again in verse 5: The remedy fits the complaint. Similarly, the verbs "forgive" and "hide" (or "cover") from verse 1 are picked up again in verse 5, and the motif of hiding or concealment is dominant: If the psalmist does not hide his sin from God (v. 5), then God hides and covers his sin (v. 1) in forgiveness of it (v. 5), and hides and conceals the psalmist, further, from all future distress (v. 7). The verb "surround" (RSV: "encompass") in verse 7 is also repeated in verse 10, and the contrast is struck between the unforgiven person, who is surrounded by sin, and the forgiven person, who is surrounded and hidden by the Lord, with the "you" of verse 7 emphasized by a separate pronoun in the Hebrew: *"You* hide me; from distress you conceal me; with shouts of deliverance you surround me."

We should also note how the psalm defines its own terms by parallel and synonymous concepts. Verse 6 speaks of "every one who is godly," and obviously such persons are those who confess their sin. But more, such persons "trust" the Lord (v. 10). They throw themselves on the mercy of God, and thus become the "righteous" of verse 11, through faith. Such persons are "happy" or "blessed" (vs. 1, 2). Covenant love ("steadfast love") surrounds them—that is, the faithful protection of God—in contrast to the sufferings that come upon the wicked (v. 10). Such persons are "upright in heart" (v. 11); there is no "deceit" in their spirit. They openly and honestly deliver all into the hands of their forgiving and faithful God. The resulting mercy and protection given by God bring with them great joy, so that the forgiven are ready to dance and sing and shout aloud in rejoicing (v. 11).

Obviously, rhetorical analysis of this psalm gets at much of its meaning. But that is not sufficient for preaching from it. We have to make the psalm the congregation's own.

Perhaps no act is more characteristic of our time than is the denial of our sinfulness. "Sin" has almost dropped from our vocabulary and our thinking. No one sins; we say we have "goofed." Or a person who commits an evil act must be sick or the product of an evil environment. "Sorry about that" is, outside of church, about as far as we will go in an acknowledgment of our corrupted natures (1 John 1:5–10 might be paired with this psalm).

Once when I was preaching in the church of a prominent university, I was told before the service that the congregation there no longer wanted the phrase "and there is no health in us" included in the prayer of General Confession. We have a hard time coming to terms with the fact that we are sinful. As Merv Griffin said one time in an interview with Billy Graham on his TV talk show, "I don't know what sin is anymore." So perhaps, to preach from this psalm, the preacher will have to define our sin—our broken relationship with our God, our failure to be what he intended us to be, our distortion of his image in us, our failure to measure up to the fullness of the stature of that true human being, Jesus Christ. The preacher also has an opportunity, preaching from this psalm, to connect the sermon with the act of confession in the liturgy.

We are, despite our refusal to acknowledge our sin, responsible to our God. He created us to conform to his image and to serve his purpose. And if we try to deny or shed that responsibility, we suffer for it.

> When I was silent, my body decayed
> with my groaning all the day;
> For day and night your hand was heavy upon me;
> You dried up my juice as in the heat of summer.
>
> (My translation)

The psalmist is literally ill with his unconfessed sin, racked with pain and dried up with the heat of a fever. Do our angers, distorted relationships, broken family ties, inabilities to perform on the job, defensiveness, selfishness, and depression have their seat in hearts harboring guilt? (The preacher will have to be careful to point out that all suffering is not the result of sin; cf. Job.) If so, there is good news for us in the scriptures. God forgave every sinful act of the psalmist, and God in Jesus Christ offers us the forgiveness of everything we have done or left undone (Rom. 8:1–11 or 2 Cor. 5:15–21 might be paired with this psalm; the pairing possibilities from the New Testament are multitudinous).

That confession, that return to the fellowship of God, gives a peace the world can never give. To be sure, it does not deliver us from any future trouble. The psalmist well knows that human life is never all sweetness and light.

> . . . every godly person will pray to you,
> In the lean time to come,
> in the rushing of many waters,
> him they will not reach.
>
> (My translation)

Fellowship with God does not deliver us from the "lean times" of trouble, but it does deliver us from the powers of chaos (rushing waters) and guilt and death. We are surrounded by the love of a God who will never let us go.

This psalmist wants to share such good news with all of us. Do not be like some stubborn beast, he instructs us, that can only be curbed in its wayward actions by the judging disciplines of God. Repent, accept the good gift of forgiveness offered, trust your Lord to heal and make whole your life. For then you will know the meaning of joy, of rejoicing in the Lord.

A Hymn: Psalm 104

Our society sometimes errs in two ways in its regard of the natural world. Either it views nature as totally devoid of God's action—existing, developing, proceeding in its cycles of birth, life, and death entirely on the basis of natural laws and forces—or it divinizes the world of nature and believes that the divine permeates everything, including us.

In its magnificent praise of the Lord of nature, Psalm 104 gives the lie to both views. The psalm is firmly anchored in the cultic creation traditions of Israel, as set forth in Genesis, and therefore there is no thought in this hymn that the world can exist or have any order apart from the creating and sustaining action of God. As in Genesis 1, God has created the world by bringing order out of the chaos or primeval deep (vs. 5–9). But God's action in relation to the natural world does not stop there, and this is particularly noted by the use of participial phrases in the Hebrew:

v. 10: "making springs gush forth in the valleys"
v. 13: "giving drink to the mountains"
v. 14: "causing grass to grow for cattle"
v. 19: "making the moon to mark the seasons"

God's action toward his creation goes on. He has not only made the world initially, he continues to make, give, cause. The psalmist perceives God's activity going on all around him. On every hand, he sees the power and majesty of his Lord at work. Thus, God makes the night come, which is appointed for the beasts of the forest to creep forth and hunt their prey (v. 20). God causes the sun to rise to provide the day for human work (vs. 22–23). God gives every creature its food at the appropriate time (vs. 27–28). God withdraws his breath of life, and death comes (v. 29). God continues to create and to bring forth each new generation of living things (v. 30).

Further, in his manifold works (v. 24), God orders all things wisely. This hymn is remarkable for its perception of the ecological order. (Note how Hebrew thought always becomes specific: Beasts of the field are mentioned, but then wild asses are singled out, v. 11; the general reference to birds is followed by specific mention of the stork, v. 17.) The "springs" (v. 10) furnish drink for all animals (v. 11) and for the trees where birds have their habitations (vs. 12, 16–17). Plants provide bread and wine for human beings (vs. 14–15); the high mountains are for wild goats, the rocks the refuge for badgers (v. 18). Time, marked by the seasons of the moon (v. 19), is apportioned for every activity of earth (vs. 19–23). The sea provides habitat for living creatures and a way for the ships (vs. 25–26).

> O Lord, how manifold are thy works!
> In wisdom hast thou made them all.

The order of the world is sustained solely because God sustains it. The psalmist knows that such order is constantly threatened by chaos, but his trust is that God by his faithfulness holds chaos in check and will never again let it engulf creation (v. 9; cf. Gen. 9:8–17).

In the theology of this hymn, however, God is not bound up with, contained in, or revealed through the natural world; and mythological thought, which divinizes the natural world, finds no place in this psalm, as it finds no place in the whole of scripture. In fact, the mythological thought of the ancient world that surrounded Israel is thoroughly demythologized. Clouds and wind, fire and flame, are not gods but only servants of the Lord (vs. 3–4). Waters are no longer primeval deities but instruments used by God to nourish his creation (vs. 10–13, 16). The sea—long a symbol of the goddess Tiamat, the primordial deep, in Mesopotamian theology—is just a body of water; and Leviathan, another name for Tiamat, is now a playful creature made by the Lord (vs. 25–26). Darkness and night are no longer associated with the divine chaos but are creations of God. The sun is his servant, the moon his creation (v. 19); the worship of astral deities and astrology has no place in the Bible. Even death, that final symbol of divinized chaos and evil, is solely God's instrument and holds no fear for the psalmist; no shrouded figure with scythe lies behind this portrayal. Life comes from the breath of God (cf. Gen. 2:7), and when God holds his breath, all living things return to dead physical matter (v. 29).

The Lord, the psalmist's God, reigns over his creation in honor and majesty. The main theme of this hymn is set forth in its first verse: "Thou art very great!" The rest of the psalm, recounting God's works, is dedicated to showing how this is so. God is so great in his majesty that the heavens form merely the curtain of his tent, the clouds merely his chariot (vs. 2–3). He clothes himself in light, for no one can see God and live (v. 2; cf. Deut. 5:25–26; 18:16). When he looks on the earth, it trembles, and the mountains smoke at his touch (v. 32; cf. Ex. 19:18; Amos 9:5; Ps. 144:5).

The majestic God of this psalm cannot be contained in any part of his creation. "Behold, heaven and the highest heaven cannot contain thee" (1 Kings 8:27). What tree, what animal, what mortal being is adequate to reveal God's nature? "To whom then will you compare me, that I should be like him? says the Holy One" (Isa. 40:25). Every attempt to divinize creation falls before the glorious majesty of this God of the Bible, who reigns over all he has made. And everything this majestic God has made and every life form that he sustains testify to his wisdom and faithfulness. All his works should cause him to be esteemed.

It is for that esteem or glorification of God forever that the psalmist finally prays in verse 31, and those who will not praise such a God, he asks to be destroyed from the earth (v. 35). "Praise the LORD" is his prayer: that is, "Hallelu-jah!" (v. 35). The psalmist, reveling in God's magnificent works, knows the purpose for which he was created.

Cannot the preacher, pointing to all God's work around us in nature, bring a congregation to the same reveling praise? Surely we have enough help from our scientists these days to spell out the magnificent orders in the natural world. And surely, in pairing a New Testament text with this psalm, we can affirm that these orders have been created and are sustained for us by God through Jesus Christ. "All things were made through him, and without him was not anything made that was made" (John 1:3). And through Jesus Christ, God faithfully, constantly, day by day, upholds "the universe by his word of power" (Heb. 1:3). He is not divorced from the natural world; neither is he contained in it or revealed by it. Rather, he rules over it as its loving Lord and majestic King. That truth is revealed to us only through the word of scripture, and it is a truth that our people need very much to hear, in order to counter the false views with which so much of our society is permeated.

To be sure, this psalm knows only a beneficent universe. There is nothing here of nature "red of tooth and claw." The struggle for survival in the natural world is part of God's appointed plan. Natural catastrophes such as drought, storm, earthquake, and famine are not mentioned, and if they pose a problem for the psalmist, he tells us nothing of it. If the preacher wants to round out the understanding of the natural world from scripture, he or she therefore may want to say something about the Bible's concept of nature also as "fallen" (cf. Gen. 3:17–18; Jer. 12:4), "subjected to futility" (Rom. 8:20) because of the sin of human beings. God does not intend the violence and destruction found in the natural world, although sometimes he uses them in judgment. But in the Bible's view, the entire creation must be redeemed (cf. Isa. 11:6–9; Rom. 8:21–23). So radical is the Bible's understanding of the corruption of the creation by sin that we could say that even our genes have been corrupted, so that we give birth to retarded and maimed and ill offspring, for whom God intended only wholeness. (It is no accident that when the Messiah comes he heals bodies and minds as well as spirits.) Nature, too, is affected by our sin—we are always leaving a "scorched earth" behind us—and the preacher may want to discuss that, in order to deal with evil in nature.

Yet, despite the fallen condition of the natural world, it manifests a marvelous "common grace," and so good is God's creation that we find ourselves surrounded by magnificent remnants of that goodness —in the beauty, order, fruitfulness of a nature wondrous beyond words. "He makes his sun rise on the evil and on the good, and sends rain on the just and on the unjust" (Matt. 5:45). The psalmist celebrates that common grace in this psalm, and preaching from the psalm can prompt a congregation also to celebrate and praise its Lord.

Other Homiletical Uses of the Psalms

The psalms are so rich in theological and devotional insights that one is tempted to devote undue attention to them. With good reason they have formed the devotional treasure of the church for centuries. However, for reasons of space, let us just discuss two other ways in which the psalms may be used in preaching.

Using a Portion of a Psalm

We need not always preach on an entire psalm. There are portions of them that furnish powerful instruction for the Christian life. For example, in a meditation dealing with God's forgiveness, I used Psalm 130:4 in connection with Romans 6:1–4, 12–14, to discuss our society's belief that God will always forgive no matter what we do.

> The psalmist, in the passage which we read for our Old Testament lesson, has a different understanding of forgiveness. He too fully expects God to forgive his sin. Indeed, he assures his fellow worshipers that the Lord will redeem them from all their iniquities. But God's forgiveness, according to the psalmist, is not without its purpose: "there is forgiveness with thee," he says, "that thou mayest be feared." There is forgiveness with God in order that he may be served in awe and obedience. There is forgiveness with God in order that his acceptance of us may lead us to a new manner of living.[18]

The preacher will find innumerable instructional passages in the Psalter that may be used to teach the congregation about the life of faith, of prayer, of obedience. To give another example, the great penitential Psalm 51 is crowded with theological insights: the fact that all sin is finally sin against God (v. 4) or that we are born into a world that is shot through with sin (v. 5); the truth that our corruption can only be done away in the mercy of God (vs. 1–2, 7–9), by his creation in us of a new heart and spirit (v. 10); the fact that we continue to fall away from God and that we need his forgiveness and cleansing and transformation of us daily by his Spirit (vs. 11–12); the realization that our praise and witness to others arise out of God's salvation of us and that, if we are saved, we always become God's "missionary" (vs. 13–14); the truth that the one attitude acceptable to God is that of total reliance on him, that we are always justified and saved by trust alone (vs. 16–17). The preacher may want to proclaim only one or two of those insights, because a thorough treatment of all of them could fill an entire book or constitute a sermon series.

If the preacher uses only a portion of a psalm as a basis for a sermon, two cautions should be kept in mind. First, the entire psalm should be read as the Old Testament lesson in order that the congregation may hear the full setting of the text. Second, the preacher must be certain that the meaning of the sermon text is not distorted by lifting it out of its context.

Pairing for New Pictures

The practice of pairing an Old Testament psalm with a New Testament passage can be carried out with a great deal of creativity and holy imagination, for the purpose of forming new pictures of the holy history.

For example, Psalm 47, which is an enthronement psalm, gives a magnificent picture of God the King over all the earth, ascending to his throne to receive the praises and pledges of loyalty from all nations. The psalm is divided into two strophes, verses 1–5 and 6–9. The figure of height dominates the entire psalm: Yahweh is "Most High" (v. 2), mounting up to his throne (v. 5), reigning over all the earth as the King who is "highly exalted" (v. 9). In the first strophe, all peoples sing joyfully and clap their hands in a cultic dance, celebrating their King, and that kingship has been manifested in God's victories over Israel's enemies (v. 3) and the gift to her of the promised land (v. 4). As in all of the Old Testament, God has shown himself Ruler by his actions in Israel, and Israel's salvation will mean finally the salvation of all the families of the earth. So the celebration of God's kingship is almost deafening in its jubilation: singing, clapping, ram's horn blaring, wild rejoicing.

In the second strophe, God takes his throne (v. 8), and all the rulers of the world gather at his feet to pledge their fealty. All now are "the people of the God of Abraham"; all now are included in the covenant (v. 9ab). Nationalistic distinctions, all divisions, have been overcome; there is one flock and one shepherd. "The shields of the earth," all weapons of war, have been turned over to God, and he reigns, in the eschatological vision of this psalm, as the King of an earth at peace (v. 9cd).

This psalm could be used in connection with any one of several New Testament passages. One thinks almost immediately of Philippians

2:9–10: The psalm portrays that coronation of Christ and the bowing of every knee and the confessing of every tongue.

To give another example, this is the psalm for Ascension Day, paired with Acts 1:9–11. "He ascended into heaven and sitteth on the right hand of God." Christ has gone up from the earth, away from us. Sometimes we tend to think it is a loss that Jesus is no longer with us, that we can no longer feel his touch and share his physical presence and hear his words from his lips. But we should rejoice, as the psalm calls us to rejoice, for Christ has ascended to rule over all the earth—to mount his throne as King of the nations, to share his Father's universal reign. Delivered now from the limitations of time and space, he no longer is "King of the Jews" alone, but King over us Gentiles as well and over all people. And there he will reign until he has put all his enemies under his feet, the last enemy to be destroyed being death. Then there will be the kingdom on earth, even as it is in heaven, in which we shall all be one flock, under our one Shepherd Christ, and there will be universal peace on earth in a kingdom that will never pass away. The stage is set by Christ's ascension; the action has begun and will be completed. Therefore (paraphrasing):

> Sing praises to God, sing praises!
> Sing praises to our King, sing praises!
> For Christ is the King of all the earth;
> Sing praises with a psalm!

Perhaps more vivid still would be the use of this psalm with the Fourth Gospel's portrayal of the crucifixion, and specifically with John 12:32: "I, when I am lifted up from the earth, will draw all men to myself." In the Fourth Gospel, Jesus' crucifixion is understood as his coronation as King, and therefore as his glorification and resurrection and ascension. "What shall I say? 'Father, save me from this hour'? No, for this purpose I have come to this hour. Father, glorify thy name" (12:27–28a). On the cross, Jesus Christ is glorified as the King of all the earth. The placard above his head, proclaiming his kingship, is written in Hebrew, Latin, and Greek (John 19:20), and even Pilate has to acknowledge that Christ is King (19:22). Jesus therefore can cry out with his last breath, "It is finished"; the purpose for which he was sent, the rule of the earth, is completed (paraphrasing):

> Christ has gone up with a shout.
> Christ reigns over the nations;
> Christ occupies his holy throne—his cross.

From that cross-throne, he will draw all peoples to himself, until all acknowledge his merciful and loving rule over them. By the cross of

Christ, the nations will be converted and become one people (cf. John 17:20–23) in covenant with their Lord.

If Psalm 47 were used in some such fashion to portray the events of Good Friday, it certainly would give that day a different tone than it often has had. No more only the sorrowful weeping over the crucifixion of our Lord—although our sin and our unbelief should remain always a source of sorrow (cf. John 12:35–36). But principally Good Friday would become, using the words of Psalm 47, the occasion of jubilation. For on Good Friday, on his cross, Jesus Christ has become earth's King (paraphrasing):

> Clap your hands, all peoples!
>   Shout to God with loud songs of joy!
> For our Lord Jesus Christ is become
>   a great King over all the earth!

Let us look at one other example of how fresh pictures of the New Testament's story emerge from pairing it with a psalm. Psalm 114 is a hymn in four strophes (as in the RSV), celebrating the deliverance of Israel by the exodus from the house of bondage in Egypt. At that event, the psalm pictures the earth trembling, the mountains skipping like rams, and the hills like lambs. All nature quakes before the power of this delivering "God of Jacob." But the exodus in the Old Testament is the parallel to the cross in the New—in both events, God redeems his people from slavery. And in Matthew's version of the crucifixion, we find the earth once again trembling: "And behold, the curtain of the temple was torn in two, from top to bottom; and the earth shook, and the rocks were split" (Matt. 27:51). Thus the questions of the psalm are appropriate:

> What ails you, . . . O mountains, that you skip like rams?
> O hills, like lambs?

They tremble before the presence of God. "Truly this was the Son of God!" confess the centurion and soldiers, in fear and awe. Here in this death on a cross, the Lord of nature and history is present, and all the earth is called to "tremble" before his power.

> Were you there when they crucified my Lord? . . .
> Sometimes it causes me to tremble.

But our psalm is a hymn praising that God who is not only awesome and powerful but also merciful, the Guide and Protector who stoops down to give drink to his chosen people as they wander through the wilderness (Ps. 114:8). And the awesome event on Golgotha is also

God stooping down to us, in his mercy providing that cleansing water that washes away our sin and that now satisfies our thirst for fellowship with him even "to the close of the age" (Matt. 28:20). The psalm helps us form new pictures of what happened on Golgotha.

CHAPTER 9

Preaching from the Wisdom Literature

We cannot understand Wisdom texts in terms of our contemporary views of reality. Old Testament Wisdom is a unique phenomenon in the Bible and in the ancient and modern worlds, and the preacher must approach Old Testament Wisdom on the basis of its own presuppositions and worldview. That is not to say that Old Testament Wisdom does not have some things in common with the Wisdom literature found in ancient Mesopotamia and especially Egypt; scholars generally acknowledge, for example, that the Egyptian *Instruction of Amenemope* was the source of Proverbs 22:17—24:22. Nevertheless, Old Testament Wisdom is distinct unto itself, shaped by the uniqueness of the biblical faith, and the preacher must try to comprehend the thought and bases of Israelite Wisdom before using it as a sermon text. Otherwise the result is likely to be a sermon more akin to the views of modern psychology or mental health than to those of the biblical faith.

The principal Wisdom document in the Old Testament is the book of Proverbs, while the books of Job and Ecclesiastes form two extended commentaries on Wisdom. But there are also a number of Wisdom psalms. Hermann Gunkel (see chapter 4) listed Psalms 127 and 133 as simple proverbial types, and Psalms 1, 37, 49, 73, 112, and 128 as longer poems. References to wise men and women, who form a special class, are found throughout the scriptures, most often as counselors to leaders and kings[1] but also as those among the populace who study and practice Wisdom.[2] In the earliest documents (Judg. 5:29) to the latest (2 Peter 3:15), Wisdom has a place in the biblical witness, and there are references to Wisdom teachings found through the scriptures.[3] Mark tells us that some regarded Jesus as a Wisdom teacher (Mark 6:2 and pars.), and certainly Jesus drew on Wisdom in a number of his teachings. In the Old Testament, Solomon especially was connected with Wisdom (1 Kings 3; 4:29–34; 5:12; 10), and so both Proverbs (1:1) and Ecclesiastes (1:1) are collected under his name, while in the New Testament, Jesus claims that "something greater than Solomon is here" (Matt. 12:42 and par.).

In the book of Proverbs, Wisdom is most often presented in the form of the *mashal*, the two-line maxim that utilizes some form of parallelism between the lines:

> A wise son makes a glad father,
> but a foolish son is a sorrow to his mother.
> Proverbs 10:1

Sometimes the two lines are expanded by the citation of the reason for the maxim:

> Fret not yourself because of evildoers,
> and be not envious of the wicked;
> for the evil man has no future;
> the lamp of the wicked will be put out.
> Proverbs 24:19–20 (cf. Ps. 37:1–2)

Sometimes the sayings are expanded in full forms of several lines (see Prov. 1:10–19 and throughout chs. 1–9), or into the long speeches that one finds in the book of Job.

Characteristic of Wisdom sayings, however, is their artistic shaping, in which one finds comparisons, contrasts, numerical listings, admonitions of sons by fathers or pupils by teachers, or phrases such as "better than," "how much more," "happy [blessed] is," "is an abomination to the Lord," all of which set forth two opposing ways of conduct. Scholars cannot agree about whether such maxims originated in folk wisdom, in the royal court, or in Wisdom schools. Probably all three environments contributed to the propagation of Wisdom. Certainly the sayings come to us in carefully framed forms that show a high degree of intellectual activity. Wisdom took shape in the time of the early monarchy, and it is generally acknowledged that Proverbs 10–29 are preexilic, while Proverbs 1–9 have sometimes been termed postexilic, a conclusion not at all certain.

We do know that Wisdom is the result of practical experience and the careful observation of both the natural and human worlds. Out of all of the chaos of experience, Wisdom finds customary "orders" in the world—ways in which human beings and natural phenomena ordinarily behave. Its aim, then, is to teach men and women these "orders," so they may know how to act in harmony with the world around them. Those who learn such Wisdom and accommodate their actions to it are "wise" and will live, and those who will not learn or who try to defy such orders are "fools," whose only end will be destruction. Thus Wisdom finally sets before human beings a life-and-death decision.

Wisdom cannot be termed a science, however, for it is not dealing with natural laws, such as the law of gravity. (If you jump out of a window, you fall.) Nor is Wisdom the observation and codification of impersonal mechanisms set into the structure of creation. Wisdom teachings in Israel, in contrast to Egyptian understandings, for example, are profoundly religious. The orders that it finds in the world are set up and sustained by God alone. In short, Wisdom embodies a doctrine of creation. God has created the world and sustains it and works in it in such a manner that there are customary ways in which human beings and nature act and react.

At the heart of Proverbs, therefore, and sounding its theme at the beginning (Prov. 1:7) is the statement, "The fear of the LORD is the beginning of wisdom" (9:10; 15:33; cf. Job 28:28; Ps. 111:10; Eccl. 12:13). Only the person who is committed to God—who desires to learn the ways of God and to obey his will, as those ways and will have been set into creation—can become "wise." Such a person trusts that God has shaped creation in an orderly and wise fashion (see Jer. 10:11; 51:15) and desires to learn that Wisdom of God with all his heart and mind and strength. Thus the wise person is at the same time pious.

Probably the most extended picture that we have in the Old Testament of such a pious wise man is that found in Job 29. Job's wise life in the past has brought him abundant life and blessings, honor in his community, prosperity and offspring, satisfaction and meaning, and a lively concern for and practice of the ways of social justice. In short, Job has been at one with his community and with his world. Wisdom is very much a communal practice that integrates one peacefully into society. Such a person, then, is termed "righteous" or "just," because he or she fulfills all the demands that community makes.

One of the important "orders" that God has set into his creation, according to Wisdom teaching, is the order of time, and this is discussed in the famous passage in Ecclesiastes 3:1–8, which is a lectionary reading. Human activity is not equally successful and meaningful at every time, and if one does not know the proper time for some activity, it can turn out very badly. "Look carefully then how you walk, not as unwise men but as wise, making the most of the time, because the days are evil" (Eph. 5:15–16). There is even a proper time to be born (Eccl. 3:2; Hos. 13:13). But especially are there proper times to say just the right word (Prov. 15:23; 25:11; 19:21). Everything has its season, and so the psalmist can pray, "So teach us to number our days that we may get a heart of wisdom" (Ps. 90:12).

According to Wisdom teaching, human beings live in a beneficent universe, and there is no reason to be afraid. God has made all things wisely (Ps. 104:24; Prov. 3:19–20). If a person will heed the words of wisdom and learn from them in commitment to God and his ways, life can be full and meaningful and harmonious. Human beings have a choice. They are responsible creatures who can choose the way of wisdom or of foolishness, of righteousness or of wickedness, of life or of death (cf. Deut. 30:15, 19). Wisdom offers to all, rich and poor, prominent and unknown, powerful and powerless, highborn and low, the possibility of abundant life. Its invitation is universal (see Prov. 8:32–36).

Obviously, there is no doctrine of the fall here. Neither nature nor human beings are corrupted by sin. Human beings can freely choose wisdom and are in no way slaves to sin. Wisdom teaching affirms the statement of Genesis, "And God saw everything that he had made, and behold, it was very good" (1:31), and it simply revels in that goodness, so that often Wisdom teaching pushes on into the joyous hymnic praise of God (as in Psalm 104).

Wisdom does acknowledge the presence of suffering in the world, but it deals with the fact by integrating such suffering into the ways of God. Thus, suffering can serve a number of purposes for the Lord. It can be a way of discipline and teaching (Prov. 3:11–12; cf. Job 5:17; 36:15, 22; Heb. 12:5–6). It can be due to hidden sins that the suffering serves to uncover (Job 22), and therefore it gives opportunity for self-examination, repentance, and return. Or very often, the suffering of the righteous and the prosperity of the wicked are only temporary, and the scales of justice will be balanced in the end (Psalms 37; 73).

Most important in this respect is Wisdom's constant appreciation of its own limits. The wise person knows that he or she does not know and can never know everything, not because the phenomena of the world are too multitudinous to master, but because God is free and Lord of creation, and God can never be mastered. "Man proposes, but God disposes"; the wise never forget that. The creation is not some mechanical machine that God has wound up like a clock and then left to run on its own, according to immutable laws. God is in charge of his creation (cf. Prov. 15:3; 22:2), and therefore there is a mystery to the ways of creation that human beings can never penetrate and finally pin down. This is set forth at length in Job 28, which uses the illustration of mining to acknowledge human technological skill and knowledge. Human beings overturn mountains, redirect streams, channel in the recesses of the earth, and discover every precious thing, but they cannot finally discover and capture wisdom for themselves, for God alone understands the way to wisdom and establishes it in the earth.

Human beings may make many plans, but finally it is God who works out his purposes.

> Many are the plans in the mind of a man,
>> but it is the purpose of the LORD that will be established.
>>> Proverbs 19:21 (cf. 16:9, 33; 21:1, 30–31; 27:1)

Human beings can deceive themselves into thinking that they have learned wisdom and are wise, much like Eve deceiving herself in the garden into thinking that eating of the fruit was desirable to make her wise (Gen. 3:6).

> There is a way which seems right to a man,
> but its end is the way to death.
>> Proverbs 14:12—16:25 (cf. Isa. 47:10)

There is constant warning in the Old Testament, therefore, against believing one's self to be wise.

> Do you see a man who is wise in his own eyes?
> There is more hope for a fool than for him.
>> Proverbs 26:12 (cf. 28:11; 30:12)

"Woe to those who are wise in their own eyes," proclaims Isaiah (5:21), "and shrewd in their own sight!" Before the purposes of God "the wisdom of their wise men shall perish, and the discernment of their discerning men shall be hid" (Isa. 29:14). God is quite capable of turning "wise men back" and of making "their knowledge foolish" (Isa. 44:25). "Among all the wise ones of the nations and in all their kingdoms there is none like" Yahweh (Jer. 10:7), and he can deal as he likes with those who claim wisdom (cf. Jer. 50:35; 51:57; Ezek. 28:2–7; 9:2). Therefore, admonishes Jeremiah 9:23–24, "let not the wise man glory in his wisdom, . . . but let him who glories glory in this, that he understands and knows me [God]."

That finally is a doctrine stemming from the profound humility before God that knows total dependence on God for one's life, one's good, one's all, and that confesses that God is free in his wisdom to work out his purposes as he sees fit (cf. Rom. 11:33–36). It is humility that trusts God to will and to do the good and therefore surrenders all things into his hands. Paul takes up much of this understanding in 1 Corinthians, when he writes of the wisdom of God that is wiser than the foolishness of men (1:25), that shames the wise of this world (1:27), and that "catches the wise in their craftiness" (3:19). The wise person relies, therefore, totally on the "hidden wisdom of God" (2:7), manifested now in Jesus Christ (1:30).

Indeed, in the New Testament, wisdom becomes totally unavailable to human beings who seek wisdom on their own. To be sure, in the

Gospel According to Matthew, Jesus taught of "the faithful and wise servant" (Matt. 24:45 and par.) and of the five foolish and five wise maidens (Matt. 25:2–13), and he admonished his disciples to be as "wise as serpents and innocent as doves" (Matt. 10:16): Our Lord utilized wisdom in his teachings. But in Luke-Acts and in the epistles of the New Testament, wisdom has become a gift given only by the Spirit (Luke 2:40, 52; 21:15; Acts 6:3, 10; 1 Cor. 12:8; Eph. 1:9, 17; Col. 1:9; 3:16). Wisdom is from "above," writes James (3:17). In Revelation, it gives the ability to interpret the Apocalypse's signs (Rev. 13:18; 17:9). In other words, wisdom is revealed by God and can only be had from that revelation.

That goes beyond what we find in the Old Testament, although it is prepared for by the apocryphal book of Sirach, in which wisdom is identified with the Torah, and by those few passages in the Old Testament itself where wisdom is made synonymous with the revealed Law (see Deut. 4:5–8; Prov. 28:4, 7, 9; 29:18; Jer. 8:8). But in most of the Old Testament, wisdom is available to human beings; it can be taught and learned by those committed to the Lord, though one must always take account of the limitations of one's own knowledge. To convey the teachings of wisdom is the purpose of these writings in the Old Testament.

Preaching from Traditional Wisdom

If the preacher has investigated the nature of the theology held by those in the congregation, he or she may be astonished to find how many there are who live their lives by a form of religious wisdom teaching. It has been my experience to encounter throughout the United States those pious folk in the church who believe that God has set into creation certain natural and moral laws that work automatically. If one eats an unhealthy diet, one becomes ill. If one steals or covets or commits adultery, one suffers automatic ill consequences. The universe, in such thought, is a moral mechanism, in which proper conduct brings its reward of health and happiness and immoral conduct reaps its punishment. There need be little thought of the action of God in such mechanistic conceptions, and indeed the world can be viewed as a totally secular sphere from which God is absent. Nevertheless, the world runs according to the laws that God has set into it, and the wise person then, as in Wisdom theology, learns and heeds those laws.

If such popular Wisdom theology has a deeper strain of piety in it, the person holding it may see God actively at work behind the laws of such a universe, but God is understood largely as a retributive Judge. As one woman expressed it, "If you do the wrong thing, God will zap you." Religious education, then, is learning the right thing to do in order not to be zapped. The theology is entirely one of works righteousness, with fear hovering always around its edges. And undeserved suffering, of course, such as that of Job, remains a total enigma, just as good fortune finds its expression in the popular phrase, "I must be doing something right."

Such popular attitudes are caricatures of the wisdom of the Old Testament, because they remain unrelated to that personal God of faithfulness and righteousness, of steadfast love and mercy, whom Israel knew her life long and to whom the pious wise committed themselves in heartfelt devotion. There is also little understanding of wisdom's limitations over against the mysteries of the universe and of God. In dealing with the Wisdom literature, the preacher needs to keep both its personal theological dimension and its humble stance before its own limits and before God in mind.

Having said that, however, preaching from any portion of Proverbs 10–29 (often called "older" or "traditional" Wisdom) can seem to confront the homiletician with enormous problems.

First, some material in that section of Proverbs appears to be totally amoral. What does one do with the statements found in Proverbs 14:20 or 17:8 or 11:16? They give no moral judgments. They are simply observations of the ways of society. (See also 13:8; 18:11, 23; 19:4, 6–7; 21:14; 22:7.)

Second, what does a preacher do with a two- or four-line text that is unconnected with what precedes and follows it? For example, Proverbs 25:6–22 is one of the stated lessons for the fifteenth Sunday of Pentecost in year C of the ecumenical lectionary. Apparently it has been chosen because it contains two sayings used by Jesus (v. 7 = Luke 14:7–11; v. 21 = Matt. 5:44), but the rest are a series of unrelated maxims. That is one of the difficulties with Proverbs 10–29; those chapters seem to have the most random order, simply listing maxims one after another. What does one do when confronted with such texts?

Third, there are maxims, sometimes placed side by side, that contradict one another (see Prov. 26:4–5). In Proverbs 6:6–11, poverty is an evil associated with laziness, but in Proverbs 15:16 we read, "Better is a little with the fear of the LORD than great treasure and trouble with it." Are these sayings to be considered as the word of the Lord or are they not? Do they have the canonical standing of revelation? If they do, what are we to do with the contradictions?

To answer these latter questions first, older traditional Wisdom has to be read on its own terms. It really does not claim the authority of prophecy. There is no "Thus saith the Lord" here, no "This is the word of the Lord." Wisdom sets forth its observations of life and offers its advice about how one can live successfully in the world, but it always hesitates, before the limitations of its own knowledge, to make absolute statements.

Wisdom therefore finds no necessity always to make moral judgments. Some of its statements can seem to be totally divorced from the will of God, because they set forth the nature of the world and of society as they are. Wisdom, in short, realistically presents what we would call the fallen nature of human life, as well as the ideal nature of that life. For example, rich people do have lots of friends (Prov. 14:20); right or wrong, that is a fact of our society.

Taken as a total body of literature, Wisdom sayings in Proverbs often discuss various topics from many different angles. There are many maxims dealing with wealth and poverty, with social justice, with the treatment of parents, with marriage and children. These represent the accumulation of several centuries of observation and experience. The task of the preacher, therefore, is to survey that accumulation. If one wants to preach on wealth and poverty, one should look at all the proverbial texts dealing with that topic. (A concordance is an invaluable tool; even better is a quick reading through Proverbs itself.) If such a survey is made and all the texts are pondered, the preacher can then ask questions of his or her text: For example, why is it that the rich have lots of friends? What does that say about the values held by our society? What kinds of friends are they? Or, going further, Are riches connected with the wise life and obedience to God? (The theological problems deepen.) When are riches evidence of foolishness? How are they to be regarded? Is it ever better to be poor? (Ella Fitzgerald once remarked, "I've been rich, and I've been poor, and rich is better.") What is the responsibility of the wealthy toward society? The proverbs treat all these questions, and they therefore afford the preacher a marvelous opportunity to examine in detail the life of our society, its standards and values, its religious beliefs and practices.

To continue the example, the final question that the preacher then asks is, How do all these wise sayings appear in the light of the New Testament's views of wealth and poverty? Do they help deepen the understandings of the subject? Must they be qualified in the light of the life of our Lord? What, finally, is the word of God for the congregation on this subject? In the context of the canon as a whole, is there not a canonical quality also to Proverbs?

In short, in dealing with traditional Wisdom, the preacher constructs a topical sermon, and, as we have said before, a topical sermon looks at the entire canon's view of the subject. Such sermons are not constructed hastily from one day's study of the scriptures. They are formed out of prolonged experience of the preacher with the biblical materials. (It has been my experience in the classroom that young preachers have difficulty writing topical sermons.) But such sermons are exceedingly rewarding in terms of instructing the congregation. One of the failures of the modern pulpit is that while it frequently exhorts congregations to live the Christian life, it much less frequently spells out the details of what that life looks like. Wisdom teachings get at the details and can be invaluable in examining everyday values and actions.

There is a greater problem facing the preacher who uses Proverbs, however, and that has to do with the understanding of Wisdom in Proverbs 1–9. Here we must expand on our discussion of the content of Wisdom theology.

Personified Wisdom

In Proverbs 1–9, Wisdom is personified and takes on the character of a person who replaces the figure of the teacher and sage to speak on her own behalf (see Prov. 1:20–33; 8; 9:1–6). In this personification, Wisdom is variously described: as one calling or preaching in the streets (1:20; 8:1); as a guide, guardian, and conversationlist (6:22); as a sister or intimate friend (7:4); as a hostess inviting to her table (9:1–6). Most important, in the famous passage of Proverbs 8:22–36, which is a lectionary text, Wisdom is described as the first work of creation (vs. 22–23), who was present with God when he made all else, who was his darling child, rejoicing and dancing before him and delighting in human beings (vs. 30–31). Such personified Wisdom is not to be viewed as a hypostasis of God or as some sort of incarnation; she is not divine but has been created at the beginning, and yet is separate and different from all God's other creations.

This personified Wisdom figure calls to human beings, inviting them to listen to her, to heed her summons, and to seek her out (Prov. 8:4–5, 10, 32–36). She woos human beings, promising them knowledge and love (vs. 9, 17), riches and honor (vs. 18, 21), righteousness and justice (v. 20), equity (2:9) and security (1:33).

> For he who finds me finds life
> and obtains favor from the LORD;
> but he who misses me injures himself;
> all who hate me love death.
> Proverbs 8:35–36

In short, Wisdom in the form of this personified figure speaks on behalf of God. No one but God can say "He who finds me finds life," for God is the source of all life. Wisdom here has become a source of revelation (cf. 30:3–5). One who finds her is given knowledge of God (2:5).

Such a view contradicts everything that we have heretofore learned about the Old Testament, because the created world has here become a source of revelation. According to the other literature of the Old Testament, God reveals himself only through his own actions and words within a sacred salvation history, or through the mediation of the cult, and he cannot be known through any part of the created world. But Wisdom has little interest in the cult (mentioned only in Prov. 2:9–10; 20:25; 21:3; 28:9); it almost totally ignores the sacred history (in later Wisdom writings, Moses and the patriarchs become models of the wise man); and the personified figure of Wisdom, the embodiment of God's order in the universe, has become that which gives knowledge of him. Von Rad has called this "the Doctrine of the Self-Revelation of Creation,"[4] "the religious provocation of man by the world"[5]—that "primeval force" for order in the creation, that "world reason" that turns toward human beings and attracts them and lures them to her ways.[6] (Von Rad identifies this—erroneously, I think—with the "speaking" of creation in Ps. 19:1–4.)[7] Thus, when Zophar asks Job, "Can you find out the deep things of God?" (Job 11:7)—that is, can you, by your own searching, discover God?—the answer would be yes. Human beings, through the instrument of Wisdom, through the observation and experience of their world, can come to a knowledge of Almighty God.

Nothing else in the Old Testament outside of the Wisdom literature supports that, and the Deuteronomists and prophets fight against such an understanding with all of their ability. Because such a doctrine is so different from the rest of the Old Testament's witness, some have therefore held—perhaps correctly—that this theology came to the fore in Israel in postexilic times, when the sacred history had come to a standstill. God no longer spoke to Israel through his prophets; the cult was impoverished; the deeds of God in Israel's history seemed to have come to an end. Israel therefore looked to the creation for the source of revelation, and specifically to the Wisdom teachings, with their personified figure of Wisdom.

In modern understanding, one finds no conception of a personified Wisdom figure, but there is the widespread belief abroad in the church that God can indeed be known through his works in creation. Two difficulties arise with such a view, however, as we have mentioned before. First, the sacred history as the source of revelation is abandoned and, in fact, has become largely unknown in the church. Second, such a search for God in his works in creation slips easily over into some form of neopantheism and nature worship. The preacher does indeed confront serious problems when attempting to preach from Proverbs 1–9.

Significantly, both Judaism and Christianity were not content to leave this Wisdom theology uncorrected. In Judaism, personified Wisdom became identified with the Torah, thus incorporating Wisdom theology once again into the sacred history and equating its revelation with those words spoken by God into the salvation history. In Christianity, both the figure of personified Wisdom and the Torah were replaced by the historical figure of Jesus Christ. Thus, in John 1, much of Wisdom's function is taken over by the incarnate Word, as Raymond Brown has shown,[8] and the statement is made that "the law was given through Moses; grace and truth came through Jesus Christ" (v. 17). Christ Jesus becomes, for the New Testament, the one source of the revelation of God. "No one has ever seen God; the only Son, who is in the bosom of the Father, he has made him known" (v. 18). In Paul's writings, therefore, Christ is "the wisdom of God" (1 Cor. 1:24, 30), and the author of Colossians desires that the Laodiceans "have all the riches of assured understanding and the knowledge of God's mystery, of Christ, in whom are hid all the treasures of wisdom and knowledge" (Col. 2:2). Christ is "the image of the invisible God" who makes God known, "the first-born of all creation" (Col. 1:15). And he is the order laid upon the universe; "in him all things hold together" (Col. 1:17). Thus, to seek wisdom, in the New Testament's view, is to seek Christ. But he cannot be known from the things of the created world. The Christian must "seek the things that are above, where Christ is seated at the right hand of God. Set your minds on things that are above," says Colossians 3:1–2, "not on things that are on earth." The figure of Wisdom in the Old Testament has now been reinterpreted and replaced by Jesus Christ, and that truth and life and knowledge of God promised by personified Wisdom can only be had from commitment to the Son of God. "I am the way, and the truth, and the life; no one comes to the Father, but by me" (John 14:6).

It is no accident, therefore, that in the Gospel According to Matthew, Jesus prays, "I thank thee, Father, Lord of heaven and earth, that thou hast hidden these things from the *wise* and understanding and revealed them to babes; yea, Father, for such was thy gracious will" (Matt. 11:25–26, emphasis added). Jesus then continues with his exclusive claim and issues an invitation to learn of him, that replaces that of Wisdom:

> All things have been delivered to me by my Father; and no one knows the Son except the Father, and no one knows the Father except the Son and any one to whom the Son chooses to reveal him. Come to me, all who labor and are heavy laden, and I will give you rest. Take my yoke upon you, and learn from me; for I am gentle and lowly in heart, and you will find rest for your souls. For my yoke is easy, and my burden is light.
>
> Matthew 11:27–30

It seems to me that in dealing with Proverbs 1–9, in order to keep the congregation from falling into egregious theological errors, this use of the canonical context for wisdom is the way open to the Christian preacher. There is a way of wisdom in this world. It is a love of God's commandments, a burning desire to follow his will, to know him intimately, and thus to find life. And that way has now been fully revealed for us in Jesus Christ our Lord. The invitation of Wisdom personified becomes the invitation of Christ:

> And now, my sons and daughters, listen to me:
>   happy are those who keep my ways.
> Hear instruction and be wise,
>   and do not neglect it. . . .
> For the one who finds me finds life
>   and obtains favor from the LORD;
> but the one who misses me injures himself;
>   all who hate me love death.
>   Proverbs 8:32–36 (paraphrase)

The Book of Job

The book of Job is so rich in Wisdom theology that we cannot begin to encompass its thought within a few pages. Nevertheless, we can perhaps give some guidance as to what we believe the book is all about.

Certainly the book is not intended to be a spiritual biography of an actual man named Job. Rather, it is a penetrating commentary on Wisdom theology and the life of all human beings within the world. The prose prologue is simply an instrument used by the narrator to set up the problems. The speeches of the three friends and of Elihu set forth those traditional Wisdom views that we discussed in the first section of this chapter, and those views can be readily identified by anyone who reads through the speeches carefully. There are tensions in the book, and the dialogue by no means moves steadily forward, nor do the individual speeches always seem integrally connected with one another. Nevertheless, there is a unity to the book, and it should be read as a whole.

The principal problem of the book of Job is not that of undeserved suffering, although certainly that forms a subtheme and is dealt with primarily by the friends. Their views are the traditional ones of Wisdom—that happiness and good result from wise accommodation to the order that God has set into the universe; that no one is completely sinless before God or can fully understand God's ways; and that therefore the one course left open to Job is to repent of his sin, to acknowledge the justice of God in afflicting him, and thus to return to

God's favor, in harmony with God's ways. Elihu adds to this the thought that God is teaching Job wisdom through his suffering (36:15, 22–23).

The problem of the book is also not one of theodicy, of justifying the ways of God to man. Both Job and the friends acknowledge that the ways of God are past finding out, and there is marvelous poetry treating the mystery and grandeur of God.

The principal theme of Job, it seems to me, is another emphasis of Wisdom theology—the fact that at the root of all wisdom is one's personal relation with God, one's commitment to him in what Job would call a divine-human friendship.

> Oh, that I were as in the months of old,
>   as in the days when God watched over me;
> when his lamp shone upon my head,
>   and by his light I walked through darkness;
> as I was in my autumn days,
>   when the friendship of God was upon my tent.
>   Job 29:1–4

This pious, righteous man is very much a participant in the school of Wisdom, but he has learned wisdom in its deepest depths. He has learned of that friendship of God, of that love for God that inspires obedience to the divine will and that informs one's actions and desires in every area of life. Out of that love for his God, Job has led an exemplary life. But the result has been that God his friend has turned against him as an enemy.

> Why dost thou hide thy face
>   and count me as thy enemy?
>   Job 13:24 (cf. 33:10;
>   16:9; 19:11)

In fact, Job feels that God has cut off all relationship with him. God has "hedged" him in so that Job cannot communicate with him (3:23; cf. 19:8; 23:17).

> Only grant two things to me,
>   then I will not hide myself from thy face:
> withdraw thy hand far from me,
>   and let not dread of thee terrify me.
> Then call, and I will answer;
>   or let me speak, and do thou reply to me.
>   Job 13:20–22 (cf. 23:3–6; 30:20; 31:35)

Job feels that God communicates with him in only one of two ways. Either he terrifies Job, cruelly watching over his every move (30:21) so that Job does not even have a moment alone to swallow his spittle (7:17–20), or God abandons Job, doing nothing whatsoever in Job's life (30:11) and refusing even to let him die (6:8–9). And Job longs for death (ch. 3), because he knows that God is Lord of life and death, and if God would let him die, that would be at least one merciful action of God toward him, out of which further communication then might grow (14:13–17). Or perhaps, Job further believes (19:25–27), after his death he might finally again find a God who is on his side—that God he has known so well as his neighbor (16:21) and friend.

One cannot deal with God in impersonal terms. He is too righteous for anyone to be blameless before him—impersonal "orders" of reward for good and punishment for evil make no sense in the light of God's justice. And God is too majestic in power for anyone to contend against him; set "orders" within creation cannot begin to encompass him (ch. 9). Only if such a God forgives and graciously allows sinful persons to approach him can human beings have dealings with their Lord (7:21; 9:14–15). And the wise life, the righteous life, consists in total commitment to such a God. That is what Job knows and what his friends do not know, and therefore God's "servant Job" has spoken of him aright, while the friends have been in error (42:7).

Job has known such a God in the past, and he clings to the hope that perhaps even after death he will know a God of such gracious mercy in the future. Though his case looks hopeless, he will not relinquish his belief in God "for him"—God his friend, God his neighbor, God his Redeemer, on his side (19:25–27).

That is also the God who finally speaks to Job out of the whirlwind in chapters 38–41. There is no softening of the former portrayal of the righteousness and power of God in these chapters. According to their account, God perfectly fulfills his covenant with his creation, and there is no way in which he can be condemned (40:8). He is glorious in his majestic power, shown forth in his works in creation, so that no human being has the remotest chance of contending with him successfully (40:2). The book of Job does not shade its presentation of the Lord in order to make the story come out successfully.

Rather, the point of the divine speeches is that it is God himself who speaks to Job. This majestic God of power and righteousness lowers himself to enter into dialogue with his mortal creature. God cares for Job. He is concerned about Job's attitude and fate. He is still God—but God *for Job, on his side.* And, indeed, he is still merciful; though the friends have been wrong, God will forgive them, through the prayerful mediation of his servant Job (42:8–9). God his friend has not abandoned him, and so Job's entire perspective is altered (42:5–6).

> I had heard of thee by the hearing of the ear,
>   but now my eye sees thee;

> therefore I despise myself,
> and repent in dust and ashes.

God, his God, has come to him, and that makes all the difference. To emphasize the fact that God is for him, not only after death but in this life also, the epilogue (42:10–17) is used to portray God's mercy in restoring Job's former prosperity—an ending which may appear rather weak in the light of all that has gone before.

God is *for* suffering humanity. God is on the side of his creaturely and mortal human beings. God the Lord, who is perfect in power and righteousness, before whom no one can stand and call into question— that God is a God who is *for* every person. That is just a story in the Old Testament, but like so much in the Old Testament account, it becomes flesh in the New. And so Paul can write his triumphant paean of praise:

> If God is for us, who is against us? He who did not spare his own Son but gave him up for us all, will he not also give us all things with him? Who shall bring any charge against God's elect? It is God who justifies; who is to condemn? . . . For I am sure that neither death, nor life . . . nor anything else in all creation, will be able to separate us from the love of God in Christ Jesus our Lord.
>
> Romans 8:31–34, 38–39

Perhaps the book of Job was written in a time when Wisdom theology had become depersonalized and its observations viewed as automatic structures of creation; we do not know. There is much uncertainty about the date, authorship, and place of origin of the book. But certainly its insistence on the personal dimension of the relation with a God who is always mighty in power and righteousness is a needed word in our age that has secularized the universe, and a needed word in all ages that want to turn religion into a magical ritual or a guarantee of success and happiness. At the heart of the biblical faith is an intimate, daily, ongoing relation with the living God that can sustain a person through all tribulation and that is the basis of Christian ethics and worship. From whatever portion of the book of Job the preacher is preaching, that is the emphasis to keep in mind.

It may be that the preacher is using one of the hymnic passages from the book to set forth the glorious nature of God. For example, Job 38:1–18 is a stated lesson for the fifth Sunday in Pentecost B. Using that, the preacher may emphasize God's majestic wisdom and might over against the puny power and understanding of mortal human beings. But the wonder of our faith is that the all-wise and powerful Lord of the universe has condescended not only to speak to foolish and weak creatures such as we, but has even sent his Son to die for us. "O the depth of the riches and wisdom and knowledge of God!" (Rom. 11:33).

The Book of Ecclesiastes

The book of Ecclesiastes also belongs firmly within the Wisdom traditions of the Old Testament, but like the book of Job it emphasizes one perhaps forgotten point from those traditions, and in the process it sometimes leaves wisdom behind altogether. Apparently the book was written in a time when Wisdom theology was flourishing, and when the advocacy of Wisdom practice was the one gospel of the day. "Of making many books there is no end, and much study is a weariness of the flesh" (12:12). But the Preacher, the author of the book (Koheleth in the Hebrew), casts a skeptical eye toward an overemphasis on Wisdom teachings (see 7:16–17). Wisdom practice is certainly a good in this writer's eyes (7:11–12; cf. 2:13–14; 7:19; 8:1, 5; 9:13–18; 10:2–3, 10, 12–15), but it has its limitations, which the Preacher has discovered in his experience.

He sets out, according to 1:13, to make a series of experiments, in which he will test the truth of Wisdom teachings. He wants to know if, in truth, wisdom will bring him happiness, satisfaction, and meaning in his life. He therefore investigates all sorts of things that might bring him abundant life: total concentration on the study of wisdom itself (1:13–18); pleasures of all sorts, and fame (2:1–11); wisdom's opposite, folly (2:12–16). His experiments take him into an observation of legal justice (3:16–22), of oppression and envy (4:1–3), of miserliness (4:7–8), of companionship (4:9–12), of the kingship (4:13–16; 5:9; 8:2–9; 10:16–17), of worship (5:1–7), of riches and poverty (5:8—6:6), of righteousness and wickedness (7:15; 8:14–15). What he finds in such observations is that one end comes to all (see 3:19; 6:6; 8:8). Therefore what is the point of trying to acquire great wisdom? "What befalls the fool will befall me also; why then have I been so very wise?" (2:15). Death is the great leveler, in the thought of Ecclesiastes.

> One fate comes to all, to the righteous and the wicked, to the good and the evil, to the clean and the unclean, to him who sacrifices and him who does not sacrifice. As is the good man, so is the sinner; and he who swears is as he who shuns an oath. This is an evil in all that is done under the sun, that one fate comes to all.
> Ecclesiastes 9:2–3

A person may be wise and have a fool for a successor (2:18–23). A king may be powerful and be scorned after death (4:13–16). A rich man may have possessions and honor and lack nothing that he desires, and yet he can take none of it with him, and he really has no lasting advantage over one who has never been born (6:1–6). There is nothing that follows after death except forgetfulness of the one who has died (2:16). And so vanity of vanities, all is vanity, says the Preacher (1:2). The pursuit of wisdom over much is a vain pursuit.

If one asks why that is so, then the ultimate answer of Ecclesiastes is that human wisdom cannot find out the ways of God, no matter how much it studies and learns.

> When I applied my mind to know wisdom, and to see the business that is done on earth, how neither day nor night one's eyes see sleep; then I saw all the work of God, that man cannot find out the work that is done under the sun. However much man may toil in seeking, he will not find it out; even though a wise man claims to know, he cannot find it out.
>
> Ecclesiastes 8:16–17

"All this I have tested by wisdom; I said, 'I will be wise'; but it was far from me" (7:23; cf. 11:5). God has indeed ordered all things, and there are set orders fixed into the creation (3:14–15). Human beings are given that knowledge. But they cannot by wisdom penetrate the ways of God to know what is wise and what is foolish, what is good and what is evil (6:10–12). They cannot know what will come after them, to determine the ultimate meaning of life (7:14; 8:7; 9:6). They cannot know the time of their death (9:11–12). And they are simply forgotten after death (2:16). Wisdom teachings cannot penetrate the ultimate mystery of God's ways.

> I have seen the business that God has given to the sons of men to be busy with. He has made everything beautiful in its time; also he has put eternity into man's mind, yet so that he cannot find out what God has done from the beginning to the end.
>
> Ecclesiastes 3:10–11

Ecclesiastes represents a devastating attack on the claims of wisdom.

Human beings cannot know the ways of God and the orders that he has set into creation, but the Preacher of this book is by no means an irreligious person. He counsels reverence and sincerity in worship (5:1–2); the prompt payment of vows to God (5:4–6); obedience to God and his commandments (8:10–13; 12:13; cf. 5:7; 7:18); mutual helpfulness in the community (4:9–12). Above all, the Preacher knows that all good things in life come from God, and that there is no joy apart from God (2:24–25). God gives human beings good gifts in life—of that the Preacher is sure.

That manner of life that the Preacher therefore advocates is one of moderation, even in the study of wisdom, of reverence and obedience, and, above all, of enjoyment of the good gifts that God does in fact give.

> There is nothing better for a man than that he should eat and drink, and find enjoyment in his toil. This also, I saw, is from the hand of God; for apart from him who can eat or who can have enjoyment?
>
> Ecclesiastes 2:24–25

This statement is sounded again and again in the book (3:12–13, 22; 5:18–20; 8:15; 9:7). Take the joy from life that God gives you, it says. If you are wealthy, enjoy your wealth; otherwise you are better dead (6:1–6); if you are married, "enjoy life with the wife whom you love" (9:9); and, above all, enjoy the work that God has given you to do, and do it with all your might; for in Sheol, the place of the dead to which you are going, there are none of these things (9:10).

Far from being a cynical work, or one of despair, Ecclesiastes' tone is largely one of gratitude and of humility before God. Human wisdom cannot penetrate the mysteries of God and of his creation; therefore we must be humble. But a good God nevertheless gives good gifts to human beings; therefore we should be grateful and joyful.

For the modern congregation, there is a lot of good advice in that. In our technological age, we sometimes believe we can know and do everything. But beyond the fringes of our knowledge there lies mystery—a fact that scientists repeatedly tell us these days—and our proper attitude before that mystery is humility. To Wisdom's surety that it could know the deep ways of God, Ecclesiastes replied, "You cannot." Human wisdom always needs that rebuke.

We further need the Preacher's counsel to enjoy God's gifts—the love of spouse and family, the beauty of the earth (3:11), food and drink and prosperity (10:19), wise and proper government (4:13; 10:16–17), and, the Preacher would say, above all else, the gift of life itself, with its work. Gratitude is the proper stance before the blessings of God poured out on us, and all joy is the fruit of his hand.

Furthermore, there is an attitude characteristic of our society for which Ecclesiastes can serve as a corrective. That attitude is summed up in the advertising slogan: "You only go around once in life, so go for the gusto." That slogan ignores the Preacher's wise insight— everything that gives true joy in this life is the gift of God. "Apart from him who can eat or who can have enjoyment?" (2:25). All that is good in life is from the hand of God.

For the Christian preacher, however, Ecclesiastes' advice does not go far enough, for the book finally sees all made meaningless in the inevitability of death. That too, of course, is wise teaching, because if death is the end, there is no ultimate meaning to anything we have done or left undone. Therefore, anyone who preaches from Ecclesiastes should also listen to Paul, as he ends his great chapter on the resurrection.

> But in fact Christ has been raised from the dead, the first fruits of those who have fallen asleep. . . . Thanks be to God, who gives us the victory through our Lord Jesus Christ. Therefore, my beloved . . . be steadfast, immovable, always abounding in the work of the Lord, knowing that in the Lord your labor is not in vain.
>
> 1 Corinthians 15:20, 57–58

There is no greater wisdom than that, and there is no better word for the church—and for its preachers.

Notes

Chapter 1: A Personal Prologue for Preachers

1. While this book consistently uses inclusive language for human beings, it follows biblical usage in the language for God. Only God can name himself. That implies nothing about the sexuality of God. Sexuality is a structure of creation, and therefore God has no sexuality. But the Bible uses masculine terminology for God in order to prevent his identification with the mother goddess and other immanental deities of ancient Near Eastern religions. I follow the same course, because so much of current feminist religion has reverted to worship of a female deity permeating all things and has thus abandoned the biblical faith.

Chapter 4: Basics of Sermon Preparation

1. I am indebted for much of this discussion to W. Eugene March, "Prophecy," in *Old Testament Form Criticism*, ed. by John Hayes (San Antonio: Trinity University Press, 1974); and to Claus Westermann, *Basic Forms of Prophetic Speech*, tr. by Hugh C. White (Philadelphia: Westminster Press, 1976). The chart is taken from a portion of a chart in Westermann, p. 174.

2. See my article, "The Use of Hymnic Elements in Preaching," *Interpretation*, January 1985.

Chapter 5: Preaching from the Narratives

1. The entire text of this sermon, entitled "The Journey—the Choice," is found in my book *Preaching as Theology and Art* (Nashville: Abingdon Press, 1984), pp. 106–113.

2. G. A. F. Knight, *Theology as Narrative: A Commentary on the Book of Exodus* (Grand Rapids: Wm. B. Eerdmans Publishing Co., 1976), p. 67.

3. Ibid., p. 80.

4. Ibid., p. 89.

5. John Bright, *A History of Israel*, 3rd ed. (Philadelphia: Westminster Press, 1981).

6. See my article "Plumbing the Riches: Preaching from Deuteronomy," *Interpretation*, July 1987.

7. Rosemary Ruether, *Women-Church* (San Francisco: Harper & Row, 1986), p. 108.

Chapter 6: Preaching from the Law

1. These comments on the individual laws of Deuteronomy were first published in a somewhat different form in my Proclamation Commentary, *Deuteronomy, Jeremiah* (Philadelphia: Fortress Press, 1978), pp. 42–45. The book is now out of print.

Chapter 7: Preaching from the Prophets

1. See, e.g., Amos 2:9–11; Hosea 11:1; Micah 6:5; Isaiah 37:35; Jeremiah 2:7; 31:2–3; etc.

2. See Isaiah 9:9; 46:12; 51:7; 63:17; Jeremiah 17:1; Hosea 7:14; 10:2; Joel 2:12; Zechariah 7:12; Malachi 2:2.

3. See also Jeremiah 2:4–13; 8:4–7; Amos 2:6–11; Hosea 11:1; 13:4–6; Isaiah 1:2–3; 65:1–2, et al.

4. T. S. Eliot "The Waste Land," lines 22–24, in *The Complete Poems and Plays, 1909–1950* (New York: Harcourt, Brace & World, 1971), p. 38.

5. This sermon has been published in *Best Sermons 1* (San Francisco: Harper & Row, 1988), pp. 285–293.

6. For a full discussion of the last six of the minor prophets, see my commentary, *Nahum-Malachi. Interpretation: A Bible Commentary for Teaching and Preaching* (Atlanta: John Knox Press, 1986).

7. The full text of this sermon was first published in my book *The Old Testament and the Proclamation of the Gospel* (Philadelphia: Westminster Press, 1973). The book is now out of print.

Chapter 8: Preaching from the Psalms

1. See C. A. Briggs, *A Critical and Exegetical Commentary on The Book of Psalms*, I (Edinburgh: T. & T. Clark, 1906), p. xciv, for a fuller discussion.

2. Psalms 2:6; 9:11, 14; 14:7; 20:2; 43:3; 53:6; 65:1; 68:16; 74:2, 4, 7; 76:2; 84:1, 7; 99:2; 122:9; 125:1; 132:13, 14; 135:2, 21.

3. Psalms 71:22; 89:18.

4. Psalms 80:1; 28:9.

5. Psalm 132:2, 5; cf. 50:1.

6. Psalms 46:7, 11; 75:9; 76:6; 81:1; 84:8; 94:7; 114:7; 146:5.

7. Psalm 89:26.

8. Psalms 85:4; 65:5; 68:19.

9. Psalms 18:31; 78:35; 95:1.

10. Psalms 5:2; 9:7; 10:16; 24:7–10; 29:1, 10; 44:4; 48:2; 68:24; 74:12; 102:12; 145:1; 146:10.

11. Psalm 22:3.

12. See also Psalms 20:1–4; 144:8; 28:3; 31:18, 20; 41:6; 52:1–4; 55:21; 63:11; 64:8; cf. 141:3; 12; 15.

13. Acts 2:34; Ephesians 1:20; Colossians 3:1; Hebrews 1:3; 8:1; 10:12; 12:2.

14. Jerusalem is described as being "in the far north" in these verses, because that was the mythic location of the mountain of the Canaanite, Jebusite deities of Salem, whom Yahweh replaced when David took Salem, or Jerusalem, as his capital city.

15. A similar concept may be found in Exodus 14:19–31; Joshua 11:20; 24:7; Judges 5:20.

16. Cf. Joshua 5:1; 10:10–11; Judges 7:22; 1 Samuel 14:15, 20.

17. Cf. Numbers 10:35–36; 1 Samuel 4:7; 5:11.

18. This entire meditation, entitled "The Purpose of Forgiveness," is published in the author's *Preaching as Theology and Art* (Nashville: Abingdon Press, 1984), pp. 28–30.

Chapter 9: Preaching from the Wisdom Literature

1. Joseph, Genesis 41:8, 33; advisers to Moses, Deuteronomy 1:13, 15; woman of Tekoa, 2 Samuel 14:2; woman of Abel, 2 Samuel 20:16; counselors to Pharaoh, Isaiah 19:11; general references, Isaiah 5:21; 29:14; 44:25; Jeremiah 8:8, 9; 9:12, 23; 10:7; 18:18; Matthew 23:34.

2. Matthew 7:24; 10:16; 11:25; Luke 10:21; Matthew 24:45; Luke 12:42; Matthew 25:2, 8, 9; Romans 1:14, 22; 16:19; 1 Corinthians 1:19, 20, 26, 27; 3:18, 19, 20; 6:5; 2 Corinthians 11:19; Ephesians 5:15; James 3:13.

3. Deuteronomy 4:6–8; Jeremiah 9:23–24; 10:12; Hosea 14:9; Micah 6:9; Matthew 7:24–27; Luke 1:17; 2:52; 11:49–52; Romans 1:18–23; Ephesians 1:9–10; Colossians 1:9–10, 28; 3:16; James 1:5–8; 3:13–18; Revelation 13:18; 17:9.

4. Gerhard von Rad, *Wisdom in Israel* (Nashville: Abingdon Press, 1972), p. 169.

5. Ibid., p. 156.

6. Ibid., p. 157.

7. Ibid., p. 162. Von Rad also points to Psalms 145:10 and 97:6.

8. Raymond E. Brown, ed. and tr., *The Gospel According to John*, vol. 1, Anchor Bible, 28 (Garden City, N.Y.: Doubleday & Co., 1966).